Education and Social Justice
in the Era of Globalisation

Education and Social Justice in the Era of Globalisation

Perspectives from India and the UK

Editors

Marie Lall

Geetha B. Nambissan

Routledge
Taylor & Francis Group
LONDON NEW YORK NEW DELHI

First published 2011 in India
by Routledge
912–915 Tolstoy House, 15–17 Tolstoy Marg, Connaught Place, New Delhi 110 001

Simultaneously published in the UK
by Routledge
2 Park Square, Milton Park, Abingdon, OX14 4RN

Routledge is an imprint of the Taylor & Francis Group, an informa business

© 2011 Marie Lall and Geetha B. Nambissan

Typeset by
Star Compugraphics Private Limited
5, CSC, Near City Apartments
Vasundhara Enclave
Delhi 110 096

Printed and bound in India by
Avantika Printers Private Limited
194/2, Ramesh Market, Garhi, East of Kailash,
New Delhi 110 065

British Library Cataloguing-in-Publication Data
A catalogue record of this book is available from the British Library

ISBN: 978-0-415-69378-3

Contents

Acknowledgements

In 2006, some of us, faculty and research scholars of the Zakir Husain Centre for Educational Studies, Jawaharlal Nehru University, New Delhi, India, and the Institute of Education, University of London, London, began a conversation on what was happening to concerns of social justice in education in an increasingly globalising world. We felt that there was much to discuss, share and learn from the experiences of India and the UK, nations which were being impacted by global economic and cultural forces in different yet similar ways. Over the next three years we embarked on what was a challenging project working together on a range of themes around social justice in education bringing in perspectives from both societies. Today we look back with considerable satisfaction at the academic and institutional collaboration that we participated in, the rich insights that emerged from our interaction with each other and the stimulating debates that we engaged in especially at the Delhi and London seminars. This book is an outcome of our work together. We are grateful to the Jawaharlal Nehru University and the Institute of Education for encouraging us to undertake this collaborative project and providing the institutional support that made it possible. We thank Professor Geoff Whitty, former director of the Institute of Education for his support of this project and the financial support from the director's fund at the Institute of Education, University of London that enabled us to undertake the study. As editors the experience has been an enriching one and we would like to thank our team — Anjali Kothari, Binay Kumar Pathak, Carol Vincent, Felicity Armstrong, Pratyasha Sahoo, Radhika Menon, Saumen Chattopadhyay, Stephen J. Ball, Srinivasa Rao and Vincent Carpentier. We also thank the Routledge team for seeing our book through.

Marie Lall, London
Geetha B. Nambissan, New Delhi

Introduction: Education, Globalisation and Social Justice

Geetha B. Nambissan and Marie Lall

Much of the scholarly work on globalisation has been framed by 'strong versions of globalisation' or what have been labelled as 'globalisation from above' perspectives. These have emphasised the powerful influence of larger structural factors and, in particular, global economic forces on education reform and policy in nation states (Maguire 2010: 59). The nation state in such accounts is viewed in minimalist terms and considered relatively powerless. Nations are seen to be left with little choice but to fall in line with the dictates of the world market and other global forces, leading to increasing convergences in policy reform. In education this is reflected in policies of parental/school choice, vouchers, as well as laying down standards and testing for 'quality control' that have come to dominate education policy in many countries today.

There are a growing number of scholars who point to the need to move away from over-generalised and macro pictures of globalisation and view it as a set of complex and dynamic processes, networks and flows that are mediated by and interface with nation states as well as institutions, cultures and practices that are historically and contextually rooted. Rizvi and Lingard (2010: x) rightly observe that 'globalization cannot be viewed as a generalized phenomenon, but rather needs to be seen as a dynamic phenomenon expressed in particular histories and political configurations'. Singh, Kenway and Apple (2007: 2) also point to the need to look 'underneath the big patterns of globalisation', to the 'dense relationship between the massive material and structural shifts associated with globalization and everyday life'. Thus 'while there are today global policy pressures and globalized policy discourses, these always manifest in vernacular ways, reflecting varying cultures, histories and politics within different nations' (Rizvi and Lingard 2010: x). This is a perspective that is not confined to looking at 'globalisation from below' but points to the interwoven and dynamic processes associated with globalisation through the 'diverse sites and spaces . . . actors linked together through flows and networks in an increasingly interconnected world' (Singh et al. 2007: 2).

The building of a 'social imaginary' (Taylor 2004), appropriate for the neoliberal project, is also an important dimension of this phase of globalisation — that is, the shared meanings and subjectivities that are critical to the project of normalising and projecting as 'inevitable' contemporary patterns of social life that, in the ascendancy of neo-liberalism, have seen the increasing penetration of market relations in all spheres of society, and redefining of institutions where the 'social' or 'public' was earlier given value (see Rizvi and Lingard 2010). Maguire says that 'globalisation is a discursive as well as material set of practices. That is, discourses of globalisation make possible certain ways of thinking, acting and being, and they displace or conceal alternatives' (2010: 59). We find this particularly important in relation to concerns of social justice that were part of the 'social imaginary' of the welfare state. The construction of neoliberal discourses, meanings and subjectivities building the 'capitalising' (Rizvi and Lingard 2010), 'possessive individual' (Apple 1982) and their circulation through networks and flows that are facilitated through globalisation are critical to the building of an ideology and social imaginary of contemporary society and social relations where social justice concerns are being increasingly marginalised and redefined.

This book has emerged from a collaborative project between faculty and research scholars of the Zakir Husain Centre for Educational Studies, Jawaharlal Nehru University, India and the Institute of Education, University of London, UK. Our concern has primarily been to resituate the debates around education and social justice in policy research and public discourse; as also to highlight the need for a more nuanced understanding of globalisation and education. We use a comparative and relational frame to study the two countries, India and the UK. We do so from vantage points within and across the two countries that have been bound historically together by colonial relationships and are linked in different ways in contemporary times as well. We felt that the flows and networks that link the two countries, one still in a position of relative economic strength (UK) and the other with a growing comparative advantage in professional skills as well as untapped markets (India), would provide insights into aspects of globalisation that have hitherto remained unexplored. Understanding the role of the state in the two nations was of particular interest as we felt that it would provide an opportunity to look concretely at its changing role in relation to education as it negotiates between global opportunities and compulsions, national interests and regional and local aspirations. Both the need to look at the 'vernaculars' of globalisation in relation to education and social justice within a broader context of macro structures and processes, and a relational frame led to the project of looking at specific themes in education and social justice from the perspective of two nations — India and the UK. In the discussion that follows, we first map the broad canvas of globalisation, social justice and education underscoring the changing role of the state. We go on to present the rationale of the India–UK comparative lens through which we look at education and social justice and finally highlight some of the themes and concerns that emerge from the contributions of the authors.

Globalisation, Social Justice, the State and Education

A lot has been written about globalisation and its effects on the relationship between the state and society. Across the social science disciplines there is an understanding that there are many differing definitions of this phenomenon; there are debates on how long it has been in existence — whether it is at all new, and how far it has actually changed the world we live in. What is clear is that the literature around globalisation discusses elements relating to increased interdependence and internationalisation as well as a rise of local structures and networks. Whilst not wanting to pin down our own definition of globalisation, we are nevertheless interested in particular in the effects of its economic dimensions — the politics of neoliberalism and how this has shifted the understanding of state responsibilities and marginalised issues pertaining to the social justice agenda.

Over the last 30 years, the income share of the richest 20 per cent of the world's population as compared to the poorest 20 per cent of the world's population increased from 30:1 to 61:1 (Brown and Lauder 2003). This widening gap — both within countries and between countries — raises questions around equality and social justice, and which sections of society globalisation is actually benefitting. Rizvi and Lingard remind us that social justice is not a term with one definition and that the liberal humanist perspective based on John Rawls' concepts of fairness and individual freedom differs from the one that believes that social justice can be achieved through market individualism where people get what they deserve, rejecting any redistributive notions. This again differs from social democratic notions of social justice which are based on social relationships and needs of people within a community.

> It is important to note, then, that market individualism and social democracy rest on very different understandings of the nature of the relationship between justice and the market. In the former the market is seen as crucial in facilitating social exchange and the exercise of individual choice, while the social democratic view suggests that the idea of justice is not entirely compatible with markets unless they are controlled (regulated) in a sufficiently rigorous manner. (Rizvi and Lingard 2010: 158)

In the post–Second World War era, European as well as many newly independent countries chose the path of social democracy and redistribution to ensure a fairer society. However, in today's globalising world, the battle lines are drawn between those who believe that the market can deliver social justice (especially with wider provision and allowing choice) and those who maintain that the market has eroded the state's ability to ensure a socially just society. In the era of globalisation, neoliberal policies have ensured the centrality of the market and this new order raises questions about the role of the state, especially since many hyperglobalists will insist that globalisation actually entails a withering away of the state. Olsen and Peters (2005) have pointed out that globalisation has not resulted in a reduction of state power, but rather in a shifting of such power to new areas whereby the state's role has moved from that of a provider of social and public services to one of a regulator. Wrigley (2007: 64–65) also explains the new role of the state:

> As David Harvey (2005) has demonstrated, neoliberalism by no means entails a diminution of state power. On the contrary, a strong state is needed to regulate the market, to combat any class resistance to it, and to eliminate/commodify any nonmarket spaces.

Consequently neoliberalism is not about less state control but rather represents a new form of state involvement. As the market logic is extended to the public sector, the state becomes a regulator rather than a provider of such services. The state is also instrumental in facilitating the market to take on these responsibilities. As such the state uses the market as a new control mechanism. Whilst there is a general withdrawal of the state it is not in the arena of control but rather in its position as responsible for safeguarding all citizens, especially the weaker sections of society. In short it is a withdrawal of the welfare state. This is underpinned by neoliberal policies.

At an economic level neoliberal policies are an element of globalisation as they structure domestic and global economic relations. Neoliberalism is, however, not identical with globalisation, only one dimension of it (Olsen and Peters 2005: 313–14). Globalisation has allowed neoliberalism to spread and it has become a western hegemonic discourse which now dominates world economic relations. In trying to understand the changing relationship between the state and society it is helpful to remember the differences between classical liberalism and neoliberalism:

> Whereas classical liberalism represents a negative conception of state power in that the individual was taken as an object to be freed from the interventions of the state, neoliberalism has come to represent a positive conception of the state's role in creating the appropriate market by providing the conditions, laws and institutions necessary for its operation. . . . In neoliberalism the state seeks to create an individual that is enterprising and competitive entrepreneur. (Ibid.: 315)

Today globalisation and international competitiveness dictate that public services, including education need to adapt to the market place and therefore the states propagate neoliberal reforms. These reforms have been particularly supported by the growing middle classes in middle-income and poorer countries such as India, as they tend to benefit most from policies of choice and have the ability to buy themselves out of the public system to the detriment of the poorer and weaker sections of society (Hill and Rosskam 2008: xvii).

The new economic realities have led to increased marketisation across the public sector, leading in turn to disaggregation, deregulation, commodification, an emphasis on measurable outputs, managerialism and accountability. Neoliberal market-oriented reforms have affected education at all levels in developed and developing countries. Primary and secondary education have opened up to the market allowing new private providers to offer educational services competing with public education provided by the state. As Bartlett et al. (2002) explain, the marketisation of education involved the introduction of market principles into the education system such as competition, deregulation and stratification. There is also a new education discourse which changes the aim of education and developing an educated society to one which is adapted to the new knowledge economy both at domestic and international levels:

> Thus, education policy discourses concerning the education-globalisation link constitute education as the essential and only strategy available for nation states to cope with the challenges, demands even, of globalisation, present and future. Education becomes the main 'insurance policy' for individuals, families, communities, countries and regions in the era of globalisation, which is invoked in terms of known (technology and skills) and unknown (the vagaries of markets) risks and insecurities. The nation state's government is thus reduced to educational formation of citizens for self-protection. The globalisation discourse of national and international education policy thus constructs the knowledge society as both problem and solution, with education advocated as the global 'vaccination'. (Gamarnikow 2009: 7)

At a global level there is an increasing convergence in discourse, values and policies resulting in policy borrowing where similar solutions are being offered for differing problems in different settings. International structures which have helped instate similar economic practices in developing countries are the World Bank and the International Monetary Fund (IMF). Their advocated structural reform programmes across developing countries have ensured that the message of the efficiency and effectiveness of the markets as providers of public services such as education has reached countries such as India, which believed in the responsibility of the state in alleviating the worst of inequalities. The World Trade Organisation (WTO) also takes part in the spreading of this economic ideology by facilitating globalisation and opening up all spheres of social life, including the public services, to international capital. The WTO 'education agenda', therefore, is to facilitate the penetration of educational services by corporate capital. The key WTO agreement for this purpose is the General Agreement on Trade in Services (GATS). This agreement incorporates the aim of unleashing progressive liberalisation of trade in services, including public services such as education. In the long-term, no area of social life is exempt from these developments. Today public services in both developed and developing countries are hostage to a marketisation process, not only endorsed but actively supported by the state. There has been a fundamental shift in the relationship between state and society as the state uses the market as a control mechanism, withdrawing from some spheres, yet remaining ever prominent.

The consequences are wide-reaching. As the power and influence of state and civil society is reduced it becomes harder for them to hold corporate power accountable and consequently democracy is weakened. In fact it also becomes more difficult for citizens to address issues of social justice as the logic of the market prevails:

> With few exceptions, the project of democratic transformation has fallen into disrepute in the popular imagination as the logic of the market undermines the most basic social solidarities. The consequences include not only a weakened state, but also a growing sense of insecurity, cynicism and political retreat on the part of the general public. The incessant calls for self reliance that now dominate public discourse betray a weakened state that neither provides adequate economic and social safety nets for its populace, especially those who are young, poor or marginalized, nor gives any indication that it either needs or is willing to care for its citizens. In this scenario, private interests trump social needs and profit becomes more important than social justice. (Giroux 2003: 180)

It is clear therefore that with increased market logic there is also an increase in democratic deficit and with it a reduction of the social justice agenda, especially in the public sector arena as new inequalities are created.

Neoliberalism manifests itself differently across different sectors, institutions and societies. However 'disparate though the phenomena constituted be they are part of the same underlying governmental change' (Harris 2007: 133). Today the way the public sector is managed has changed markedly. There has been a shift away from old-style public sector bureaucratic administration. Managerialism has been the key mechanism in the cultural re-engineering of the public sector. The elevation of effectiveness and efficiency as the sole criterion of legitimacy reflects the increasing dominance of an ethic of managerialism and a concomitant emphasis upon measuring and improving performance (performative strategies). The accounting logic 'produces an aura of factual representation, promoting a general perception that it generates neutral, objective information'. But professional 'outputs' are not easily standardised and measurable. This is particularly the case in education. While there have been different effects in different countries, the focus has shifted to an instrumentalist thinking with measurable outputs. The new policy discourse is constraining and restricting (Harris 2007). Giroux explains the lack of concern for issues of ethics, equity and justice by the fact that corporate concerns are narrow in nature (Giroux 2003: 187).

The influx of new educational providers has led to increased opportunities for students from poorer backgrounds to attend school. Nevertheless, as Roberts (2001 in Reay 2006) argues, this transformation has created the illusion of a fairer society while it creates a stratification along the system which relegates the working classes to different trajectories as compared to the middle classes (Reay 2006). The underlying assumption of market-oriented policies is that free market allows parents to choose the school that aligns with their expectations and needs. The possibility of choosing a school would act as a natural selection process through which unpopular schools will be forced to change or to close if they do not adapt to clients' expectations (Ball 1993). Policy makers have seen a marketised education system as an ideal solution because it allows parents to choose and compels schools to improve regardless of their resources (ibid.). However, the rhetoric of choice assumes that all parents have equal cultural capital and are equally informed and capable of making such a choice for their children. The middle classes benefit whilst the lower classes have to make do with the leftovers (Leathwood 2004; Reay et al. 2001). As a consequence of the new policies and the focus on choice the vision of a collective good has given way to individualism where every individual and every family is having to develop strategies to compete with others. Those who are weaker and poorer are left to lose out:

> In the social democratic era, education was constructed as a public good and a collective form of welfare provision, a key element of Marshall's social citizenship (Marshall, 1950). In the current neo-liberal era, by contrast, policy discourses construct education as a positional good for individuals, and as the site for human capital formation for the globalised economy. What has not changed is the importance ascribed to education. (Gamarnikow 2009: 13)

There have been similar effects in the higher education sector. Marketisation across the sector has made performativity and accountability cornerstones of higher education policies today. The pressure to increase the number of students, account for how time is spent and the general concern with national and international rankings are all effects of the changing understanding of what higher education stands for. The role of the university is no longer that of a 'public interest institution' but that of being a site of 'knowledge production in light of the economic imperatives of the "knowledge economy"'. As academics are ranked according to the number of their publications their universities compete internationally for those students who will bring in the highest fees. We are reminded of Hatcher's observation:

> the starting point has to be the recognition that there are two distinct logics at work. One is a logic of education, based on social and individual need, and notions of equity and democracy. The other is a logic of business, whose bottom line is profit. Not everything business wants to do is incompatible with education interests. But the logic of business is incompatible with the logic of education. (2001: 58)

As a number of scholars have argued, 'economic globalisation has not been experienced as a homogenous phenomenon' (Maguire 2010: 60) and market forces have penetrated some public sector systems more than others. Referring to the fact that countries are located 'differently in relation to the unfolding of late capitalism' (or are early/later developing societies), Maguire observes that 'it is evident that changes in capitalist relations and policy production are tempered by specificities of local histories and cultures (economic, political and social) and are recalibrated over time' (ibid.). We now turn to two differently located societies — India and the UK — to study their experiences of education and social justice in the era of globalisation.

India and the UK

We look at education and social justice in India and the UK, historically linked by 200 years of colonial rule that left a deleterious impact on India's economic and social development. Education was particularly affected as British rule destroyed the network of indigenous schools and left in their place a poorly developed education system that had an extremely narrow base.[1] Soon after India's independence in the 1950s, barely 18 per cent of children in the relevant age group were in school. While India had to rebuild her educational system, legacies of British rule such as the public (private) schools (on the British model) established for the Indian middle-class elite, and

English, the language of the colonial power, as a cultural resource left a deep imprint on education in the post-independence period. Both India and UK have social groups that experience structural exclusion because of their location in the social hierarchy — race/caste, tribal/ethnic identity and minority status (see Lall and Rao in this volume).

The newly independent Indian state in 1947 was committed to social justice and equality and education was seen as an important channel for economic and social advancement. This was written into the Indian Constitution and translated through legislative action into policies for affirmative action through reservations in educational institutions and public employment as well as other incentives and programmes initially for communities such as the scheduled castes (SC) and tribes (ST). These are communities that have been historically socially discriminated and marginalised. In the 1990s reservations were extended to the other backward classes (OBC) and the disabled. Post-war welfare state education policies in UK brought in institutional reform and programmes to facilitate equality of opportunity. There were also significant shifts in policy in relation to education of the disabled (see Armstrong and Sahoo in this volume). However, as Lall and Rao observe (in this volume), policies of the state in the UK were assimilationist and colour blind till the 1970s and the multiracial policies were incorporated in education policy only subsequently.

Economic restructuring was initiated in the UK in the 1970s following the international oil crisis. In education this saw the introduction of market principles (competition and school autonomy) in state education to increase efficiency and achievement and curtailment of public funding for education. De-regulation and 'choice' in education became part of education policy in the 1990s to raise the standards and accountability of schools (Maguire 2010). It is important that the UK had already achieved universal secondary education when it began carrying out reforms in education. When India was forced to carry out structural adjustment policies and liberalise its economy in 1991, more than a third of the population was not literate and less that 50 per cent of children in the relevant age group completed primary education. The economic reforms did not directly impinge on resources for primary education in India and the 1990s saw the launching of massive state-sponsored programmes to universalise primary schooling (District Primary Education Programme [DPEP] in 1994) and elementary education (Sarva Shiksha Abhiyan in 2000). A major policy shift was the bringing in of external aid/grants to supplement funds for elementary education. Foreign funders who supported the DPEP included the World Bank, European Union (EU), the Department for International Development (DIFD, UK) as well as other multilateral organisations. That the Indian state should seek foreign funds to meet its constitutional obligation of providing elementary education to all children came in for criticism that included the charge that this provided space for organisations such as the World Bank that espoused neoliberal ideology to influence Indian education policy (Kumar et al. 2001). Higher education felt the brunt of the economic reforms as budgets were cut and ways to bring in private sources of funding became part of the policy discourse.

UK and India are increasingly drawn into global markets for education and labour in which they participate in similar and yet different ways. State policies in education are influenced by global economic agreements such as the GATS and WTO, and the setting in place of internationally comparative standards for education and skill development. Compulsions to maintain a competitive edge, pressures from economic and social interests, and local aspirations, histories and cultural traditions are some of the factors that influence education policy. At a more global level we see the construction of a neo-liberal discourse and advocacy networks which directly link the two countries (Nambissan and Ball in this volume).

Both India and UK are signatories to international commitments to children's rights and social justice in education and are linked through global networks and alliances built to address issues related to the right to education, especially of marginal groups. However, today both nations are confronted by widening social inequalities with large sections of the population denied equitable opportunities in education. Aspects of the social structure (race in the UK and caste in India) underlie the historical experience of disadvantage and continue to influence contemporary educational outcomes and life chances to varying degrees in both societies. The middle classes are distinctly advantaged in both countries; there are interesting contrasts and yet parallels in the way they build cultural and social capital for success in education and social mobility. Though the ideology of the market was never absent from policy and public discourse it was more on the periphery. Today it is becoming increasingly dominant in state policy and civil society.

Both in India and the UK, the state–education relationship that emerges from our discussion is extremely complex. The state still plays a central role in educational provision and in addressing educational disadvantage through specific policies and programmes for different groups as well as in facilitating the process of marketisation. Since 2004 India's public spending has quadrupled and significant anti-poverty programmes such as the country-wide rural employment guarantee scheme and the midday meals programme have been implemented by the state. In the education sector we see what appear to be contradictory tendencies whereby increased public spending on specific programmes is coupled with both managerialist policies in higher education and an encouraged private sector provision — even for the very poor in school education. In the UK education is still largely state provided — but both at school and in higher education, the private sector penetration is far greater than what is immediately visible (Ball 2007). In a recent reflection on the early pronouncements of the new Conservative–Liberal government (following the defeat of New Labour), Exley and Ball (2010: 14) observe that 'the disarticulation of the state education system in England is already underway, and the Conservative Programme will perhaps take this process further and further'. Thus while there are state-led programmes with social democratic tendencies (more clearly seen in India), they sit side by side with neoliberal policies (more pronounced in the UK). UK and India thus offer an opportunity to look below the larger picture of globalisation to understand how it has played out in the two countries that began neoliberal reforms at different points of time. In the sections that follow we present some of the broad themes that run through the essays in this volume focusing mainly on social justice and education.

Changing Discourses and Practices

Equality and social justice in education have been dwelt upon by all authors in their areas of enquiry. They have voiced concern about the changing discourse on social justice with the ascendance of the neoliberal paradigm in education, pointing to widening disparities between social groups while emphasising emerging and deepening inequalities as a result of new state policies and programmes.

There has been a significant volume of research as well as official statistics that show that groups that experience discrimination and disadvantage because of identities of race, caste and ethnic identity show lower participation and achievement rates in schools and higher education in India and the UK. From Lall and Rao we learn that while access has increased at all levels of education (in terms of enrolment) in the last three decades, disparities (between Black and Minority Ethnic [BME] and their White peers in the UK, and SCs and STs as compared to the general population in India) have widened in relation to school completion and achievement. They emphasise the need to go beyond broad literacy and enrolment figures to look at intra-group inequalities that are increasing. Further, they point to newly emerging labels ('model minorities' in UK and the 'creamy layer' in India) that have been brought into the social justice discourse and are being used on the one hand as the basis for unfair comparisons among and within groups. On the other hand these labels tend to deflect attention away from larger structural exclusions on the basis of caste, class, race and minority status. Categories such as 'model minorities' and 'creamy layer' also appear ad hoc and lack descriptive and analytical robustness, but they are evocative and build into discourses that suggest that disadvantage and advantage are located within communities and families and are not linked to wider structures and processes or policy changes (Lall and Rao in this volume).

Regimes of competition that include standardised testing of high skills (within and across nations) are becoming widespread as nations strive to make their school systems more efficient in order to gain a competitive edge in the global market for education and labour. In the UK, 'league tables' that are regularly published, categorise state schools according to the performance of children on standardised tests. This is seen as one way to introduce elements of efficiency into the state system of education, as schools are compelled to improve achievement in tests if they wish to appear attractive to parents of prospective students, and thereby access state funds that are linked to enrolment. Lall and Rao cite research to show that the emphasis on league table performance has widened the achievement gap between Black (other than Asian Indians) and White pupils. The former may not only fail to get the attention they need from the school, but may actually be excluded from being entered for exams as they may depress the school's league table standing.

The growing preoccupation with testing and competition and the resulting narrowing and fragmenting of the larger objectives of education lead to the neglect of inclusive cultures and practices.

Armstrong and Sahoo (in this volume) observe that this is a cause of concern in the education of children with disabilities. In their chapter they acknowledge the pioneering steps that UK has taken to bring about inclusion in education as against segregation based on a medicalised perspective of disability as individual impairment. In an environment of growing competition among schools to improve their league table performance and the resulting institutional selectivity, children with disabilities are marginalised and become educationally especially vulnerable.

Efforts by the state to expand access to higher education are visible in both the UK and India — in policy pronouncements and new programmes and in the increase in public funding (in India since early 2000). In India, enrolments in higher education are targeted at 15 per cent (from the current 11–12 per cent) of the relevant age group. As Carpentier, Chattopadhyay and Pathak (henceforth Carpentier et al.; in this volume) indicate, the challenge in India is one of expanding provision to meet the growing demand for higher education as well as ensuring quality. This is an enormous challenge as a mere 3 per cent increase in enrolment in the post–school going age group in India translates into as many as 7 million students! In the UK the thrust has been on expanding enrolment among BME and these communities are the focus of special attention in the Widening Participation programmes initiated since early 2000.

As in the case of schooling, enrolment in higher education has increased but there are disparities in participation according to class/caste/race and gender in both countries as highlighted by Lall and Rao as well as by Carpentier et al. More crucial and often not adequately highlighted is that there is unequal access to the more prestigious institutions of higher education which enable better job opportunities. For instance, both sets of authors note that while participation rates have increased among BME, a larger proportion of them as compared to their White counterparts are found in the newer 'post-1992' (polytechnics and colleges of higher education) group considered less prestigious than the older 'Russell group' of institutions. This is another dimension of 'new inequalities' in education that lead to unequal advantage in the labour market/occupational placements.

Funding is a key issue for ensuring quality and social justice in higher education. Carpentier et al. point to differences in UK and India in relation to the source of funding for the expansion of access to higher education. In the UK, expansion of higher education provision has been primarily in the state sector and at the time of writing, there were four private universities. However, there has been an increasing dependence on private resources (raising fees and other charges) especially in the post 1990 era thereby increasing household expenditure on higher education. This has equity implications for access to higher education as emphasised by the authors. Altbach's comment (1998: 2) cited by Carpentier et al. is also pertinent: 'with tuition and other charges rising, public and private institutions look more and more similar'.

Private educational institutions have had a growing presence in Indian higher education in the post-independence decades especially in relation to professional education. However, the state was seen as the major provider of education at this stage. The 1990s saw a questioning of the 'public/quasi public good' nature of higher education. Policy discourse centred on redefining it as a 'private'/'non-merit' good and bringing in the 'user fees' principle (Carpentier et al.). This was the precursor for the state to downsize higher education budgets and look to private resources to expand this sector, by raising tuition in state institutions, and calling for the greater participation of the private sector and public private partnerships. There has been a rapid increase in the establishment of private colleges and universities in India. Carpentier et al. underscore the fact that a regulatory framework to govern private institutions and those that are being established under public–private partnerships (PPPs) has not been set in place.

Markets, Choice and Schooling

The growing marketisation of education in the last two decades has been emphasised by commentators on globalisation. However, markets have entered the education system in UK and India very differently and our work suggests that while there are generalised policy discourses that circulate and suggest policy convergence, there is need for in-depth study of specific contexts within a comparative and relational frame. A key feature of neoliberal reform in education has been to bring markets into state education through programmes of choice and vouchers. The UK did not adopt the policy of vouchers and in fact rejected it in the early 1980s. As mentioned earlier, parental choice linked to per capita funding of students to bring about competition among schools and improve efficiency were free market principles introduced in the UK within the state system of education which is still the major provider of school education — only 7 per cent of children are enrolled in the private and non-state sector (Vincent and Menon in this volume).

India in contrast has seen growing private provision in education with as many as a quarter of its children (more at the secondary than at the primary stage) in private unaided schools. The private school sector has a range of schools that include the high-end elite private (more recently 'international') schools, the middle-range public/ private schools and Christian missionary schools, and at the bottom, the low-cost private/'budget' schools that are unregulated. Unlike in the UK, the Indian middle classes (middle fractions) and increasingly those belonging to lower middle-class fractions have moved out of the state system of education and into private schools. 'Budget schools' run on a bare minimum of resources and with teachers on contract. As they profess to provide 'English-medium' education they are accessed by poorer families who are willing to pay the fees they charge so that their children acquire knowledge of English (Nambissan and Ball in this volume).

Parental choice and vouchers are still not elements of school reform in India, however, they are becoming part of discourses and discursive practices that are being constructed to influence education policy. Nambissan and Ball discuss one transnational advocacy network for choice and vouchers in India in which the UK is implicated. UK academics (Tooley), organisations (CfBT, University of New Castle) and think tanks (EFI, Cato) are key players along with local actors and organisations. It is ironic that a reform that was not accepted in the UK (vouchers) and is not backed by research evidence as to its positive outcomes is being advocated for India. It is the unregulated low-cost private/budget school sector accessed by poorer sections in India that is largely being targeted. Though couched in the language of equity and responding to parental choice (that state-funded vouchers be given to poor parents who aspire to send their children to private schools), unregulated school markets for the poor are also projected as a business opportunity where profits can be reaped (Nambissan and Ball in this volume). Armstrong and Sahoo (this volume) also point to 'a new presence on the special education scene' of for-profit organisations and observe that this reflects the 'commodification of disability, and the disabled through the adoption of marketing strategies'.

The quality of education on offer is also an issue that has been discussed by different authors. Widening participation in higher education in both countries has been observed by Carpentier et al. (this volume). However, they observe that the provision of higher education is not only inadequate in terms of provision, but the quality of education offered in general (other than in a minority of institutions under the central government) is poor. They observe that higher education under the purview of the states in India has been allowed to languish — starved of resources as well as faculty. Quality concerns are pertinent in the private sector too as adequate regulatory frameworks are not in place and they are poorly governed as evident from the prevalence of corrupt practices (Carpentier et al.). The relational dimension is important here. Inadequate provision and the indifferent quality of education on offer in India along with the opportunities for status and prestige that a 'foreign degree' brings with it have been responsible for increasing student migration to universities in other countries. India's globalising middle classes are today looking to world markets in education for a 'global experience', to become global citizens and access opportunities that have come with the new economy. As state funding for universities in the developed world is being downsized, they are looking at international students as a critical source of private resources for higher education.

The UK is one of the preferred destinations of Indian students who migrate for higher education. In 2008 around 15 per cent of all Indian students studying abroad were in the UK (UNESCO 2010).[2] International students have been charged full tuition in UK institutions since the 1970s (Carpentier et al. in this volume). The charging of full tuition from students from India and other developing countries to meet the resource crunch in higher education in the UK raises larger equity concerns. UK universities are also major providers of higher education abroad and India is an important market for such cross border trade. Private providers offering their own or accredited degrees are also emerging as players in the business of trade in education. Carpentier et al. note that research on private educational institutions is in its infancy and little is known about them. They emphasise that given the growing marketisation of higher education, even the introduction of regulatory mechanisms are likely to be inadequate in adressing equity issues.

The non-state sector has played a key role in the spread of education in most countries. In India, the church, indigenous community efforts and philanthropic groups played an important role in spreading education to different social groups during the colonial period and in the early decades after Independence. In the area of special education they were among the first to work with disabled children and are today carrying out innovative work in both India and the UK (Armstrong and Sahoo in this volume). What has been highlighted especially in the contemporary period of globalisation is the marketisation of education — commodification and commercialisation which is seen as inequitous and detrimental to the very purposes of education (Carpentier et al. in this volume).

The Middle Classes and Advantage in Education

The middle classes have been seen to access the lion's share of opportunities that have come with the new economy, using education as a key cultural resource. Vincent and Menon's essay which focuses on the middle classes in England and India suggests that broad generalisations about middle-class advantage would be simplistic. The middle classes have their historical roots, cultural traditions and institutions which influence what constitutes 'middle classness' — respectability, status and opportunity as well as the elements of cultural capital. The origins of the Indian middle classes can be traced to colonial rule when occupations and professions that emerged during the period were accessed through formal education, initially in the medium of English. The post-independence development trajectory and subsequently the new globalising economy has led to the emergence of complex and heterogeneous social groups that comprise fractions of what could be termed 'middle classes'. These include middle-class fractions that have emerged among the SC/ST and OBCs in India and the BME groups in the UK.

The 'making of the middle-class child' in the UK and India is discussed by Vincent and Menon and explored by Kothari (this volume) in a study of a family in a city in India. They show how families strategise to give their children an edge in education and subsequently in the increasingly competitive new economy. The impact of globalisation can be seen in the changing mobility strategies employed by the mother-daughter duo, the focus of Kothari's study. Thus, for instance, the interface between biography and history plays out differently for the mother (old middle class) who raised her daughter in the pre-globalisation period and her daughter who is doing so in the era of globalisation as a member of the new middle class. As members of the middle classes (though belonging to two fractions) they strive to give their children the best that they can by drawing upon economic, cultural and emotional resources within the family. The gendered nature of middle-class advantage in education and the key role of 'mother's work' in building cultural, symbolic and emotional capital for children also finds mention in Vincent and Menon's work as well as Kothari's. There are parallels as well as differences that emerge in the two contexts. This is an area of research that is yet to receive attention in India. Kothari's insights point to the importance of studying the changing 'micro practices' of the middle classes in specific contexts in order to understand the advantages in education and future life chances that children from these families receive.

One of the key cultural resources that give the Indian middle classes advantage in education and occupational opportunities is the knowledge of English language. This links back to the legacy of colonialism and has been critical in accessing of opportunities in post-Independence decades and crucially so after the opening up of the economy. In the global division of labour the flourishing of Business Processing Organisations (BPOs) in India is linked to the knowledge of English that a small (in proportion) but significant (in numbers) section of the population has. English has always created a social divide in India and with the new economy this divide has deepened. English-medium education is seen as important for international migration not only to better educational and occupational opportunities but also for enhanced marriage prospects — with the UK, US and Canada as the preferred destination (Kothari in this volume; see also Chopra 2005).

The State and Education Policy — Convergences and Networks

An important tenet of neoliberalism is the rolling back of the state as the market is seen to be best equipped to take care of the needs of society. The state is seen to be subject to global economic and political pressures and 'education policy is increasingly subordinated to and articulated in terms of economic policy and necessities of international competition' (Ball 2008: 53). From our work we find that both in India and the UK the state is still the main provider of education. Though the marketisation of education has been growing and there are international pressures and commitments that impinge on national education policy, the state has had to also contend with and address aspirations and challenges from within society.

While India is seen as a rising economic power making a presence in the global arena, the state has to contend with democratic politics, pending international social commitments, an increasingly vocal civil society as well as remnants of an ideology of equity/social justice that informed the post-independence developmental project in which nation building has been prominent. We have already referred to the affirmative action programmes, more specifically the reservation policy in educational institutions for SC and ST communities. These policies continue to be implemented during the period of globalisation, in fact, far more stringently than earlier. In the 1990s when the structural adjustment programme was being implemented in India, the government also brought into force the Mandal Commission recommendations for reservations for the OBCs in employment and more recently in educational institutions as well (Lall and Rao in this volume). An earlier commitment of the state, the poor representation of these groups in education and employment, the growing economic and political dominance of sections within the OBCs and larger political considerations of democratic politics were among the factors that were responsible for the implementation of OBC reservations (see Lall and Rao in this volume). Recently, the Right to Education Bill was enacted in the Indian parliament (2009) and has come into force from April 2010. Here again the Indian state was compelled to legislate as it had to contend with and negotiate pressures and commitments — global, national and from civil society. On the other hand Lall and Rao cite Gillborn (2008) to state that 'education in Britain has remained fundamentally racist as none of the policies developed by the government have in any way redressed racial inequalities, largely due to a structure favouring white supremacy.'

Armstrong and Sahoo show how national policy making (in India and UK) in relation to the education of the disabled in the period of globalisation has been influenced by their specific socio-historical experiences, and more clearly by the global disability movement in the last two decades. Inclusive policies are now incorporated within policy texts and legislations in the two countries. However, while policies on education for the disabled today incorporate the language of inclusion, we have seen that they have also to contend with policies that seek to make education systems more competitive leading to selective institutional practices that individualise success and marginalise those who are different. Further, policies of inclusion of the disabled in regular schools are often at variance with local beliefs, norms and practices that may continue to view disability as an individual impairment and family misfortune. Thus Armstrong and Sahoo's essay cautions on the ease with which 'policy borrowing' is made possible by global discourses and translates into national policy without regard for local specific contexts, shared meanings and interpretations.

A complex network of economic and political interests that are linked through transnational networks are driving the advocacy for a policy shift in favour of de-regulation and state-supported choice and vouchers for expanding education among the poor in India (Nambissan and Ball in this volume). Nambissan and Ball's essay suggests that the failure of the Indian state to meet (Education for All) EFA targets for universal primary education is likely to make it increasingly vulnerable to pressures for education reforms such as vouchers. However, as elementary education is still viewed within the discourse of rights and social justice the state is treading cautiously in its official policy documents though unregulated markets continue to expand. Though the state sector is still the main provider of education in the UK, there has been a far greater magnitude of what Ball (2007) refers to as 'endogenous' privatisation especially in England. Commenting on education policy at the end of the first decade of the 21st century in the UK, Maguire (2010: 60) observes that 'Currently, there is a focus on a "for profit element' in state education (Ball 2007) and an approach towards individualising and personalising provision (Clarke et al. 2007). . . . All these different policy shifts are still firmly set within the regulating discourses of economic necessity and of the need for international competitiveness'.

Conclusion

The eclipsing of the social justice discourse in education by one increasingly based on the neoliberal ideology of the market is a reflection of deep-seated changes that are going on in contemporary societies as they are drawn into processes of globalisation and increasing privatisation. In our discussion on education and social justice in India and the UK, we have focused on the 'vernaculars' of globalisation in two countries that share a historical past as also contemporary linkages. While individual contributions show that the state–education relationship is changing in both countries and neoliberal policies in education (more so in the UK) are impacting national education systems, they also highlight the importance of understanding the complex ways in which the 'imperatives' of globalisation are mediated through diverse historical, socio-cultural and policy contexts. On the one hand the state in both countries is bringing in market forces in education not only to maintain a competitive edge globally, but also because of the profit-yielding potential of education as a 'private good'. However, it has also to contend with structural limits to the promise that globalisation and the expanding knowledge economy was projected to offer. Inequalities across and within nations have increased and vast sections of the population in both societies are experiencing the downside of globalisation and changing state policies. In education, social conflict and tensions are likely to increase not only among those who have been historically excluded from education and those who lack the required cultural and social capital, but also among the middle classes who are finding that the returns to higher levels of education are diminishing.

Our contributors have voiced concern about the narrow perspective of human capital and comparative advantage in the global economy that is driving national education policy and the lip service being paid to social justice mainly in terms of expanding provision for hitherto excluded groups. The increasingly differentiated systems of education, the spread of for-profit schooling and tight controls and accountability structures and standardised assessment practices that schools are being drawn into have grave consequences for the purposes of education and social justice. In the contemporary era of globalisation, there is urgent need to reflect on the purposes of education, to build a larger social imaginary in which the public good nature of education (beyond markets, competition and instrumental concerns) finds space. Further to address through evidence-based research, the challenges that state and society face in bringing social justice to education.

+

Notes

1. It was with reference to the destruction of the indigenous system of education that Mahatma Gandhi, speaking before a select audience at Chatham House, London, on 20 October 1931, had observed: 'I say

without fear of my figures being successfully challenged that India today is more illiterate than it was before a fifty or hundred years ago, and so is Burma, because the British administrators when they came to India, instead of taking hold of things as they were, began to root them out. They scratched the soil and began to look at the root and left the root like that and the beautiful tree perished.' See http://voi.org/books/hsus/ch4. htm (accessed 20 March 2010).

2. According to informal estimates after a spate of attacks on Indian students in Australia the proportion of students opting for UK could be higher, around 25 per cent. See http://www.siliconindia.com/shownews/5060_percent_Indian_students_now_prefer_UK-nid-57688.html (accessed January 2011).

References

Altbach, P. G. 1999. *Private Prometheus: Private Higher Education and Development in the 21st Century*. London: Greenwood Press.

Apple, M. 1982. 'Curricular Form and the Logic of Technical Control: Building the Possessive Individual', in M. Apple (ed.), *Cultural and Economic Reproduction in Education*. London: Routledge Kegan Paul.

Ball, S. 1993. 'Education Markets, Choice and Social Class: The Market as a Class Strategy in the UK and the USA', *British Journal of Sociology of Education*, 14 (1), 3–19.

———. 2007. *Education plc Understanding Private Sector Participation in Public Sector Education*. London: Routledge, Taylor & Francis group.

———. 2008. *The Education Debate: Policy and Politics in the 21st Century*. Bristol: Policy Press.

Bartlett, L., M. Frederick, T. Gulbrandsen and E. Murillo. 2002. 'The Marketization of Education: Public Schools for Private Ends', *Anthropology and Education Quarterly*, 33 (1), 1–25.

Brown, P. and H. Lauder. 2003. *Globalisation and the Knowledge Economy: Some Observations on Recent Trends in Employment, Education and the Labour Market*. Cardiff: University of Cardiff.

Chopra, R. 2005. 'Sisters, Brothers and Migration', in Radhika Chopra and Patricia Jeffreys, *Educational Regimes in Contemporary India*. New Delhi: Sage Publications, pp. 299–315.

Exley, S. and S. J. Ball. 2010. 'Something Old, Something New . . . Understanding Conservative Education Policy', available at http://www.social-policy.org.uk/lincoln/ball_exley.pdf (accessed January 2011).

Gamarnikow. E. 2009. 'Education in Network Society: Critical Reflection', in R. Cowen and A. M. Kazamias (eds), *International Handbook of Comparative Education*. London: Springer, vol. 1, pp. 619–31.

Gillborn, D. 2008. *Racism and Education, Coincidence or Conspiracy*. London: Routledge.

Giroux, H. A. 2003. 'Selling Out Higher Education', *Policy Futures in Education*, 1 (1), 179–200.

Harris, S. 2007. *The Governance of Education — How Neoliberalism is Transforming Policy and Practice*. London: Continuum.

Hatcher, R. 2001. 'Getting Down to Business: Schooling in the Globalised Economy', *Education and Social Justice*, 3 (2), 45–59.

Hill, D. and E. Rosskam (eds). 2008. *The Developing World and State Education: Neoliberal Depredation and Egalitarian Alternatives.* New York: Routledge

Kumar, K., M. Priyam and S. Saxena. 2001. 'Looking Beyond the Smokescreen: DPEP and Primary Education in India', *Economic and Political Weekly*, 36 (7) (17–23), 560–68.

Leathwood, C. 2004, 'A Critique of Institutional Inequalities in Higher Education: (Or an Alternative to Hypocrisy for Higher Education Policy)', *Theory and Research in Education*, 2 (1), 31–48.

Maguire, M. 2010. 'Towards a Sociology of the Global Teacher', in Michael W. Apple, Stephen J. Ball and Luis Armando Gandin (eds), *The Routledge International Handbook of the Sociology of Education*. London and New York: Routledge, pp. 58–68.

Olsen, M. and M. A. Peters. 2005. 'Neoliberalism, Higher Education and the Knowledge Economy: From the Free Market to Knowledge Capitalism', *Journal of Education Policy*, 20 (3), May, 313–45.

Reay, D. 2006. 'The Zombie Stalking English Schools: Social Class and Educational Inequality', *British Journal of Educational Studies*, 54 (3), 288–307.

Reay, D., M. David and S. Ball. 2001. 'Making a Difference? Institutional Habituses and Higher Education' (Online), *Sociological Research Online*, 5 (4), available at http://socresonline.org.uk/5/4/reay.html (accessed 20 January 2009).

Rizvi, F. and B. Lingard. 2010. *Globalising Educational Policy.* London: Routledge, Taylor & Francis Group.

Singh, M., J. Kenway and M. W. Apple 2007/2005. 'Globalizing Education: Perspectives from Above and Below', in M. W. Apple, J. Kenway and M. Singh (ed.), *Globalizing Education: Policies, Pedagogies & Politics.* New York: Peter Lang.

Taylor, C. 2004. *Modern Social Imaginaries.* Durham, NC: Duke University Press.

Wrigley, T. 2007. 'Rethinking Education in an Era of Globalisation', *Journal for Critical Education Policy Studies*, 5 (2).

1

Revisiting the Equality Debate in India and the UK: Caste, Race and Class Intersections in Education

Marie Lall and S. Srinivasa Rao

The transition from the post-War welfare state to the neoliberal modes of governance has been accompanied by changing and contested discourses as to what constitutes 'equality' in different societies. Though there have always been disagreements over the definitions and focus of equality, today new groups are demanding inclusion, and developing strategies and demands to define and expand the bases of equality. This has resulted in direct confrontations between beneficiary groups and non-beneficiary groups, which in turn have implications for the way equality is interpreted. This essay thus aims to discuss the shifts and discourses in the way issues of equality are perceived in the realm of education in the United Kingdom and India within the larger backdrop of globalisation and the rise of neoliberal policies. The essay will address the issue of formal labelling and how labels have often subsumed and camouflaged emerging inequalities. Whilst there are differences in the labelling processes and the remedial policies in the UK and in India, there are still notable and interesting similarities in both contexts. The focus here is on how the effects of globalisation, mainly driven by neoliberal forces of privatisation, have caused changes to policies and institutions and to the labelled groups themselves exacerbating the existing inequalities or introducing claims of new inequalities, and how the issues of caste, race and class intersect to further these new claims as well as the persisting inequalities in both school and higher education (HE) in both the countries.

Globalisation is associated with the increasing adoption of market forms for the delivery of services which were once organised by the state and financed through taxation (for example, education, health and other welfare provisions). Many writers such as Ball (2004), Apple (2001), etc., point to the increasing 'commodification' of these services and their penetration by a private sector ethos, either in provision or in sponsorship, or through the organisation of services according to market principles by the introduction of consumer choice. Globalisation has led to the restructuring of the education system at a global level, with the state increasingly taking a back seat, acting more as a regulator rather than a provider (Carnoy 2000). Governments attempt to justify opening up education to corporate capital on the grounds that private sector management methods are best, and that business people are needed to 'modernise' education for a 'knowledge economy' based on information technologies.

There is increased 'policy borrowing' across countries (Halpin and Barry 1995), even if the policies promoted have little relevance to the new context they are being applied to. In this light both India and the UK have experienced increased market logic in their education systems, where results have to be measured and efficiency and effectiveness are the buzzwords of the day. However, many scholars have pointed out that globalisation has led to greater economic and social inequality (UNDP 1999; Apple 2001; Rikowski 2002, etc.). Though educational access has expanded, it has become unequal in quality. As Martin Carnoy (2000) argues, greater decentralisation and privatisation has generally not increased the quality of educational services and has produced more educational inequality. Beyond this we argue here that the effects of globalisation have caused changes to policies, institutions and to the labelled groups themselves exacerbating the existing inequalities.

Caste and Race: Are they Comparable?

Caste and race are both socially constructed systems/institutions of inequality. Caste is the most pervasive dimension of social strati-fication in India. Estimated to be more than 2000 years old, the caste system has undergone several transformations. It is a hereditary, endogamous, usually localised group, having a traditional association with an occupation, and a particular position in the local hierarchy of castes. Relations between castes are governed, among other things, by concepts of 'purity-pollution', 'division of labour', 'segregation', etc.

Those at the top are said to be the most clean and pure such as Brahmins and those at the bottom of the hierarchy are most impure or unclean, like the ex-untouchables.[1] Lower castes are denied equal opportunities in all aspects of social life, including education. However, the recent assertions of dalit identity have raised the level of awareness and consciousness among these groups (Bhambri 2005) to claim their rights as equal members of the democratic society.

Race, like caste is a socially constructed difference, whereby physical and cultural characteristics are used to distinguish one group from another. Whilst the apprtenance to a particular caste group cannot generally be deduced from physical characteristics, race focuses largely on skin colour. The social construction of race has underpinned regimes of domination and control throughout history and across the globe, epitomised by the colonial system. Today critical race theory (CRT) looks at how racism has become a part of society and underpins the domination of the White ruling classes. As Britain undergoes demographic changes with increased migration from different ethnic groups, the question of racism and racial equality has become politically salient.

Berreman (1960) suggests that the two systems are structurally similar though they differ in content and origin. He compares the relationship between 'touchable', especially 'twice-born' and ex-untouchable castes in India with that between African-Americans and Whites in the southern United States. According to him, in both the systems, 'there are rigid rules of avoidance and certain types of contacts are defined as contaminating, while others are non-contaminating' (Berreman 1960: 122). He argues that the ideological justification for the rules differs in the two cultures, as do the definitions of the acts themselves, but these are cultural details. The essential similarity lies in the fact that the function of the rules in both cases is to maintain the system with institutionalised inequality as its fundamental feature. Institutional inequalities are furthermore entrenched through the education system. As Berreman (1960) points out, colour is a conspicuous mark of caste in the west, while in India there are complex religious features which do not appear in the west, but in both cases, dwelling area, occupation, place of worship, and cultural behaviour and so on are important symbols associated with caste status and race. Some other scholars do argue that, 'while the categories of caste and race may not be exactly equatable, nevertheless there can be notable parallels between racism and casteism, both based in ideologies about birth groups, involving notions of purity, and often resulting in social and occupational segregation' (Jenkins 2004: 748).

The debate over comparability of race with caste and racism with casteism took place in the context of the United Nation's World Congress on Racism, Racial Discrimination, Xenophobia and Related Intolerance in 2001. Scholars such as Béteille (2001) argued that racism was based on false science and there are no genetically and biologically different races among human beings. They maintain that caste has nothing to do with race and therefore to include caste in a discussion of racism was erroneous (Béteille 2001). But this view is severely contested by scholars like Gail Omvedt (2001). For her, neither caste as a social system nor racism is based on actual biological differences among human beings. Both, though, are systems of discrimination that attribute natural or essential qualities to people born in specific social groups (Omvedt 2001). She argues that while caste may have nothing to do with race, the justifications of caste discrimination have a lot to do with the social phenomenon of racism.

In both India and the UK the state officially has developed policies to address the discrimination and inequalities vis-à-vis these marginalised caste and racial groups. The paradox of labelling remains as the state tries to overcome discrimination through policies targeted at the labelled groups. Whilst the labelling process is in itself a discriminatory act, it also emerges that certain discrimination and disadvantage falls 'through the policy gaps' whilst simultaneously raising consciousness among the other new groups who aspire to be included into the special state protection regime.

Background to Caste and Race Labelling

In India, the state-sponsored formal labelling process began during the colonial period. The British in India formally introduced the principle of equality of all citizens before law through the Caste Disabilities Act of 1850. As far back as in 1885, the provincial Madras government made a provision for education of children from disadvantaged sections. Later, as a consequence of the non-Brahmin movement, the Madras government reserved positions for the non-Brahmins in government services. Another significant development in the early part of the 20th century was the appointment of a committee (1918) by the Maharaja of Mysore for the upliftment of the non-Brahmin sections of the society under the chairmanship of Sir Lislie Miller.[2] Further, the Montague-Chelmsford Reforms (1919) envisaged representation of deprived sections in several local self-governments and public bodies. Further, the Government of India Act (1935) provided for reservation to the depressed castes in the legislative assemblies of different provinces.[3]

At independence, in India, the caste system and the practice of untouchability was officially abolished and the idea of 'casteless' society was advocated by the newly adopted Constitution. However, the ex-untouchables were formally labelled as 'Scheduled Castes' by the state by incorporating these groups in a Schedule of the Indian Constitution and identifying them on the basis of their economic exploitation, social segregation, occupational stratification and hierarchy based on ritual purity and pollution and socio-cultural oppression. Scheduled Castes are a large and important segment of the total Indian population (around 17 per cent in 2001), which is heterogeneous and whose problems differ from region to region, from urban to rural, and among various sub-castes.

The middle-class intelligentsia from among these groups prefer to describe themselves by the label 'dalit' (depressed), indicating their depressed position as a marker of a new identity. The newly emerging dalit consciousness is complex and encapsulates deprivations stemming from the inhuman conditions of material existence, powerlessness, and ideological hegemony (Oommen 1984: 47).[4] One manifestation of such labelling by the group itself has led to the consolidation of the group internally and emerges as a single unit that could withstand the previous exclusions. A case in point is the emergence of a dalit party, Bahujan Samaj Party (BSP), as a ruling party in the northern state of Uttar Pradesh. Despite such achievements of dalits in the political arena, the practice of untouchability is reported even today in certain parts of the country.

Another social group formally labelled by the state is the Scheduled Tribes, which constitutes around 8 per cent of the total country's population. However, the problems of STs are different from those of SCs. Scheduled Tribes have been traditionally separated in terms of territorial communities. Some of the tribes still live in geographic isolation and are wandering communities, though in recent times, there appears to be an effort at cooption of STs into the fold of settled village social structure and Hindu society.[5] Today, the Scheduled Tribes in certain forest and hilly areas face serious threats of displacement from the mining industry promoted by the neoliberal state. As a result, there has been a huge migration of tribals from their habitat into the urban metropolitan cities, leading a life of misery and deprivation in strange socio-cultural settings. The early categorisations of SCs/STs were largely used to differentiate broad categories from each other; however, the policies were unable to address the diverse needs of these heterogeneous groups. As the economic livelihood of certain small sections of SCs/STs have improved, new, economically less fortunate groups (but not pertaining to the SC/ST categories) have become more vocal, demanding reservations for themselves. This is particularly the case for the Other Backward Classes (OBCs), who are slightly above the SCs and below some of the intermediary peasant castes and are artisan castes such as blacksmiths, barbers, cow herders, washermen, etc. These artisan castes are labelled by the Constitution as 'educationally and socially' backward classes, rechristened as OBCs in popular parlance.

The OBCs are part of the caste Hindu society and suffer less deprivation and exclusion from opportunities compared to SCs/STs. In certain parts of India OBCs are better off than even some of the so-called forward castes in terms of their land holdings, economic well-being, and representation in political power. The current proportion of OBCs in the total population is not known exactly as India stopped recording data pertaining to caste background in the national census after 1931, except for the two labelled categories, namely, Scheduled Castes and Tribes.[6] Despite the presence of credible data, the OBCs' clout in the political elite made them advance their interests in labelling themselves as backward or most backward for coverage under the affirmative action (AA) policies. The Indian case is unique in that the backward/disadvantaged groups are numerically important and have increasing clout, especially in the electoral process. It is interesting to note that the labelling process has helped certain groups to mobilise politically.

The UK, on the other hand, has a history of immigration, which greatly increased after the Second World War as the empire slowly disintegrated. This meant that the many industrialised countries of Europe, including the UK, were in need of labour in the 1950s and 1960s and as a result had to incorporate immigrants from the former colonies such as the Caribbean, the Indian subcontinent and Sub-Saharan Africa. The influx of immigrants from the ex-colonies has changed the demography of the United Kingdom, though the influx has never amounted to more than 4 per cent of the total population of the country during the 1960s (Tomlinson 1984: 23). However, over the last few decades ethnic minority groups have become an important and growing proportion of the population in the UK. The 2001 Census for England and Wales shows that the Black and Minority Ethnic (BME) groups make up almost 10 per cent of the population (Table 1.1). Around half of the BME population lives in Greater London and groups are unevenly spread around the rest of the country with many areas remaining almost completely White.

Table 1.1:   Ethnic Origin in the 2001 Census (England & Wales)

Ethnic origin	Proportion of population
White	91.3%
South Asian (includes Indian, Pakistani and Bangladeshi)	4.4%
Black British (includes Black Caribbean and Black African)	2.2%
Mixed Race*	1.4%
Chinese	0.4%
Other	0.4%

Source: Adapted from BBC News (2003) cited in Lall and Gillborn (2005, NDC report).

Notes: *This is the formal designation as used in the Census although (as noted earlier) there is no such thing as an 'un-mixed race': some commentators prefer the term 'dual heritage'.

The new group of immigrants brought with them their unique cultures and patterns of living into a predominantly homogeneous White Britain and new stereotyped labels began to emerge in British society, the most popular of them being 'Asian' and was mainly 'West Indian'. Moreover, much of the academic literature produced during the 1960s, as Tomlinson (1984) calls it, was 'simplistic' and 'paternalistic' towards minorities, reflecting the general notions of the White majoritarian society. Such a view 'often took a static view of minority cultures, with customs brought by minorities assumed to be unchanging and some of it encouraged stereotyping ... rather than cultural attributes to be respected' (Tomlinson 1984: 22). This has forced the government to start special policies and programmes for the ethnic and racial minorities.

Government policy with regard to race and ethnic minorities went through five policy phases between 1945 and 1997 (Gillborn 2008). Until the late 1950s race was largely ignored by policy. In the subsequent decade assimilationist policies which attempted to reduce to a minimum any ethnic and cultural differences were accompanied by widespread violence against non-White groups. Cultural pluralism became the policy aim in the 1970s and the Race Relations Act (1976) was put in place seemingly improving the situation (but according to Gillborn not altering the fundamental structures). The 1980s were characterised by cultural pluralism and multiculturalism with the first inquiry into race and education acknowledging that racism in schools and society is a factor in Black under-achievement. Under Margaret Thatcher, 'colour-blind' policies which ignored racial diversity were advocated as the new fair way, leading to a new form of racism. According to Gillborn (2008), education in Britain has remained a fundamentally racist system and none of the policies developed by the government have in any way redressed racial inequalities. This is due largely to a structure favouring White supremacy.

In the late 1990s the murder of Stephen Lawrence shed light on a new form of racism, which went beyond the cruder and more violent forms of racism and could not be picked up by labels; this was institutional racism. Institutional racism refers to racism taking place within public services (including the police, housing and education) and was described for the first time in the *Stephen Lawrence Inquiry Report* (Macpherson 1999).

> [Institutional racism consists of the 'collective failure of an organisation to provide an appropriate and professional service to people because of their colour, culture, or ethnic origin. It can be seen or detected in processes, attitudes and behaviour which amount to discrimination through unwitting prejudice, ignorance, thoughtlessness and racist stereotyping which disadvantage minority ethnic people.' (The Stephen Lawrence Inquiry, Macpherson 1999: 28)

Most generally individuals working in those public bodies will not see themselves as racist or recognise that their institution discriminates on the basis of race against others. One of the most significant outcomes of the Stephen Lawrence Inquiry was the extension of race relations legislation to place a positive duty on all public authorities to pro-actively pursue race equality (through the provisions of the Race Relations [Amendment] Act 2000). Regardless of local demographics, all public authorities (including schools, councils and the police force) now have a statutory duty to create a race equality policy, to monitor its effects, and to take action to ensure race equality. This includes keeping a detailed record of the ethnic origin of all staff, students and employees.

When racial monitoring started in the 1980s, the labels were quite crude, with, for example, one general label for all Asians. The disaggregation of racial groups only started in the late 1990s. Full ethnic monitoring of race groups in education and employment started in 2002 and had as a basic purpose of monitoring the inequalities in employment and education. Prior to that, every statistic was based on either separate Local Education Authority data or on research samples. The disaggregation of racial groups has brought about new problems, as various minority groups are compared with each other. This, as shall be seen in the following text has had a particular effect in education.

Yet another form of labelling that is often referred to in the case of the UK is in terms of social class. Social class divisions continue to figure in the public and policy discourses in terms of the varying linguistic and cultural capital, social networks, occupational and educational deprivations or advantages. In fact, it must be recorded that the class connotations continue to dominate the sociological literature on education in the UK. Thus, in predominantly dominant White British society, the labels of working class, middle class or the elite also have serious connotations for the way the issues of equality are understood. The social class analysis of educational contexts in the UK is also often used to examine similar phenomena within the Indian social science discourses reflecting applicability of concepts, theories and policy labels in both the countries.

In the pre-1939 British society, it is known that up to 88 per cent of young people left school by 14 years (Tomlinson 2001a: 2–3). In India, the data on literacy in terms of caste and poverty show the relevance of class analysis to the issue of educational under-achievement. The most significant commonality in both the contexts of the UK and India is that in both countries there is some amount of predictability of groups in terms of their group behaviour in education. For instance, the elite and the middle classes prefer, select and stream into superior and prestigious educational opportunities whereas the working-class minorities are left with or have opted for less prestigious and inferior educational opportunities.

Caste, Race, Class and the Issues of Educational (Dis)advantage

In both India and the UK the state has a commitment to social justice and equality, though the application of specific policies addressing these issues differs widely. In both countries education is seen as a

vehicle for social justice and social mobility. In India, this has resulted
in affirmative action or reservation policies in both higher education
institutions and public sector employment for the SCs/STs, with
the intention of helping them overcome structural discrimination and
social disadvantage. Till 2007, there were no reservations for OBCs
in the higher educational institutions at an all-India level. However,
from the 2008 academic session, a 27 per cent quota for OBCs in
central higher educational institutions across the country expanded
the scope of coverage of preferential policies.[7] In the UK, despite the
absence of a written constitution, an insistence of inclusive education
for all groups developed over the past three decades. The National
Curriculum was introduced in 1988 to which all children and young
people are entitled regardless of ethnicity, linguistic and cultural
background. The state moved away from elite grammar schools to
comprehensive schools, and the discourse of inclusive education was
developed to include the disabled as well as children of all ethnic
backgrounds. However, unlike India, the UK did not develop a set
of affirmative action policies to help those most disadvantaged close
the gap.

The educational achievements of different social groups in India
vary in terms of caste, place of residence (rural and urban), and gender
(Table 1.2). The differences in literacy rates between the SCs/STs
and non-SCs/STs are graded depending on their relative position
in the social structure. One striking fact is that the literacy levels of

**Table 1.2:   Graded Inequalities in Literacy Rates among SCs, STs and
Non-SC/STs in Terms of Rural — Urban and Gender Categories**

Categories	2001	1991
Rural Female ST	32.4	16.0
Rural Female SC	37.6	19.5
Rural Female Non-SC/ST	50.2	35.4
Rural Male SC	53.7	46.0
Rural Male ST	57.4	38.5
Urban Female SC	57.5	42.3
Urban Female ST	59.9	45.7
Rural Male Non-SC/ST	74.3	63.4
Urban Female Non-SC/ST	75.2	67.5
Urban Male ST	77.8	66.6
Urban Male SC	77.9	66.5
Urban Male Non-SC/ST	87.6	83.4

Source: NCERT (2007: 32).

the labelled categories remain far behind the literacy levels of the non-labelled categories indicating uneven access and opportunities to basic education.

The single most important factor for the uneven distribution of educational achievements is the absence of schools in areas which are accessible to SCs and STs. However, in recent years, there has been a thrust on more effective coverage of areas where there is a concentration of SCs and STs in the primary and secondary education programmes in order to provide equal opportunity and access for these hitherto historically excluded groups.

In the UK an achievement gap between White and non-White groups was noted since the time of ethnic monitoring in the late 1980s. In a similar manner to India's labelled categories, the structural inequalities of the system made it impossible for BME groups to achieve on par with their White peers. 'Colour-blind' policies officially seen as 'fair' actually made things worse and forms of affirmative action were needed. The 'achievement gap' between White and Black groups has actually widened between 1989 and today moving from 12 percentage points in 1989 to 21 percentage points in 2004 (Gillborn 2008: 59–67).[8] The emphasis on exam performance and league tables during the 1990s helped widen the achievement gap considerably. Whilst the UK is not measuring educational inequalities on the basis of literacy, inequalities of achievement often mask low levels of literacy and numeracy, especially amongst the most disadvantaged groups.

Research by Gillborn and Mirza in 2000 showed that Local Education Authorities (LEAs) had different views on how to deal with the inequalities of achievement, mostly focusing on increased attainment across all racial groups, yet with no strategies allowing for BME students to be able to catch up or close the gap. In fact, Black pupils suffered considerably from ability setting in the class and a form of 'triage' employed by schools to try and maximise their success on the league tables through improved exam results. In India too, ability streaming and institutional selectivity have become unwritten practices in school education in the wake of competition for monopoly in the educational market. A consequence of such practices is the exclusion of disadvantaged caste, race and class groups. Often pupils, who are perceived as underachieving, do not only not get the help they need, but are not even entered for the same GCSE exams as their White peers (Gillborn and Youdell 2000).

Data from the Department for Education & Skills (DfES) in 2003 shows that Bangladeshi and Pakistani pupils continued to achieve results in school examinations that were, on average, significantly less than those of their White counterparts. The situation was worse for Black (African Caribbean) pupils whose results in the statistics were *less* than they had achieved in the same survey two years earlier (against a backdrop of year-on-year improvements by White pupils) (DfES 2003b and c).

The disaggregation of racial groups, in particular the disaggregation of the 'Asian' group has shown that whilst Black and Afro-Caribbean boys are generally still at the bottom of the pile, they are now joined by Pakistani and sometimes Bangladeshi boys. In *Racism and Education — Coincidence or Conspiracy*, Gillborn (2008) argues that the achievement gap between White and Black pupils has been 'locked in' and that race inequality has today become a permanent feature of the education system.

Figure 1.1: 5 or more GCSE Higher Grade (A*–C) Passes by Gender (Selected Ethnic Groups) England, 2003

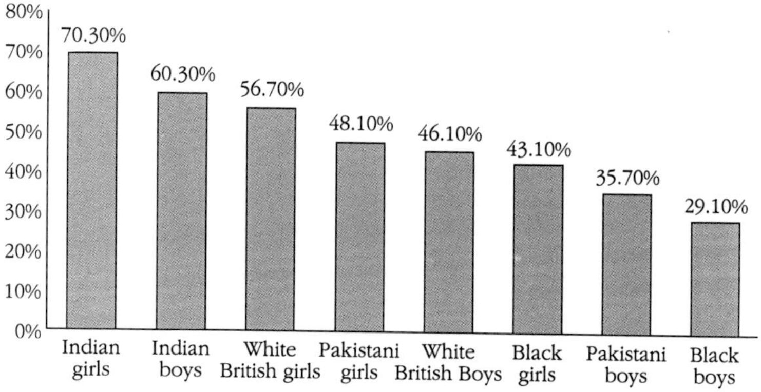

Source: Developed on the basis of Pupil Level Annual School Census (PLASC) data (2003).

Similar issues are apparent in both countries in higher education where the disadvantaged groups who access higher education tend to go to the less prestigious universities.[9] There are, however, also significant differences as certain BME groups are comparatively over-represented in HE. In India there has been a far lower participation of SCs/STs than non-SCs/STs and figures are even worse when looking at their distribution in prestigious faculties and institutions in higher education which are in demand for high salaried jobs (Rao 2002a; Rao 2006; Chanana 1993). A majority of the SC and ST students enrolled at the undergraduate and graduate levels are in the liberal arts faculty. The enrollment in the professional courses for which the job market is attractive is extremely low and the proportion of SC/ST students in the emerging areas of information technology, bio-technology, etc., is negligible. The enrollment of SCs/STs in the central universities and elite institutions such as IITs and IIMs is very low. Thus, inequality has a particularly pronounced characteristic in Indian higher education (Rao 2002a).

In part this is due to the fact that higher education in India is largely urban and the bulk of the SCs/STs live in rural areas and their children are first-generation learners (Rao 2002a). Their parental occupations and education is generally low and they are often engaged in wage-earning agricultural labour or artisanship. Therefore, poverty and lack of economic resources in the family and the utility of extra hands for earning to eke out a living, to some extent, affect the educational chances of the SCs/STs. The stigma of caste/tribe further accentuates the unequal access to educational opportunities among these groups (Velaskar 1992).

Table 1.3: Enrollment of SCs, STs and non-SCs/STs in Higher Education

Year	Scheduled Castes	Scheduled Tribes	Non-SC/STs
1978–79	7.03	1.6	91.35
1988–89	7.29	1.8	90.90
1996–97	7.77	2.73	89.49
2004–05	10.7	3.68	85.60

Source: Rao (2002a: 47) and Government of India (2005).

In the UK the staying on rates in higher education for BME groups is proportionally higher than their White counterparts, in particular for women of Indian origin and men of South Asian (Indian, Pakistani and Bangladeshi) origin. With regard to Black Afro-Caribbean and Pakistani/Bangladeshi women the staying on rates are similar to their White peers in the 16–19 age group (Modood et al. 1997: 76). Modood et al. (1997) attribute this to a desire to acquire qualifications and seeing these qualifications as a means of improving their social standing. The study also brings evidence that children of parents with higher qualifications are more likely to pursue such qualifications themselves. Those of Indian origin were more likely to have parents who had qualifications as opposed to those of Afro-Caribbean, Pakistani or Bangladeshi origin (ibid.: 81). However, especially Pakistani and Bangladeshi students tend to access the new universities as opposed to Oxbridge or the more prestigious Russel group universities (Leathwood 2004; Reay et al. 2005).

In part this is due to the fact that many of the new universities are located in areas where BME communities live (such as East London, or the Midlands belt), allowing students to study whilst living at home. In part it is due to the perception that the elitist universities will not provide the kind of help these students might need in order to finish their degrees. The net result is that once qualified, BME students from new universities are seen as holding second class degrees and are therefore discriminated against in the workplace.

It is important to note in this context that the class barriers among the racial and ethnic minorities further accentuated divisions among groups in terms of their educational achievements. For instance, in the 1960s, the ethnic immigrant minorities were generally from the working class backgrounds irrespective of their place of origin (Caribbean or Asian). A small number of migrant parents attained 'middle-class' status in terms of occupation and income by the 1980s, though a large number continued to be of the working-class background. The shift has also influenced the way a few minorities have come to view education in comparison to others of their own groups. One must, however, understand that the class position of ethnic and racial minorities is complex and is not easily equated with the class position of White parents and that 'the expectations and views of education attributed to working class indigenous (*white*) parents are often not necessarily shared by minority working classes' (Tomlinson 1984: 33).

Overall, it must be noted that the opportunity structures for the elite and middle classes as well as the Whites, on the one hand, and the working-class and immigrant minority groups in education are divergent. Consequently, these divergent opportunity structures prepare both the groups for two different kinds of occupational roles and social class membership in the future, reproducing the very same social structure. As discussed earlier, in the UK, it was only after the 1944 Act came into implementation that the educational opportunities for the working classes widened. The school systems also began to be comprehensive. However, with the introduction of neoliberal reforms in the late 1970s under the market forces, social and economic inequalities dramatically increased and disadvantages enhanced for particular groups (Tomlinson 2001a: 3). In India, as stated before, though the affirmative action policies of the state helped working-class and caste minorities to enter prestigious institutions and courses of study in higher education, there is much to be desired. School education also continues to discriminate against these groups in the neoliberal era which will be discussed in detail later in the essay.

Thus, in both India and the UK, the groups which are most socially disadvantaged have had this disadvantage compounded by the structures in place, despite government discourse to the contrary. Policies — either of reservation or inclusive education — have not led to a substantial change for the majority of these groups. There are of course exceptions — as the next section will discuss. In both countries, the governments have been keen to point to sections of these groups who have moved beyond their original position of disadvantage — the creamy layer and the model minority.

Labels within the Labelled Categories — The *Creamy Layer* in India and the *Model Minority* in the UK

Though there is no notion of a 'model minority' as in the UK, in India, there are certain groups within the disadvantaged, who are far ahead of other members of their own caste/tribe in terms of their economic and occupational status as a result of their access to the educational and employment opportunities through the policy of reservations. They have advanced as a group and have achieved a higher level of mobility compared to others in the group, and are referred to as a 'creamy layer' (Jaffrelot 2003). According to Weisskopf (2004: 35) they are:

> those members of the underrepresented groups eligible for reservations who are very well off in socio-economic terms and who, according to the critics, monopolise the opportunities opened up for reservation policies. Especially, among those who are not eligible and who are concerned about being displaced by the beneficiaries of reservation policies, there is a widespread belief that the beneficiaries come from a 'creamy layer', that is, if anything, more privileged in socio-economic terms than those whom they displace.

In other words, the concept of a creamy layer indicates reproduction within the beneficiary class of exactly the same kind of clustering the reservation is meant to remedy. The policy of reservations in India is found to particularly favour the urban and male students from among the first and second generation beneficiaries of reservations. Thus, the government uses the notion of 'creamy layer' to leave out members of the same caste who acquired economic, social and cultural capital and limits access to opportunities to those who do not possess such capital.[10] In this sense, to a certain extent, caste and class intersections are duly recognised in identifying the potential beneficiary group and non-beneficiary group. The creamy layer principle is applicable only to the OBC category, but not to the SC, ST categories, because the nature and extent of disadvantages and stigma among SCs, STs and OBCs differ.[11] The incidence of poverty is one indication of the relative deprivation that these communities experience (Table 1.4).

Table 1.4: Poverty Ratios among SCs, STs, OBCs, and Others (1999–2000)

Area	SCs	STs	OBCs	Others
Rural	36.3	45.9	27.1	15.2
Urban	38.5	34.8	29.5	15.4

Source: Government of India (2006: 105).

Further, if we look at the caste–class interface in terms of gross enrollment ratios (GERs) in higher education, it becomes amply clear that the enrollment among the poor working-class SCs, STs, OBCs is lower than the non-labelled categories (poor as well as non-poor). For instance, in 1999–2000, the GER of poor SCs was 1.89, poor STs was 1.55, poor OBCs was 2.30 and poor non-SC, ST, OBC categories was 3.58 and the corresponding figures for non-poor among these groups was 6.68 (SCs), 9.70 (STs), 8.69 (OBCs) and 19.73 (non-SCs, STs, OBCs) (Srivastava and Sinha 2008: 107). Such differences in access to higher education lead to the demands for exclusion of the urban, middle and elite class creamy layer, who have already bene-fitted from the higher education provisioning through quota policies, from the state labelling and benefits.

In the UK the labelling of racial groups has been accompanied by the phenomenon of comparing different racial groups with each other. In education in particular, the government has been at pains to point out that certain groups achieve better than others and that con-sequently government policies were not to blame for the continuing and widening achievement gap. This is particularly the case for children of Indian and Chinese origin who tend to perform better than their White peers in GCSE examinations. Official data, for example, confirm that Indian pupils are more likely to achieve five higher grade passes regardless of gender and receipt of free school meals (usually taken as a proxy indicator for family poverty). This is frequently referenced by practitioners and policy makers and there is a danger of Indians being cast in the role of a 'model minority' (Min 2004). This presents considerable problems because first, it risks assuming that Indian pupils face no problems in school, and second, it can be taken to indicate that any relative under-achievement by other minorities must signal an inherent problem with that group rather than a school system which apparently serves the Indian minority so well. It also assumes the heterogeneity of the Indian group, not allowing for differences between those who migrated from East Africa, and those who came from India, or in fact making allowances for class differences.

Earlier the Swann Report referred to a composite 'Asian' group and, whilst criticising the lack of national data, remarked on the apparent similarity between the performance of White and 'Asian' pupils (Swann 1985: 65). The failure to disaggregate 'Asian' populations continued to mask differences in attainment until well into the next decade (Drew 1995). However, an emerging pattern suggested that Indian pupils were the most successful of the 'Asian' groups and, in many areas, achieved results in excess of those of their White counterparts (Gillborn and Gipps 1996: 23–24). This pattern was repeated in the only nationally representative sample of school leavers' attainments, the Youth Cohort Study (YCS), which first disaggregated 'Asian' respondents in its 1992 cohort.

The YCS data paints an interesting picture of growing disparities in performance during the 1990s. In 1992, for example, Indian pupils were just 1 percentage point ahead of Whites in the proportion attaining the benchmark of at least five higher grade GCSE passes, but this gap continued to grow throughout the decade reaching 10 percentage points in 2000 (DfES 2003a). What is more, the gap remains significant even when the data is broken down by gender and indicators of family economic background.

The PLASC data indicates that Indian pupils are more likely to achieve the GCSE benchmark than their White peers of the same gender and free school meal (FSM) status. Indeed, the difference is such that, despite the existence of a 'gender gap' in each group, Indian

Table 1.5: **Five or More Higher Grade GCSE Passes By Ethnicity, Free School, Meals and Gender (2003)**

Group	Non-FSM		FSM		Total	
	Boys	Girls	Boys	Girls	Boys	Girls
Indian	63%	73%	42%	52%	60%	70%
White[15]	50%	61%	17%	40%	46%	57%

Source: DfES (2004: table 40a).
Notes: 'White' is used here to refer to pupils designated officially as 'White British'.

boys achieve better results on average than White girls of the same FSM status. This pattern of relative Indian success has been noted in several reviews of the field (DfES 2003b; Gillborn and Mirza 2000; Richardson and Wood 1999) and is now well established. Indeed, Indian success (along with that of their Chinese peers) is often cited in policy documents, where it is frequently contrasted with the much lower attainments of other minority groups: for example,

> Many minority ethnic pupils have benefited significantly from our focus on standards. The first ever census data on minority ethnic achievement confirms that Chinese and Indian young people achieve better than average GCSE results. But it also shows a long tail of underachievement for many Black and Pakistani pupils . . . (Stephen Twigg MP, foreword to DfES 2003c: 1)

Similar processes have been analysed in the US in relation to Asian Americans, especially those with family origins in Japan and China. Despite its continuing appeal to the US mass media, the 'model minority thesis' (Min 2004) has been heavily criticised by minority scholars, community activists and practitioners. In addition, the 'myth' of Asian success can work against groups who do not achieve so highly (including working-class Whites) by promoting the idea that educational success is solely a product of 'culture' and/or self-discipline and determination (Chang 2000). In India, the application of a creamy layer to the SCs/STs is resisted as it is argued that the economic betterment had not eliminated or reduced the historically entrenched stigmas, which reproduce discrimination in education and employment. The argument of John Ogbu (1992) is interesting in this context. He argues that the minority children do not fail in school because of mere cultural/language differences or succeed in school because they share the culture and language of the dominant group. For example, in the case of Britain, he cites the case of students of Asian origin, for whom the British language and culture are different, who do considerably better, as discussed earlier, than the West Indian students, who have long been privy to the British language and culture.

Thus, the notions of 'creamy layer' or 'model minority' need to be applied carefully if these labels are used as mechanisms of exclusion of certain individuals and groups within the labelled categories from certain affirmative and anti-discrimination provisions of the state. Again, Ogbu's (1991: 6) explanation of variability of academic performance and attainments across caste and racial minority children may help us understand the differences among various groups better. First, the wider societal forces encourage or discourage the ethnic and caste minorities from striving for school or academic success. Second, the dominant explanations ignore the group's collective orientations towards schooling and striving for school and educational success as a factor in academic achievement. They assume that school and educational success is a matter of family background and individual ability and effort. Third, the theoretical explanations and popular arguments fail to consider the minorities' own notions of the meaning of and the 'how-to' of schooling and education in the context of their own social reality.

Globalisation, Social Inequalities and Education

This section will look at the effects globalisation has had on education in both India and the UK, focusing in particular on how the disadvantaged groups discussed in the preceding sections have been affected. The essay argues that policies, institutions and the groups themselves have been affected, with major changes in discourse and state priorities. In both countries those who should be most protected by government policy are those who, despite the labelling regime, have in effect fallen in-between the policy planks.

Effects on Policies and Institutions

Global competition has resulted in an increase in neoliberal policies favouring private sector involvement in both the countries and consequently a shrinking of the state. Assessment has become highly standardised through the introduction of Standard Assessment Tests, and the publication of national performance tables (often referred to as 'league tables' in the UK and institutional accreditation in India) which show the differences between institutions in terms of the achievements in reaching different levels of attainment, creating greater competition among them. The notion of 'parental choice' has become a key theme in government rhetoric, and divisions between schools in terms of social class, performance, and as agents for selective distribution of desirable cultural capital, have become wider and deeper. In the UK, rigorous inspection procedures have been introduced, with poorly performing schools under the constant threat of being taken into 'special measures' or even closed. There have been recent indications of moves to partially privatise sectors of the state education system by transforming some schools, often those deemed to be 'failing' and in economically disadvantaged areas, into quasi-independent 'Academies' and 'Trusts' under the control of managers representing business interests, religious groups and 'philanthropists'.

The introduction of league tables and school inspections has meant that schools now use a form of triage to ascertain their place or increase their success vis-à-vis other schools (Gillborn and Youdell 2000). By setting students according to ability, the school can focus the teacher's resources on the group of students which are seen as to be able to improve their standard with some help. Those at the bottom of the pile are overlooked as they are seen as 'hopeless cases'. However, research data has shown that ethnic minority groups and especially Blacks, Afro-Caribbean and Bangladeshi as well as Pakistani children are over-represented in the lower sets (Gillborn and Youdell 2000). In higher education the labelling policies have resulted in the disproportionate representation of certain groups in the less pre-stigious, post-1992 universities (Leathwood 2004; Reay et al. 2005). In both cases this reinforces the structure that perpetuates inequalities as BME (those not part of the model minorities) groups are not given the required help to overcome the hurdles. The government, however, can point to a widening of access, especially at HE level, which allows larger number of students to study at university. The problem here is that the increased numbers can no longer be separated from the quality.

In India, policies initiated by the state advocate more or less the withdrawal of the state from the business of education in the era of neoliberal reforms. There have been efforts to discredit public educational governance and to introduce public–private partnerships in both university and school education. Certain segments of Indian industry and business, such as the Confederation of Indian Industry (CII) and Federation of Indian Chambers of Commerce and Industry (FICCI) backed by the National Knowledge Commission, actively advocate such models even in primary education, now a fundamental right, which is universal and is completely the state's responsibility. At the same time, the state, in order to meet its political agenda, advocates policies for expanding quota-based affirmative action policies. Since the 1990s, there has been an indiscriminate expansion of private professional higher education in several states which expanded opportunities for the burgeoning middle classes from among the non-labelled castes. The private institutions of higher education are statutorily not bound to implement the quota policy, as a result of which the disadvantaged castes are excluded from the attractive professional education driven largely by the private sector. Though there have been demands for reservations in the private sector higher education and employment (Thorat 2004; Kumar 2005), neither has the state brought in any legi-slation nor has the private sector paid any heed to the demand.

At the school level, access to quality private schooling is denied or restricted to the economically weaker labelled castes as the policy of reservations is not applied to school education. However, there have been demands from civil society groups for a provision of access for deprived groups to elite private schools on the pretext that the state provides free land to private schools. Once the land is provided, schools ignore their commitment to the government to provide schooling for the poorer families in return. This has led to judicial intervention in certain states like Delhi and the state is now asked by the courts to implement a 20 per cent quota of seats in the private schools to provide quality schooling and infrastructure to underprivileged caste and social classes. The provision has been subsequently adopted into the Right to Education Act, which reserves 25 per cent of seats in private schools to children of these groups. However, the experience so for has been that the schooling delivered for those admitted on quota and for those from the privileged home backgrounds is entirely different. The timings of schools and teachers teaching these two groups of children are different, with the less-qualified teaching poor children and the better qualified teaching privileged children of the same school.

In India, increased private sector involvement has also led to an increased hierarchy of institutions between those financed by the state, the private sector and those not for profit. The international competition keeps the pressure on for further expansion, especially in HE in both countries. In both countries the focus is on the achievement of the middle classes as opposed to reaching out to those who are seen as potentially dragging down the achievement levels. Whilst expansion of HE institutions in India and the UK seem at the surface to serve the social justice agenda, the effect on the ground is far more complex. In India the complexity is clearly pronounced in the way the caste and class groups are represented in the private and public institutions, the elite professional and liberal arts and science institutions. For instance, the upper-caste and middle-class children attend the private and professional institutions of higher education and the lower-caste and lower-class children attend the government and liberal arts and science institutions. In the UK a similar effect is taking place as the middle classes monopolise the Russell Group institutions.

Effects on Groups

The main effects of the changes talked of here both at policy and institutional level have resulted in disadvantaged groups no longer being as homogeneous as previously, widening the inequalities across these groups as well as creating intra-group competition. A part of the disadvantaged groups has moved up the class ladder, resulting in changed state behaviour.

The UK is today still deeply divided by class. As the middle classes have developed strategies to harness the benefits of globalisation, the demographic profile of the middle classes has changed as well (Ball 2004). In the UK, for instance, there are certain BME groups, especially those of Indian origin, now belonging to the middle classes. As a result policies which are meant to help disadvantaged groups are seen by the White majority as discriminatory towards them and consequently have led to a backlash. More recent investment in social exclusion by the UK government has in effect focused on White working classes. One example of this has been the high profile New Deal for Communities (NDC), funded by the Office of the Deputy Prime Minister and rolled out across some of the most disadvantaged areas of England. The national evaluation, however, found that apart from the NDC partnerships based in London most of the areas targeted were White with hardly any BME groups benefiting from the funding meant to bring housing, education, health, worklessness and the physical environment up to the standard of the surrounding communities.[12] This was seen as a direct response to demands by the White working class whose discontent had been noted during the Oldham race riots a few years previously.

As such the disaggregation of the BME group with regard to education has also helped the state justify its policies, pointing out that BME under-achievement is limited to certain groups, and therefore is not a reflection on government policy. The model minority thesis, however, masks the increasing inequalities experienced by those outside this new label as well as differences within this group.

In India, globalisation has created strong and aggressive polar opposites of those who support and those who oppose the very idea of caste-based affirmative action as a reaction to the policies. For those who reject AA, the measure is inherently inegalitarian as such a measure favours the less endowed and hence it is a clear case of negation of meritocracy and that caste cannot be the measure of backwardness (Chaudhury 2005). These arguments are accentuated in the light of globalisation as the ideology that governs globalisation itself is premised on such meritocratic principles and nothing else.

Today, the debate is primarily about the very basis of judging disadvantage. There are some who argue that social backwardness is presumed more important than economic backwardness and vice-versa. Most often such debates are politically motivated and there have been no empirically validated arguments or factual data. The opposition to caste as an indicator of backwardness and measure of equality is due to the exclusionary character of the market-driven process of economic globalisation, which is said to be widening the gap between the rich and the poor. Further, an important trend observed in recent times is the expansion of the Indian middle classes manifold and also the expansion of millionaires in the post neoliberal era. For this group, the caste-based reservations work against their interests in two fundamental ways: First, they feel that the reservations would dilute the merit of incumbent employees of their establishments, and second, the middle class, upper castes feel that their cake in the access to higher education is shrunk with the continuing and expanding reservation regimes.

One aspect that seems to be clearly manifested in India at present is the gap between the dalits and the non-dalits in accessing quality school education. While the slightly better-off non-dalit parents send their sons/daughters to the private schools that have sprung up in remote villages, the dalit children are left with no option but to attend the low-quality, poorly equipped, multi-grade, single classroom state-run schools. Nambissan (2006: 243) puts it rightly,

> poor infrastructure, lack of basic amenities, and facilities, as well as adequate number of teachers is a feature of schools that dalit children encounter as they enter government (local body managed) schools. In addition, curriculum is dominated by conventional pedagogy based on the textbook, chalk and talk and absence of relevant teaching aids. . . . This provides an unattractive learning environment for dalit children (the majority of whom enter government schools) and contrasts with the quality of schooling in 'public-private' institutions enjoyed by the more privileged strata.

Wider implications of new state policies in both the UK and India have resulted in claims of exclusion and inclusion and have also increased the competition between various labelled groups as well as competition inside the labelled group. In the case of India, the inter-group inequalities (SC/ST/OBC and non-SC/ST/OBC) are so far given more prominence leaving out the intra-group inequalities. Similarly, in the UK the focus is on comparing Black, Afro-Caribbean, Bangladeshi and Pakistani groups to their Indian counterparts. These broad categories, however, mask internal differences and inequalities, which in the UK are not taken into account. In India, however, inequalities are allowed to persist between sub-groups within each of the categories giving rise to demands for sub-classification of the labelled groups. If one looks at the beneficiary groups within these categories, one finds that some sub-castes are more advanced than the other castes in the same category.[13]

Increasing demands for labelling in India by new groups include disadvantaged religious minorities such as Christians and Muslims. Moreover, there have been demands for inclusion of women into the quota regime, which is promised by every government at the centre, but they fail to deliver due to certain political parties, who argue that there was no such need or that the quota must be further sub-classified in terms of caste as the degrees of deprivations experienced by women of different castes vary. This makes the state policy making a highly complex process, wherein the old groups demand correction of discrepancies in the way the egalitarian policies are implemented and the new groups demanding their inclusion into the special privileges. The contestation is interestingly restricted to the public education and employment sectors whereas, as mentioned earlier, the bulk of expansion is taking place in the private sector in the context of globalisation.

As the state shrinks in both India and the UK, the interests of the upper caste and middle class groups remain intact, whilst the interests of the disadvantaged are competing evermore over an increasingly smaller part of the public pie. Thus, as Tomlinson argues, 'the new framework for funding, administering, and monitoring all aspects of education, and the competition between schools based on parental choice of school . . . gradually introduced new ways of disadvantaging minorities' (2001b: 196). The intention of the educational market in the era of globalisation therefore is to change the balance of power from producers to consumers of education; choice and competition ensure that good '*private*' schools prosper while weaker '*state*' and '*public*' schools close, and ostensibly free consumers are allowed to embrace the laws of the market and the values of self-interest and personal and familial profit (Tomlinson 2001b: 196) (emphasis in italics added). No amount of labelling can remedy this fact as long as the state reduces rather than increases its involvement in education or any other public service.

Conclusions

The focus of this essay has been on how globalisation has affected the discourse and policies around disadvantaged groups in India and the UK in the realm of education. Caste and race are still the key indicators for inequalities in educational access and outcomes. The move of parts of these labelled groups across the class divisions has resulted in elite/well-to-do groups being separated out by the state for different reasons. In India this has resulted in increased conflict within the groups and in the UK a greater neglect for the most disadvantaged in society.

Whilst there are differences in the labelling process and the remedial policies (in the UK race labelling and achievement is monitored at school level, whilst in India the reservation system has more influence at higher education level), there are still notable and interesting similarities. In the UK the labelling of ethnic groups served the purpose to show that certain communities were underrepresented in certain professions, did less well at school or were less well-represented in higher education. Government policies based their logic on the statistics collected across the country in schools, higher education institutions and jobs. These numbers were collected in order to show where things needed to be remedied. In a similar way India's perpetuation of the caste labels has been promoted as the guarantor for groups who have been discriminated against to be granted access in education and employment. However, these very same labels have helped some and, in the case of others, served to increase discrimination and create a new, even more underprivileged, minority.

In the UK as ethnic groups are further disaggregated, the government increasingly justifies its policies as sound as not all groups suffer in the same way. This is particularly the case in the education sector, where Indian and Chinese young people's success is used to vindicate government policy. This has resulted in a pathologisation of those who do not achieve as well, and who are often seen as being at fault for their own plight. In India caste reservation has resulted in a creamy layer in the post-liberalisation era in the 1990s whereby certain sub-groups hold on to the privileges accorded to them by the law, yet not allowing for the trickle down effect to take place in order for the policies to have a more equitable outcome in society. However, the basis of such exclusion is their relative economic well-being and achievement of a middle-class status.

Interestingly, exclusion of the creamy layer of individuals in India or model minority groups in the UK is thought to be ending the effects of caste or race stigma and discrimination, thereby making it possible to achieve a casteless or colour-blind society in respective societies. This argument is contested by the dalit and racial minority groups because caste or racial status is ascribed and will remain with the individual till the end. The complexity of the problem is compounded when globalisation gives rise to the internal inequalities within each of the labelled castes or racial groups.

Further, in the era of globalisation, the educational institutions must expand as well as become socially inclusive (Béteille 2008). The expansion of human capital cutting across racial or caste lines would only enhance the potential of diverse societies such as India and UK to lead the knowledge economies and societies of today and tomorrow. The challenge for both the Indian and the British state is to combine expansion with equity and excellence. This is unlikely to happen if the state's role shrinks further in light of globalisation.

✛

Notes

1. 'Varna' divides the entire Hindu society into four categories in a hierarchy in terms of their occupation. They are Brahmins (the clergy), Kshatriyas (the warriors), Vaishyas (the traders) and Shudras (the peasants). The untouchables are outside the varna system.

2. The Committee recommended that within a period of not more than seven years, not less than half of the higher and two-thirds of the lower appointments in each grade of the service and so far as possible in each office, are to be held by members of the communities other than the Brahmins, preference being given to duly qualified candidates of the depressed classes, when such are available. ('Report of the Karnataka Third Backward Classes Commission', Volume I, Government of Karnataka, Bangalore, 1990, p. 12).

3. The reservations for SCs were made for the first time in 1943 when 8.33 per cent vacancies in government services were reserved for them through a Government Order. In June 1946, this was raised to 12.5 per cent to correspond with their proportion in the population (Chanana 1993: 122).

4. However, Oommen (1984) argues that the dalit consciousness is qualitatively different from the general caste consciousness.

5. In 2002, there was an attempt at the Bhopal conclave of the dalit intelligentsia to bring tribals also into the fold of dalit nomenclature in order to fight jointly against the injustices in the name of caste and tribe (Rao 2002b).

6. However, after a renewed demand and political pressure, the Government of India had in principle, in May 2010, accepted to include caste enumeration as part of the national Census 2011. This may give exact proportions of all the labelled and non-labelled categories in the total population and their relative socio-economic deprivations.

7. While it is for the first time that the OBCs are provided with reservations in admissions to higher education at the national level, different states had varying percentages of reservation for OBCs in their respective states.

8. The only comparative data available to draw comparisons is the Youth Cohort Study which reports on a sample of 16-year-olds and has been collecting data since the late 1980s. The more recently available PLASC (Pupil Level Annual Schools Census) data has only been available since 2002.

9. In the UK less prestigious universities are generally former polytechnics which have been transformed into universities in the early 1990s and which are known as 'new' universities.

10. For instance, children of senior administrative government servants, those employed in public sector undertakings, armed forces, banks, insurance organisations, universities, judiciary, etc. and professionals

such as doctors, lawyers, chartered accountants, income tax consultants, engineers, architects, etc. or big land lords, whose annual income does not cross ₹ 450,000 per annum, form the creamy layer.

11. These parameters were implemented since 1991 when the job reservations for OBCs were introduced by the V. P. Singh government.
12. The national evaluation of the education strand was conducted by Gillborn and Lall between 2002 and 2005. The reports can be found at http://extra.shu.ac.uk/ndc/ndc_reports_01.htm (accessed May 2008).
13. For instance, there has been vertical mobility among members of some castes such as Malas (SC), Patidars (OBC), Okkaligas and Lingayats (OBC), Meenas (ST), Kurmis and Yadavs (OBC), Nadars (OBC), etc. in terms of their occupational and educational status, which led to the creation of a middle class as well as the political and business elite.

References

Apple, M. W. 2001. 'Comparing Neo-liberal Projects and Inequality in Education', *Comparative Education*, 37 (4), 409–23.

Ball, S. J. 2004. *Class Strategies and the Education Market: The Middle Classes and Social Advantage*. London: Routledge Falmer.

Berreman, Gerald D. 1960. 'Caste in India and the United States', *American Journal of Sociology*, 64 (2), 12027.

Béteille, Andre. 2001. 'Race and Caste', *The Hindu*, Chennai, March 10.

———. 2008. 'Access to Education', *Economic and Political Weekly*, 43 (20), May 17, 40–48.

Bhambri, C. P. 2005. 'Reservations and Casteism', *Economic and Politicial Weekly*, 40 (9), 806–8.

Carnoy, Martin. 2000. *Globalisation and Educational Restructuring*. Paris: International Institute of Educational Planning.

Chanana, Karuna. 1993. 'Accessing Higher Education — The Dilemma of Schooling: Women, Minorities, Scheduled Castes, and Scheduled Tribes in Contemporary India', in Suma Chitnis and Philip Altbach (eds), *Higher Education Reform in India: Experience and Perspectives*. New Delhi: Sage Publications.

Chang, R. S. 2000. 'Toward an Asian American Legal Scholarship: Critical Race Theory, Post-Structuralism, and Narrative Space', in R. Delgado and J. Stefancic (eds), *Critical Race Theory: The Cutting Edge*. Philadelphia: Temple University Press, pp. 354–68.

Chaudhury, Pradipta. 2005. 'Does Caste Indicate Deprivation?', *Seminar*, 549, 26–29.

Department for Education & Skills (DfES). 2003a. Youth Cohort Study: *The Activities and Experiences of 16 Year Olds: England and Wales*. SFR 04/2003. London: DfES.

Department for Education & Skills (DfES). 2003b. *Minority Ethnic Attainment and Participation in Education and Training: The Evidence*, Research Topic Paper RTP01-03. London: DfES.

———. 2003c. *Aiming High: Raising the Achievement of Minority Ethnic Pupils*. London: DfES.

———. 2004. *National Curriculum Assessment and GCSE/GNVQ Attainment by Pupil Characteristics, in England, 2002 (Final) and 2003 (Provisional)*, SFR 04/2004. London: DfES.

Drew, D. 1995. *'Race', Education and Work: The Statistics of Inequality*. Aldershot: Avebury.

Gillborn, D. and H. S. Mirza. 2000. *Educational Inequality: Mapping Race, Class and Gender — A Synthesis of Research Evidence. Report #HMI 232*. London: Office for Standards in Education.

Gillborn, D. 2008. *Racism and Education, Coincidence or Conspiracy*. London: Routledge.

Gillborn, D. and C. Gipps. 1996. *Recent Research on the Achievement of Ethnic Minority Pupils*. London: Office for Standards in Education.

Gillborn, D. and D. Youdell. 2000. *Rationing Education*. Buckingham: OUP.

Government of India. 2005. *Selected Educational Statistics 2004–5*. New Delhi: Ministry of Human Resources Development.

———. 2006. *Final Report of the Oversight Committee on the Implementation of the New Reservation Policy in Higher Educational Institutions*. New Delhi: Planning Commission.

Government of Karnataka. 1990. *Report of the Karnataka Third Backward Classes Commission*, Volume I. Bangalore: Government of Karnataka.

Halpin, D and T. Barry. 1995. 'The Politics of Education Policy Borrowing', *Comparative Education*, 31 (3), 303–10.

Jaffrelot, C. 2003. *India's Silent Revolution: The Rise of the Lower Castes in North India*. London: Hurst.

Jenkins, Laura Dudley. 2004. 'Race, Caste and Justice: Social Science Categories and Antidiscrimination Policies in India and the United States', *Connecticut Law Review*, 36, 747–85.

Kumar, Vivek. 2005. 'Understanding the Politics of Reservation: A Perspective from the Below', *Economic and Political Weekly*, 40 (9), 803–6.

Lall, M. and D. Gillborn. 2005. *Beyond a Colour-blind Approach: Addressing Black and Minority Ethnic Inclusion in the Education Strand of New Deal for Communities*, New Deal for Communities (NDC) Evaluation Report. Sheffield: Hallam University.

Leathwood, C. 2004. 'A Critique of Institutional Inequalities in Higher Education: (Or an Alternative to Hypocrisy for Higher Educational Policy)', *Theory and Research in Education*, 2 (1), 31–48.

Macpherson, W. 1999. *The Stephen Lawrence Inquiry*, The Stationary Office, London. Available at http://www.archive.official-documents.co.uk/document/cm42/4262/4262.htm (accessed May 2008).

Min, P. G. 2004. 'Social Science Research on Asian Americans', in J. A. Banks and C. A. M. Banks (eds), *Handbook of Research on Multicultural Education*. 2nd edn. San Francisco: Jossey-Bass, pp. 332–48.

Modood, T., R. Berthoud, J. Lakey, J. Nazroo, P. Smith and S. Virdee. 1997. *Ethnic Minorities in Britain*. London: Policy Studies Institute.

Nambissan, Geetha B. 2006. 'Terms of Inclusion: Dalits and the Right to Education', in Ravi Kumar (ed.), *The Crisis of Elementary Education in India*. New Delhi: Sage Publications, pp. 224–65.

NCERT. 2007. *Position Paper of the National Focus Group on Problems of Scheduled Caste and Scheduled Tribe Children*. New Delhi: National Curriculum Framework 2005.

Ogbu, John U. 1991. 'Immigrant and Involuntary Minorities in Comparative Perspective', in Margaret A. Gibson and John U. Ogbu, *Minority Status and Schooling: A Comparative Study of Immigrant and Involuntary Minorities*. New York and London: Garland Publishing Inc, pp. 3–33.

———. 1992. 'Understanding Cultural Diversity and Learning', *Educational Researcher*, 21 (8), 5–14 and 24.

Omvedt, Gail. 2001. 'The UN, Racism, and Caste II', *The Hindu*, Chennai, 10 April.

Oommen, T. K. 1984. 'Sources of Deprivation and Styles of Protest: The Case of Dalits in India', *Contributions to Indian Sociology (n.s)*, 18 (1), 45–61.

Rao, S. Srinivasa. 2002a. 'Equality in Higher Education: The Impact of Affirmative Action Policies in India', in Edgar Beckham (ed.), *Global Collaborations: The Role of Higher Education in Diverse Democracies*. Washington D. C.: Association of American Colleges and Universities, pp. 41–62.

———. 2002b. 'Dalits in Education and Workforce', *Economic and Political Weekly*, 37 (29), 20 July, 2998–3000.

———. 2006. 'Engineering and Technology Education in India: Uneven Spread, Quality and Social Coverage', *Journal of Educational Planning and Administration*, 20 (2), 205–25.

Reay, D. M. David, and S. Ball. 2005. *Degrees of Choice: Class, Race, Gender and Higher Education*. Stoke-on-Trent: Trentham Books.

Richardson, R. and A. Wood. 1999. *Inclusive Schools, Inclusive Society: Race and Identity on the Agenda*. Report produced for Race on the Agenda in partnership with Association of London Government and Save the Children. Stoke-on-Trent, Trentham.

Rikowski, Glenn. 2002. 'Globalisation and Education', a paper prepared for the House of Lords Select Committee on Economic Affairs, London.

Srivastava, Ravi S. and S. Sinha. 2008. 'Inter-group Disparities in Access to Higher Education', in University Grants Commission, *Higher Education in India: Issues Related to Expansion, Inclusiveness, Quality and Finance*. New Delhi: UGC, pp. 103–10.

Swann, Lord. 1985. *Education for All: Final Report of the Committee of Inquiry into the Education of Children from Ethnic Minority Groups.* Cmnd 9453. London: HMSO.

Thorat, Sukhadeo. 2004. 'On Reservation Policy for Private Sector', *Economic and Political Weekly*, 39 (25), 2560–563.

Tomlinson, Sally. 1984. *Home and School in Multicultural Britain.* London: Batsford Academic and Educational Ltd.

———. 2001a. *Education in a Post-welfare Society.* Buckingham and Philadelphia: Open University Press.

———. 2001b. 'Some Success, Could Do Better: Education and Race 1976–2000', in Robert Philips and John Furlong (eds), *Education Reform and the State: Twenty Five Years of Politics, Policy, and Practice.* London and New York: Routledge Falmer, pp. 192–206.

UNDP. 1999. *Globalisation with a Human Face.* New York: Human Development Report, UNDP.

Velaskar, Padma. 1992. 'Unequal Schooling as a Factor in the Reproduction of Social Inequality', *Sociological Bulletin*, 39 (1&2), 131–46.

Weisskopf, Thomas E. 2004. *Affirmative Action in the United States and India: A Comparative Perspective.* London and New York: Routledge.

2

The Educational Strategies of the Middle Classes in England and India

Carol Vincent and Radhika Menon

> This increasingly interconnected world — of commerce and capital coupled with new patterns of emigration — means that social class is being produced and realigned everywhere. (Weis 2008: 4)

Lois Weis, an American sociologist, here highlights the effects of globalisation on the way in which social class is produced and maintained in different sites around the world. In this essay, we wish to explore social class — specifically the characteristics and behaviours of the middle classes in England and India — against the backdrop of a globalising world. We agree with Weis when she argues that class is an indispensable focus for analysis because it 'organises the social, cultural and material world in exceptionally powerful ways' (2008: 2). We are focusing on the middle classes because of their role in creating hegemonic discourses, which value and legitimate only certain people, certain ways of being and behaving, and certain attitudes (Sridharan 2004, Skeggs 2004, Kothari this volume). The two countries provide a useful contrast — one, England, with established middle-class groupings, the other, India, with a burgeoning middle-class populace. It has been suggested that the sheer size and vitality of the 'new' middle classes in India presents a labour market threat to the middle classes in established industrialised countries such as the US and the UK (Weis 2008; Fernandes 2006). As Weis (2008: 3) comments,

> This evolving set of international economic and human resource relations affects the educational aspirations and antipathies of younger generations in a variety of [labour] exporting and importing countries. . . . The push and pull dynamics of globalization (in the sense of pushing certain kinds of jobs outside the borders of first wave industrialized nations whilst simultaneously pulling such jobs to nations such as China and India) exert particular class-linked forms of pressure on schools,

families and youth — forms of pressure that are shared in a wide variety of nations, although locally specific iterations are obviously important.

Weis's words draw attention to the way in which perceptions of changing labour markets influence the education of the young. In order to give some form and colour to 'locally specific iterations' we will in this essay interrogate class-based attitudes, and specifically, the practices, priorities and preoccupations of the middle classes in India and England with regard to education. We consider some of the ways the middle classes in India and England seek to prepare their children for life in a global market place, a market place that is frequently perceived as congested, but also as offering opportunities to participate in and benefit from the profits of capital mobility. Education is commonly seen in developing and developed countries as the key to reaching and then staying in the middle classes. However, parental perceptions, both in England and India, of acute competition in education and labour markets result in much anxiety, insecurity and strategising around education. This essay will focus on the following issues: the definitions of the middle classes in use in both countries, their prioritising of education and the results of that prioritising on the character and functioning of school systems in England and India, with particular reference to parental choice of school, and finally, the ways in which parents seek to develop and support their child's skills and abilities in order to 'make up' the middle-class child. The essay draws on recent research conducted in England and India, including data collected by Carol Vincent and Stephen Ball on the extracurricular activities arranged for young middle-class children, and exploratory work on schooling and extracurricular activities amongst the middle class conducted by Radhika Menon.[1]

Identifying the Middle Classes

The recent history of class analysis and class theory is fraught, disputatious and complicated, but not altogether unproductive (see Savage 2000 for an excellent overview). Within this history there has been a particular and growing attention paid to the examination of the middle class, as 'the new collective subject on the historical stage' (Lockwood 1995: 10). This attention is not simply focused on England. The emergence of a 'new' middle class in some of the world's key developing countries has also been up for economic and social comment, with India providing a major example of this global development (Sridharan 2004; Fernandes 2006; Scrase 2006).

In both England and India identifying the 'middle class' is complex and contested. Even the terminology is contested, although many theorists in both countries argue that the middle class is internally differentiated so that the term 'middle classes' is more accurate (Fernandes 2006; Savage et al. 1992; Deshpande 2003).

In India, the measurement of 'middle class' in economic surveys uses both purchasing power as indicated by income as well as consumption expenditure.[2] Deshpande (2003: 132–40) argues that consumption categories make problematic classifications in India and estimates that the size of this class hovers around 10–15 per cent of the population (ibid.: 138). Arun Kumar (2008) estimates this to be even less, at around 3 per cent, arguing that far from the middle, it is actually the elite of the Indian society. In India defining difficulties extend beyond the actual location of the middle class, its size, to inequities that exist as a result of privileges generated from gender, caste, regional, religious and linguistic locations.

Globalisation and economic liberalisation have increased the internal differentiation of the middle classes (Deshpande 2003; Fernandes 2006) with the fractions periodically facing conflicts of interest (Scrase 2006). During the early years of Indian independence the middle class mostly consisted of professional and commercial classes working with the government sector and only a small section came from the industrial entrepreneurs (Mishra 1961). In contrast to this, the post-liberalisation middle class substantially includes those sections of the entrepreneurial class who have gained from the downsizing of the government sector and the restructuring of the Indian economy. Fernandes (2006: xviii) defines this 'new' middle class as that section which 'largely encompasses English-speaking urban white collar segments of the middle class who are benefiting from new employment opportunities (particularly in private sector employment). It is a section that is marked by its social and cultural visibility in present day India.'

A key definition of middle class in the English context is Goldthorpe's classification of 'the service class' (Marshall 1998). These are managers and professionals, who enjoy a high degree of flexibility, autonomy and discretion. They have a first degree and often some post-graduate education. However, this categorisation has been criticised for being too broad, amalgamating a capitalist elite and a wider body of professional and managerial employees at different levels of seniority (Marshall 1998), and later theorisation concentrates on defining class fractions within the service class (see below).

There is also, in the UK context, the 'intermediate' class, positioned between the middle classes and the working classes. This is a class grouping much neglected in research. These are people (the category includes a higher percentage of women) who work in routine non-manual jobs, clerical and administrative work. The intermediate class is in itself heterogeneous, and therefore some groups within it may be closer to the middle classes or alternatively to the working classes. In one of the few pieces of recent qualitative research which considers the intermediate class, Ball et al. (2008) argued that those within their group of respondents who had 'intermediate' class jobs had other characteristics, other forms and volumes of (social, economic, cultural) capital which placed them closer to those respondents whose (semi/unskilled) occupation categorised them as working class. These characteristics included, for example, close and local family networks, shaky and uneven knowledge and resources with which to negotiate, for example, school choice systems and procedures, limited financial resources, and dependence on state benefits. This uncertain class position, this 'inbetween-ness', reflects some of the emerging social groups in India, precariously seeking (see reference to 'seekers' and 'strivers' later) but not always succeeding in attaining and maintaining a new middle-class identity.

As implied earlier, social class is routinely 'read off' from occupation and/or income. However, it is important to note that more complex definitions rely on an understanding of class as more than an objective social category. Stephen Ball (2003: 175–76) argues,

> Class identities are not to be found within talk about categories, but in practices and accounts of practices — in practices of distinction and closure. . . . This is a view of class as relational, emergent, contextualised, dynamic, localised and eventualised. Class is not the membership of a category or the simple possession of certain capitals or assets. It is the activation of resources and social identities, or rather the interplay of such identities in specific locations for particular ends.

It is our contention from the evidence available to date in England and India that the social field of education is one whereon 'practices of distinction and closure', that is practices of differentiation and exclusion, are played out by differently situated families. In the field of education, for example, our argument is that families use their different cultural social and economic resources in order 'to preserve their relative social standing and capacities for upward mobility' (Fernandes 2006: xxx). We will consider the specific strategies in which they might engage later. Liechty takes up Ball's notion of understanding class through the study of such practices, and argues for the importance of the concept of 'cultural space'.

> The experience of class is bound up with ways of doing and being, practice and performance, then the outcome of that doing and being — the product of class cultural practice — is cultural space. (Liechty 2003: 255)

He defines cultural space as 'a space in which specific claims to value, meaning and reality are lived out and naturalised in everyday practice. Thus class is never a thing, always a process' (2003: 85). As Skeggs (2004: 3) notes, 'class is in continual production'. She continues 'class is not a pre-existing slot to which we are assigned but a set of contestable relations' (2004: 117). This means the middle classes are involved in a struggle to validate themselves and their way of life as normative, whilst making clear the distinction and separation between themselves and the working classes. Education is a key arena for that struggle.

Class Fractions

Some of the recent key debates around the definition of the middle classes take up this question of how class is performed, and whether there are variations in values, lifestyles, political preferences and social relations, and if so whether these are significant enough to identify a set of distinct fractions (the 'middle classes', rather than 'the middle class'). Debate has also focused on how such fractions can be understood. Research in England has explored differences in values, behaviour and attitudes stemming from occupations (e.g., Crompton 1995; Devine 2004) and more recently from lifestyles (Savage 2000; Savage et al. 2003), and the localities in which people choose to live (Butler and Robson 2003). All these variables appear useful analytically. The nuances of difference within the middle classes are expressed occupationally, through consumption patterns, and also spatially, as different localities appeal to different middle-class groups (ibid.).

Market-oriented research, in India, focusing on lifestyle and consumption of middle classes has also produced descriptions of behaviour, particularly consumer behaviour, of various fractions (McKinsey 2007; Farrell and Beinhockcr 2007). These studies link income differentials with concomitant consumer behaviour. 'The seekers' are said to range from young college graduates to mid-level government officials, traders and business people who possess a television, a refrigerator, a mobile phone and perhaps even a scooter or a car. Their budgets are stretched but they scrimp and save for their children's education and own retirement. The 'strivers' are said to be senior government officials, managers of large businesses, professionals and rich farmers who are successful and upwardly mobile and are highly brand conscious, buying the latest foreign-made cars and electronic gadgets. They are likely to have air conditioning, and can indulge in an annual vacation within India. The third category is of the global Indians, whose tastes are indistinguishable from those of prosperous young westerners (see Farrell and Beinhocker 2007 for this classification).

Consumption-based classifications of the middle classes are contested in the UK (see Chan and Goldthorpe 2007; Le Roux et al. 2008 for discussion). In India, as pointed out earlier, there is a great deal of dispute over the reliability of identifying social class on the basis of consumption and lifestyle given the cultural complexity and diversity in the country. It has been observed that the outcome of the same economic process could have different cultural responses depending upon socio-political factors. For instance, Hasan and Menon (2005) found Muslim middle-class women increasingly adopting the veil as they began to access education and employment and entered the public sphere. Other dimensions, in addition to occupation, that affect lifestyle and consumption in India include the rural/urban divide and differentiation based on the language commonly adopted for social interaction (Deshpande 2003). Most notably there is caste, although caste and class do merge in India, with the middle classes of the higher echelons coming predominantly from the upper caste. However, policies of positive discrimination like 'reservations' have made a dent and led to some social mobility for those lower down in the caste hierarchy (see Lall and Rao in this volume).

Thus in both countries we see that occupation and income remain major categorisations for classifying the middle classes. However, in both countries, these measures alone are inadequate and education, locality, lifestyle and consumption, besides language use and caste in India, remain crucial to the understanding of social location.

The Morality of the Middle Classes

In India, the post-liberalisation period has led to tremendous changes within the social fabric and concomitant class behaviour and attitudes, with a number of commentaries being written on the subject. Nandy (2008), in a highly polemical public debate, suggested that there is a crisis of values emerging from the urban middle class's conservative social-political positioning; Fernandes (2004) has referred to a 'politics of forgetting', that is, forgetting the marginalised sections of society that have not benefited from the market. Wessel (2004) notes an acceptance of increased consumption but with tremendous amount of moral unease, thus indicating a conflict with the high morality of traditional social norms. Therefore, though tentative, the descriptions available of the behaviour of the middle classes indicate a tendency to place the individual or self before the collective.

The morality of the middle classes has also been a topic of interest for sociologists in the UK (e.g., Skeggs 2004; Lawler 2005; Sayer, 2005). In England, Bill Jordan and colleagues (1994) and Stephen Ball (2003) have argued that middle-class families' moral narratives are underpinned by an individualistic discourse of 'putting the family first'. Jordan and colleagues note that this can be understood as a 'distinctive culture — one that prioritized the family as a . . . setting for the pursuit of self-making', that is, making something of oneself, and by extension, one's children (Jordan et al. 1994: 6). A key part of 'putting the family first' is securing children's access to a 'good' education, and it is to this that we now turn.

Education and School Choice

State/private schooling

Education is understood by the middle classes (and others) to be of crucial importance to life chances. In the context of an increasingly globalised world, and perceived congestion in labour markets, the task of finding the 'right' kind of education and school generates anxiety and uncertainty in middle-class families (Ball 2003). The privileging of private schooling — understood as promising exam success and the company of other similarly advantaged peers — is an issue affecting the education systems of both countries. In the

UK private education is largely the preserve of privileged elite, and therefore state education is still widespread. There are approximately 7 per cent of pupils nationwide in the private system, although this varies considerably from area to area. In London, for example, 20 per cent of school children are in the private system (Machin and Wilson 2005). Middle-class parents in state schools typically feel that they have to compensate for any perceived educational inadequacies by monitoring their children's progress and by being ready to intervene if necessary — a process Vincent and her colleagues refer to as 'risk managing' (Vincent 2001).

In India, the choice of private schooling was historically a means for educating children for a position in public/government service at the higher echelons (see John Sargent's Report of 1944 for a comment on the product of such schools). But in the last couple of decades, increasing awareness of education's role in social mobility alongside neglect in the state provisioning of free and compulsory education of equitable quality have made parents resort to private schools for securing education for their children. The overall student enrolment in privately managed schools (both aided and state-aided) is claimed to be 22.5 per cent (ASER 2008). Earlier NCERT (2002) had estimated 19.5 per cent of all secondary schools as being private and 26.25 per cent of the schools as private-state-aided schools. In the meantime, there has been an expansion in the kinds of private schools available in India (Nambissan and Ball, this volume). Fernandes (2006: 131) argues that the middle classes in India have 'increasingly resorted to privatized strategies designed to give individual benefits rather than through organized political pressure on the state' and that 'everyday forms of privatization in arenas such as education and healthcare are part of the broader pattern of privatized middle class strategies designed to give upward mobility through the acquisition and deployment of various forms of social, cultural and economic resources' (ibid.: 132). Béteille (2008: 44) comments that the middle classes are enthusiasts of differentiated schooling as it equips their children with better credentials, thereby giving them an edge in the employment race. In the UK the same middle-class desire for differentiation is apparent, and has affected the policies of the recent Labour government, keen to keep the middle classes within the state education system. Thus successive policies have encouraged differentiation in state school type, and schools choosing a specialism (in a particular area of the curriculum). The coalition government elected in May 2010 is intensifying the focus on differentiated provision, by making it easier for parents, teachers, businesses and charities to establish their own schools. State policy prescriptions have swerved around similar lines in India too, particularly after the National Policy of Education 1986, when differentiated educational provisioning under the category of Pace Setting Schools was introduced within the state system for 'talented children' from rural areas (see National Policy of Education 1986: Section 5.14 and 5.15). In recent years differentiation has increased on a number of counts both within the state as well as in the private sector. Initiatives vary from the infrastructure provided, to the medium of instruction, to curriculum and examination boards, to fees charged (Kumar 1987; Velaskar 1992). This has led to social class differentiation within the school composition and increasing homogenity of each type of school as a result of costs of schooling and medium of instruction (Velaskar 1992; Chitnis 1987). A fall out of this school differentiation has been the greater involvement from parents in decisions associated with school education.

Possessing and Activating Resources for Choice-making

The research on school choice presents a clear picture of opportunities shaped by differential parental resources, attitudes and values. Qualitative studies in England show that the concept of choice of school has, in the 20 years since the reforms of the 1980s which mandated parental choice, become embedded. Thus most parents are familiar with the idea that they can choose a school.[3] The argument that choice is a chimera is also familiar. Parents can see how popular schools in any one locality become heavily oversubscribed, attracting potential pupils away from less popular ones. Thus parents anxious to secure a place at a particular school can become involved in a variety of legal and non-legal strategies in order to do so.[4]

Parents choosing schools in England have access to 'cold' data (Ball and Vincent 1998), that is, apparently objective and publicly available data. This includes 'league tables' which list school performance in nationally administered exams and tests, the reports of the school inspectors, Ofsted, and the brochures and prospectuses of individual schools. However, research into school choice also suggests that 'hot' knowledge is highly influential (Ball and Vincent 1998; Ball 2003). The term denotes knowledge and information gleaned from networks of friends and acquaintances, and deals with more intangible indicators like whether other similar families use the school, a school's 'feel', its parent–teacher relationships, and the characteristics and behaviour of the potential peer group. Perceptions of the latter are particularly influential (Ball 2003).

Similarly, in India, school differentiation has meant that parents are increasingly required to deliberate on suitable schools for their children and different fractions of the middle classes have found different ways to engage with this task. In a study of upper middle-class parents in Delhi, Waldrop (2004: 208) found that parents started their search for an appropriate school for their child early and keenly followed school reputations based on 'all-India exam results' and 'rumours of the cultural taste of the families of children admitted in the school'. They also mobilised their social networks and worked towards getting admission to a particular school where an elite homogeneity was maintained. Nambissan (2010) has cited studies by Donner (2005), Benei (2005), Drury (1993), Scrase and Scrase (2009) and Upadhya (1987) to describe the middle classes' ways of 'choosing a right school' for their child. This includes choice of English-medium schools (Drury 1993) amongst wealthy business families of Kanpur city (in the northern Indian state of Uttar Pradesh) and the movement of the lower middle classes to private unrecognised schools away from state-funded schools. She also points to the selection of English-medium schools over Bengali-medium schools by the middle classes of Kolkata (in the eastern state of Bengal) as indicated by the studies of Scrase and Scrase (2009) and Donner (2005) along with a growth of private tuitions for English learning to keep up with this rage for English-medium schools. At the same time though, in India the resources available for school choice appear to be influenced by caste and gender factors within the same middle-class group. Dreze and Gazdar (1997), in a study of Uttar Pradesh, find that school attendance in private schools is 'significantly male dominated as parents are more willing to pay for male children'. This gender bias is affected by the traditional view that boys will enter the employment market and it is their occupation that would impact future class position of families. (For a discussion on middle-class girls and education, see Kothari in this volume). Balagopalan and Subrahmaniam (2003) have indicated exclusions and clustering of children from specific caste groups in certain kinds of schools. (For a discussion on caste and education see Lall and Rao in this volume.)

Choice policies have come in for widespread criticism in England, as parents bring differential forms and kinds of social, economic and cultural resources to bear on the issue of choosing a school. For example, there is a body of English research which shows that middle- and working-class parents are differently oriented towards choice (e.g., Gewirtz et al. 1996; Reay and Ball 1997; Reay and Lucey 2003; Vincent et al. 2010). In research carried out in London in the early 1990s, Ball and colleagues (1996) drew a distinction between middle-class 'cosmopolitans' willing to research several schools from a wide area, and able to manage the transport implications of the child attending far-flung schools, and working-class 'locals', who did not consider schools outside their immediate area, and typically started with a choice of two institutions.

The same team later put forward a threefold division of parents based on their ability and willingness to engage in school choice (Gewirtz et al. 1996). Parents came from both middle- and working-class backgrounds. In their sample, the *privileged/skilled choosers* were overwhelmingly middle class. These parents valued choice of school and considered their options over a long period of time, and they had the economic, social and cultural capital necessary to engage with the possibilities of choice. They discussed school practices and policies in detail. They often found trying to choose a school anxiety-provoking, and were uncertain as to what to decide. The *semi-skilled choosers* were a mixed social class group who had 'strong inclination but limited capacity to engage "effectively" with the market' (Gewirtz et al. 1996: 40). They did not have the knowledge or contacts around education and schools that the first group often had, and felt themselves to be 'outsiders' looking in on the education system (ibid.: 43). The third group who were working class were termed '*disconnected*', not inclined to engage with the market in education, and prioritising instead the facilities of the school, the safety of the journey there, the convenience of the school's location and its familiarity (e.g., if the child had friends going there, or family members/neighbours attended). They were less likely to visit schools in advance of their choice, or identify a large number of schools to choose between. All groups, however, if they did visit schools, highlighted their affective responses as an important part of their decision.

Mike Savage and colleagues (2003) conducting research in different localities within Manchester, found similar differences. They argued that in comparison to middle-class parents in affluent areas of Manchester, for the less mobile and affluent residents of another locality, Cheadle, 'education provoked much less debate with a more passive acceptance that the local schools were "ok" or even good' (ibid.: 70). Therefore this body of research clearly illustrates that as a result of cultural, social and economic resources which are differentially distributed throughout society, some parents are in a better position than others to make a choice of a 'good' school and to see that choice realised. As a result choice policies are responsible for a new set of inequities impacting on families.

Choosing a Particular Type of Education

In post-colonial India, education, and in particular, familiarity and ease with English, represents an indispensable tool for advancement. A command of English is widely regarded in India as a tool of social mobility, but also a 'requirement to maintain social status' (Dewey 2006: 222; Liechty 2003). Therefore, for many middle-class parents a key requirement for their children's education is that their children emerge fluent in English (Kothari in this volume; Nambissan 2010). A recent ethnographic study of an elite school in Bombay highlights the way in which 'English language schools, commonly referred to in India as "English medium", function as symbolic capital' (Dewey 2006: 215). 'In many ways English language education serves as the primary means by which the dominant social order maintains and reproduces itself in India' (ibid.: 217). Dewey also discusses the way in which English is positioned as the language of the urban elite, marginalising Hindi as the language of the rural, lower status 'other' (also see Kumar 1987; Velaskar 1992). As a result of this emphasis on the need for fluent English for success in a global economy Fernandes (2006: 133) notes a steep decline in local vernacular municipal schools.

Choice research in England suggests that 'matching' the interests and personality of the child with a school is important to many middle-class parents. However, there is a limit to the degree to which this can be done within a state sector dominated by the National Curriculum. Some secondary schools have specialist status in a particular area (e.g., performing arts, business, etc.) which means they have specific resources and expertise in that area, but despite this there is an overall similarity rather than a diversity of provision. There is more diversity in the private system, but the most elite private schools are heavily academically oriented. In India, Waldrop (2004) observes that within the private sector, academics and other professionals with higher university degrees preferred schools for their children that were of a 'new attitude', with 'an equal stress on maths and music', with less academic orientation and which discouraged learning by rote.

The primary data tables of a study (Pramanik 2007) located in the eastern Indian state of Orissa indicate that of the three kinds of schools with different public examination boards and syllabus, the middle- and higher-income groups with small families chose private ICSE and CBSE schools while lower-income groups with larger families chose state-funded HSC schools — this is also seen by Jeffery and Jeffery (2005), who found an increased preference for private schooling amongst small-town middle-class people of Uttar Pradesh.[5] The ICSE and CBSE offered education in English and a larger number of students participated in academic and sports activities. Children of these schools also had private tutoring apart from home and class work and students spent a substantial part of their time at home studying. The students in HSC schools on the other hand were engaged in a greater number of religious activities and household chores. The HSC students got either no additional skill training or attended singing and dancing classes while ICSE and CBSE students attended computer and karate classes. It could safely be assumed that the extracurricular interest in computers has its origins in the association of computers with employment prospects in India. Pramanik's study (2007) seems to indicate that higher-income parents, by choosing ICSE and CBSE for their children, are possibly consolidating their social and economic resources in order to give their children a competitive edge.

Exclusion

In terms of exclusion, there are issues in both countries. Selective admissions to schools derive both from parental strategising and also from the actions of schools themselves, as staff try to identify the most desirable pupils. In England, there has been a long-running debate arguing over the extent to which schools — particularly those in urban areas where the density of population requires several schools in one locality — are becoming more socially polarised, as a result of parental choice and competition over places (e.g., Allen and Vignoles 2007). State schools' ability to select pupils is now heavily restricted as a result of a Code of Practice on school admissions, put in place by the last Labour government to try and stop schools 'cream skimming' desirable pupils. These are children assumed to be the most worthwhile investment as pupils, in terms of the ratio between teacher effort and success measured in exam results.

In relation to India, Waldrop (2004) concludes, based on the Delhi study, that there is a class segmentation, as early as nursery admissions (see Vincent and Ball 2006 for a similar argument on social segregation in the early years in London). The admission criteria used by the schools Waldrop studied focuses on shared values between parents and the school, a process which then eliminates children from other backgrounds.[6] Similarly, Tilak (1990) notes that private institutions in India maintain their exclusivity by charging high tuition fees and asking for large 'donations' at the time of admission. The interviews of parents by the schools also aim to maintain parental homogeneity.

Exclusionary practices have also found their way into state-funded schools in recent years, as part of the search for talented children. In Delhi, for instance, in 2006, 8,000 students were studying in the better-provisioned model schools, which had been set up for select students from state-funded schools.[7] The success of these schools is presented as at par, if not better, than that of private schools that have a homogeneous set of students. However, it is clear that the success of these schools is also due to the homogeneity that they seek to maintain. In a newspaper interview, the Minister of Education, Delhi, reported that the accomplishments of the Rajkiya Pratibha Vikas Vidyalaya (RPVV) — one such model school, run by the Delhi government — was because it had ensured screening through entrance examinations of students in addition to the selection of specially skilled teachers.[8] Accounts are also found of student selections being practiced in England, notably in the faith schools which have disregarded the Code of Practice. As a result, the government took steps in 2009 to tighten the regulations of the Code under which state schools operate (Moorhead 2009).

As the competition for attaining and retaining middle-class status becomes increasingly strained, the implementation of public policies that aim to combat social discrimination has been hotly contested, particularly when they have access implications to prized educational institutions. In India, the judicial attempts to put an end to nursery school admission tests based on recommendations of progressive educational groups have routinely been violated by the private schools. This kind of blockading also was visible when private schools in Delhi that had taken government subsidy for acquiring land, went out of the way to keep out non-fee-paying children from under-privileged backgrounds, who they were supposed to admit under a 25 per cent clause. The parents of the fee-paying students from the middle classes were often reported in the media to be in agreement with the school's exclusionary practices. As we have shown so far, parents think of education as fundamental for the future life chances of their children, which then makes selection of a school for their ward a crucial exercise for those parents who have enough advantage to be able to enact such a choice. Consequently, the process of choosing becomes a repository of anxiety, strategising, principle and prejudice.

'Making up' the Middle-class Child

Education also goes on inside the home of course, and as part of this, educational tasks may be delegated by affluent parents to particular experts in the form of tutoring, or the extracurricular activities in which middle-class children commonly take part. As the French sociologist Pierre Bourdieu notes, it is not sufficient to attend to the education system alone. 'Academic capital is in fact the guaranteed product of the combined effects of cultural transmission by the family and cultural transmission by the school (the efficiency of which depends on the amount of cultural capital directly inherited from the family)' (1984: 23). In other words, in order to fully come to grips with the distribution of academic capital we must look at the work done inside the family in the transmission of cultural capital and in particular 'in its earliest conditions of acquisition . . . through the more or less visible marks they leave' (ibid.: 18) This is, Bourdieu argues, 'the best hidden and socially most determinant educational investment' (ibid.: 17). The role of enrichment activities therefore is to supplement the inherited capital with that produced by bought-in tuition in a variety of areas. These activities contribute to the cultural capital held by and embodied in the family itself and are part of an accrual of class resources (Skeggs 2004). Eventually, of course, the conditions of acquisition are obscured and the skills involved are simply seen as 'legitimate competence', viewed as natural and essential qualities of the individual child.

Annette Lareau's recent study in the US on class-related differences in the 'cultural logics of childrearing' (2002: 772) is helpful here as her work illustrates the way in which social class influences the 'rhythms of family life'. She identifies the 'cultural logic of middle class parents' as emphasising 'concerted cultivation' of their children. 'They enrol their children in numerous age-specific, organised activities that dominate family life and create enormous labour, particularly for mothers. The parents view these activities as transmitting life skills to children' (2002: 748). Lareau argues that the childrearing strategies of the working class and poor parents in her study emphasise by contrast, the 'accomplishment of natural growth'. 'These parents believe that as long as they provide love, food and safety, their children will grow and thrive. They do not focus on developing their children's special talents' (2002: 748–49).

There appears to have been a boom in enrichment activities over the last 10–15 years in England, and the availability and range of activities is still increasing. Commercial providers are both local or franchised nationally and they advertise in local newsletters and magazines. The summer 2005 edition of *Families North* (a London newsletter) contained advertisements for drama, dance, music, art (several different providers for all of these), singing, karate, yoga, gym, cooking, football, mixed sports, swimming, computing, French, basketball and pottery. The spring 2006 edition included life coaching and sewing (not together!). Children can start most of these activities from 3 or 4 years onwards, although there is also a thriving market in classes in baby gym, movement, music and art for the under 3s. These activities are replicated outside London, although possibly not in such density and variety (see Vincent and Ball 2007).

We also find this search for a competitive edge amongst the middle classes of India. On the academic front, this is seen in the increasing recourse to private tuition. The exploratory research done by Menon indicates that children from professional middle-class families studying at the upper primary stage take private tuitions as much for getting assistance with homework as they do for gaining an edge in Mathematics and Sciences, long before they face the public examination at the secondary level.[9] The programmes that these children attended included Mathematics foundation-building exercises like Abacus. However, non-academic activities also were pursued seriously, so much so that the children were spending a substantial amount of time in activities planned by their parents; in one case, a 6-year-old child was learning ballet and music while her 12-year-old brother went for Martial Arts classes in addition to tuitions. During their vacations the children were enrolled in swimming classes, summer camps, activity clubs and a privately run experiential learning programme.

Menon found that middle-class parents were often uncertain about the utility of the courses but went ahead anyway and enrolled their children. They made decisions based on what their friends reported and discussed. Thus one of the families began by sending their children for singing classes, followed by dancing lessons and special Mathematics classes every day after school. In the vacations, apart from all this, children were sent for swimming coaching. Keeping abreast of any new programmes and activities became an additional mothering responsibility. One parent commented on how she had once gone to meet another mother, a stranger, because her child had told her of a Maths strengthening programme that another child attended. Thus parenting included constantly being on the look-out for activities that may give the child an edge. This 'lookout' meant taking their cues not only from amongst family and friends but also from far-off sources and mass media. Almost like the 'other-directed' Levittowners of H. J. Gans (1967).

All the parents in Menon's study pointed out that their upbringing had been dramatically different from the way they were rearing their children. All of them had been brought up to be engineers or doctors if possible. Though only a couple actually took up these occupations in adulthood, their childhood was spent in academic work that avoided 'wasting time' on other activities. However, as parents now they were keen that their children be exposed to various structured or planned unstructured activities. The choice of these activities differed from parent to parent depending upon their own inclinations. For instance, three sets of parents who liked being outdoors and had read up on child development ensured activities where they could 'be with nature', like participating in summer camps, going for nature walks or bird watching. Other parents did what was familiar to them by enrolling them in swimming, singing and dancing classes. The respondent parents felt abashed if they had to cut costs on some of these additional activities. This also was in stark contrast to their own upbringing wherein firm limits had been set on what could be spent on children. Cutting costs on these additional activities — that were perceived as an investment for providing a competitive edge to the child — was never discussed when the families interacted with each other, though complaints did come up about fees. One child had even attended a parent-funded international exchange programme. In some cases, enthusiasm for these extra-curricular activities also reflects the parents' own sense of having missed out on a field in which they perceive they could have excelled. A mother of a 6-year old, an academic, says that she realised how much she had missed out on the opportunities provided by structured activities only when she began her search for suitable activities for her child.

For most parents their investment in these myriad activities reflected class-related beliefs about 'appropriate' activities for children. A mother who is a school teacher tells Menon how she is bringing up her two children: 'the way the upper middle class does'. This she explained was by sending her children to an expensive pre-nursery programme and a school offering academic activities in English. She spoke to her children in English at home, though it was not her mother tongue and took them for skating classes at the age of 3. This group of respondent parents had their own intellectual dispositions, which made them lean towards one or the other particular belief systems but the childrearing methods that they adopted were similar in that they promoted ample scope for the child to develop his/her 'individuality'. The parents took pride in their child's difference, provided that this difference meant being above normal, perhaps 'the best' in a particular field. There were, however, exceptions to this, as one set of parents allowed their two children to be as they pleased and even admiringly acknowledged their children's run-in with the school administration, their peer group and with school authorities. They were willing to pick up a fight for their children when required as they held that their children's natural disposition was being damaged, indicating that the middle-class child also was one with a strong individuality.

Thus, we can see the fundamental role played by concerted cultivation in middle-class families in London and Delhi, as parents sought to 'make up a middle class child' with considerable social and cultural resources. The aim of concerted cultivation appears to be the formation of middle-class 'omnivores' (Skeggs 2004; Vincent and Ball 2007), or as one of us has referred to them elsewhere, 'Renaissance children', with skills in intellectual, physical and creative arenas (Vincent and Ball 2007).

Conclusion

'Fear of falling' (Ehrenreich 1989) appears strong within the middle classes in England and India, and education — both within and outside the school — is a key site in which parents try and ensure their children's reproduction within the relative security of the middle classes. Education is seen as the selection of the 'right' kind of schooling — manifested in school choice — as well as the selection of a number of activities that will maintain and reproduce cultural capital with the aim of further consolidating the family's social class position.

These efforts engender increased parental (maternal) responsibilities, considerable parental anxiety, and shifts in child care practices. In the race to get ahead, gain an edge on the competition, parental efforts are focused on the 'cultivation of the individual' within the child. The daily time-table of a child can become tightly packed with activities, minimising their time free from adult direction. The pressures of the race, 'putting the family first' and educational strategising to those ends makes the middle classes reluctant to enter into any action that would jeopardise their position. As a result (in India) one can witness the flight of the middle classes from state-supported schools, or the fierce opposition of private school management and parents to the reservation of 25 per cent of school places for children from disadvantaged backgrounds or to reservation policies in general. In England, one can witness the polarisation of the state school system in urban areas into schools with sufficient children from families 'like us', and schools attended by the poor, often ethnic minority, 'other'. Choice policies privilege the logics of individualised families and the maximisation of their self-interest. Thus, in both countries the retreat into individualism renders unlikely any sustained collective action in support of the state education systems. What we see instead is the middle classes creating and maintaining class boundaries through education, in order to preserve and protect social privilege. This conclusion does not apply only to India and England. Parental choice is a global policy discourse, to be found shaping education systems worldwide, through voucher schemes and other initiatives. As choice policy spreads, and with it the requirement for strategic and individual enterprise on the part of parents, new forms of inequity will surely result.

✛

Notes

1. This included an exploratory work on educational choices exercised by 16 middle-class professional families (earning between ₹ 45,000 and 2 lakh a month) and was based on open-ended interviews and supplemented with group discussions, observations in a private international preschool, a post-school Mathematics strengthening programme and a paid sports

ground. The mothers (aged between 30 and 47) included college and school teachers, NGO professionals, a banker, an advocate, a journalist, and homemakers by choice. Among the fathers, five held corporate jobs at the middle managerial levels, three were technical specialists, three were journalists and there was an academician, a scientist, an administrator, a lawyer and a filmmaker. All had postgraduate degrees and necessary professional and academic qualifications required for the job. None of the parents were original residents of Delhi and had come to the city either for education or employment and had then stayed on. The families spoke at least two languages apart from English at home.

2. Income as in National Council of Applied Economic Research, Market Information Survey of Households data. The expenditure figures refer to NSSO data.

3. The legislation actually only offers parents the right to express a preference for a particular school.

4. For example, your chances of attaining a place at school in most localities still comes down to how close you live to the building; therefore lying about your address would be an example of an illegal strategy to obtain a place, moving house to be nearer the school a legal one. House prices of properties near 'good' schools clearly demonstrate a premium. Faith schools are often in demand, but require evidence of religious practice. Abundant anecdotal evidence tells of parents finding their faith a few years before their child is due to start school.

5. Schools in India can opt for recognition by getting their school affiliated to different boards of education, which have their own syllabus and conduct public examinations. The Indian Certificate of Secondary Education (ICSE) examination is conducted by the Council for the Indian School Certificate Examinations, a private, non-governmental board of school education in India. The Central Board of Secondary Education (CBSE) is an autonomous organisation that conducts two major examinations every year, the All India Secondary School Examination (AISSE) for Class X and a school-leaving examination for class XII, the All India Senior School Certificate Examination (AISSCE). The High School Certificate (HSC) examinations are conducted by boards that operate at state levels. A large number of private schools have opted for recognition from the ICSE and CBSE while a majority of the state-funded schools are with the HSC board.

6. The admission of children on the basis of examinations has been highly contested. The conflict is powered by different sections of the middle class taking on each other. While a section of the middle classes upheld selection processes for nursery admissions, another section has refuted this through multiple litigations. The conflict of interest over seats subsequently led to the tabling of the Ganguly Committee Report which calls for putting a stop to the school's interaction with parents for deciding nursery admissions (http://www.karmayog.org/socialjurist/socialjurist_2630.htm).

7. *The Hindustan Times*, 'Government Schools Get Better by the Years', 25 May 2006.
8. Ibid.
9. See endnote 1 for details of interviewees (Menon 2008). 'Curricular and Co-curricular Activities of Children: An Exploratory Study of Professional Middle Class's Educational Habits', a study undertaken for filling gaps in the existing literature on enrichment activities and the middle classes in India. Unpublished.

References

Allen, Rebecca and Anna Vignoles. 2007. 'What Does an Index of School Segregation Measure?' *Oxford Review of Education*, 33 (5), 643–88.

Annual Status of Education (ASER) Report. 2008. Delhi: Pratham.

Balagopalan, S. and R. Subrahmaniam. 2003. 'Dalit and Adivasi Children in Schools, Some Preliminary Research Themes and Findings', *IDS Bulletin*, 34 (1), 43–54.

Ball, S. J. 2003. *Class Strategies and the Education Market Place*. London: Routledge Falmer.

Ball, S. and C. Vincent. 1998. 'I Heard it on the Grapevine': 'Hot' Knowledge and School Choice, *British Journal of Sociology of Education*, 19 (3), 377–400.

Ball, S. J., R. Bowe and S. Gewirtz. 1996. 'School Choice, Social Class and Distinction: The Realisation of Social Advantage in Education', *Journal of Education Policy*, 11 (1), 89–112.

Ball, S., C. Vincent and A. Braun. 2008. 'Is There an Intermediate Social Class? Trajectories of Longing and Liminality', Internal project paper, unpublished.

Benei, Veronique. 2005. 'Of Languages, Passions and Interests: Education, Regionalism and Globalization in Maharashtra, 1800–2000', in Jackie Assayag and C. J. Fuller (eds), *Globalising India: Perspectives from Below*. London: Anthem Press, pp. 141–64.

Béteille, A. 2008. 'Access to Education', *Economic and Political Weekly*, 43 (20), 40–48.

Bourdieu, P. 1984. *Distinction: A Social Critique of the Judgement of Taste*. London: Routledge.

Butler, T. with G. Robson. 2003. *London Calling*. Oxford: Berg.

Chan, T. and J. Goldthorpe. 2007. 'Social Stratification and Cultural Consumption: Music in England', *European Sociological Review*, 23 (1), 1–19.

Chitnis, S. 1987. 'Education and Social Stratification', in Ratna Ghosh and Mathew Zachariah (eds), *Education and the Process of Change*. New Delhi: Sage Publications.

Crompton, R. 1995. 'Women's Employment and the "Middle Class"', in T. Butler and M. Savage (eds), *Social Change and the Middle Classes.* London: UCL Press.

Deshpande, S. 2003. *Contemporary India: A Sociological View.* New Delhi: Penguin Books.

Devine, F. 2004. *Class Practices: How Parents Help their Children Get Good Jobs.* Cambridge: Cambridge University Press.

Dewey, S. 2006. 'Imperial Designs, Post-colonial Replications: Class and Power at Cathedral and John Connon School in Bombay', *Ethnography and Education*, 1 (2), 215–29.

Donner, Henrike. 2005. '"Children are Capital, Grandchildren are Interest": Changing Educational Strategies and Parenting in Calcutta's Middle-class Families', in Jackie Assayag and C. J. Fuller (eds), *Globalizing India: Perspectives from Below.* London: Anthem Press, pp. 119–39.

Dreze, Jean and Haris Gazdar. 1997. 'Uttar Pradesh: The Burden of Inertia', in Jean Dreze and Amartya Sen (eds), *Indian Development: Selected Regional Perspectives.* New Delhi: Oxford University Press.

Drury, David. 1993. *The Iron School Master. Education, Employment and the Family in India.* New Delhi: Hindustan Book Company.

Ehrenreich, B. 1989. *Fear of Falling: The Inner Life of the Middle Class.* New York: Pantheon Books.

Farrell, Diana and Eric Beinhocker. 2007. 'Next Big Spender: India's Middle Class', *Business Week.* Available online at http://www.mckinsey.com/mgi/mginews/bigspenders.asp (accessed 5 April 2009).

Fernandes, L. 2004. 'The Politics of Forgetting: Class Politics, State Power and the Restructuring of Urban Space in India', *Urban Studies,*. 41 (12), November, 2415–430.

———. 2006. *India's New Middle Class.* Minneapolis: University of Minnesota Press.

Gans, H. J. 1967. *The Levittowners: Ways of life and Politics in a New Suburban Community.* Referred Morningside edition, 1982. New York: Columbia University Press.

Gewirtz, S., S. Ball and R. Bowe. 1996. *Markets, Choice and Equity.* Buckingham: Open University Press.

Hasan, Z. and R. Menon. 2005. *Educating Muslim Girls: A Comparison of Five Indian Cities.* New Delhi: Women Unlimited.

Jeffery, R., P. Jeffery and C. Jeffrey. 2005. 'Social Inequalities and the Privatisation of Secondary Schooling in North India', in Radhika Chopra and Patricia Jeffery (eds), *Educational Regimes in Contemporary India.* New Delhi, Thousand Oaks and London: Sage, pp. 41–61.

Jordan, B., M. Redley and S. James. 1994. *Putting the Family First: Identities, Decisions and Citizenship.* London: UCL Press.

Kumar, Arun. 2008. 'Identifying the Elite: Air Travel is Not the Right Indicator', *The Tribune*, 1 April 2008.

Kumar, K. 1987. 'Reproduction or Change? Education and Elites in India', in Ratna Ghosh and Mathew Zachariah (eds), *Education and the Process of Change*. New Delhi: Sage Publications.

Government of India. 1986. National Policy of Education. New Delhi: Ministry of Human Resource Development.

Lareau, A. 2002. *Unequal Childhoods*. Berkley: University of California Press.

Lawler, S. 2005. 'Disgusted Subjects: The Making of Middle-class Identities', *The Sociological Review*, 53 (3), 429–46.

Le Roux, B., H. Rouanet, M. Savage and A. Warde. 2008. 'Challenging Class: Class and Cultural Divisions in the UK', *Sociology*, 42 (6), 1049–71.

Liechty, M. 2003. *Suitably Modern: Making Middle-Class Culture in a New Consumer Society*. Princeton, NJ: Princeton University Press.

Lockwood, D. 1995. 'Marking Out the Middle Class(es)', in T. Butler and M. Savage (eds), *Social Change and the Middle Classes*. London: University College London Press.

Machin, S. and J. Wilson. 2005. 'Public and Private Schooling Initiatives in England', Paper prepared for 'Mobilizing the Private Sector for Public Education'. Kennedy School of Government, Harvard University, 5–6 October.

Marshall, G. 1998. 'Goldthorpe Class Scheme', *A Dictionary of Sociology*. Oxford: Oxford University Press.

McKinsey Global Institute. 2007. *'The Bird of Gold': The Rise of India's Consumer Market*, May 2007. Available online at http://www.mckinsey.com/mgi/publications/india_consumer_market/index.asp (accessed 5 April 2009).

Menon, R. 2008. 'Curricular and Co-curricular Activities of Children: An Exploratory Study of Professional Middle Class's Educational Habits'. Unpublished.

Mishra, B. B. 1961. 'The Indian Middle Class: Their Growth in Recent Times', New York: Oxford University Press.

Moorhead, J. 2009. 'Admission "Still Too Complex"', *The Guardian*, 3 March.

Nambissan, G. B. 2010. 'The Indian Middle Classes and Educational Advantage: Family Strategies and Practices', in Michael Apple et al. (eds), *The Routledge International Handbook of the Sociology of Education*. London and New York: Routledge, pp. 285–95.

Nandy, A. 2008. 'Gujarat: Blame the Middle Class', *The Times of India*, 14 January.

NCERT. 2002. *Seventh All India Education Survey*. New Delhi: NCERT.

Pramanik, R. 2007. *Overburdened School-Going Children*. New Delhi: Concept Publishing Company.

Reay, D. and S. Ball. 1997. '"Spoilt for Choice"? The Working Class and Education Markets', *Oxford Review of Education*, 23 (1): 89–101.

Reay, D. and H. Lucey. 2003. 'The Limits of Choice', *Sociology*, 37 (1): 121–42.

Savage, M. 2000. *Class Analysis and Social Transformation*. Buckingham: Open University Press.

Savage, M., G. Bagnall and B. Longhurst. 2003. *Globalisation and Belonging*. London: Sage Publications.

Savage, M., J. Barlow, P. Dickens and A. Fielding. 1992. *Property, Bureaucracy and Culture: Middle Class Formation in Contemporary Britain*. London: Routledge.

Sayer, A. 2005. *The Moral Significance of Class*. Cambridge: Cambridge University Press.

Scrase, T. 2006. 'The "New" Middle Class in India: A Re-assessment'. Paper presented at 16th Biennial Conference of the Asian Studies Association of Australia in Wollongong, 26 June–29 June. Available on-line at http://coombs.anu.edu.au/SpecialProj/ASAA/biennial-conference/2006/Scrase-Tim-ASAA2006.pdf (accessed March 24 2009).

Scrase R. G. and T. J. Scrase. 2009. *Globalisation and the Middle Classes in India. The Social and Cultural Impact of Neoliberal Reforms*. London and New York: Routledge Taylor & Francis Group.

Skeggs, B. 2004. *Class, Self, Culture*. London: Routledge.

Sridharan, E. 2004. 'The Growth and Sectoral Composition of India's Middle Classes: Its Impact on the Politics of Liberalization in India', *India Review*, 1 (4): 405–28.

Tilak J. 1990. 'The Political Economy of Education in India', *Special Studies in Comparative Education*, No. 24. Graduate School of Education and State University of New York.

Upadhya, C. 1987. 'Culture, Class and Entrepreneurship: A Case Study of Coastal Andhra Pradesh, India', in Mario Rutten and Carol Upadhya (eds), *Small Business Entrepreneurs in Asia and Europe· Towards a Comparative Perspective*. New Delhi: Sage Publications, pp. 47–80.

Velaskar, P. 1992. 'Unequal Schooling as a Factor in the Reproduction of Social Inequality in India', *Sociological Bulletin*, 39 (1&2), 131–46.

Vincent, C. 2001. 'Social Class and Parental Agency', *Journal of Education Policy*, 16 (4), 347–64.

Vincent, C. and S. J. Ball. 2006. *Childcare, Choice and Class Practices*. London: Routledge.

———. 2007. '"Making Up" the Middle-Class Child: Families, Activities and Class Dispositions', *Sociology*, 41 (6), 1061–77.

Vincent, C., S. Ball and A. Braun. 2010. 'Local Links, Local Knowledge: Choosing Care Settings and Primary Schools', *British Educational Research Journal*, 36 (2), 279–98.

Waldrop, A. 2004. 'The Meaning of the Old School-tie: Private Schools, Admission Procedures and Class Segmentation in New Delhi', in A. Vaugier-Chatterjee (ed.), *Education and Democracy in India*. New Delhi: Manohar and Centre De Sciences Humaines.

Weis, L. 2008. (ed.), *The Way Class Works: Readings on School, the Family, the Economy*. New York: Routledge.

Wessel, M. V. 2004. 'Talking about Consumption: How an Indian Middle Class Disassociates from Middle-Class Life', *Cultural Dynamics*, 16 (1), 93–116.

3

Globalisation, Economic Reforms and the Lives of Urban, Middle-class Women in India

Anjali Kothari

This essay explores how two women from a middle-class Indian family have responded to economic, social and cultural changes brought about by the restructuring of India's economy in the early 1990s. It focuses specifically on the period since 1991, when the largely protected Indian economy opened up to the outside world, signalling its most remarkable shift since independence from Britain in 1947 (Das 2002). Import substitution, which had been central to the economy until then, was lifted and the country opened up to foreign investors, resulting in a significant increase in the availability and variety of consumer goods on the market. This period also saw the launch in India of the News Corporation–owned Satellite Television Asia Region (STAR) network in direct competition with local, state-run television. With its 'western' content of programmes, STAR saw its name 'become inextricably linked with the entire debate surrounding cultural change in India in the 1990s' (Butcher 2003: 13) and its emergence as a symbol of the country's new 'post-liberalisation generation, melded in the convergence of East and West' ibid.: 13).

Carol Vincent and Radhika Menon's essay in this volume looks at the middle classes in India and the UK, particularly at how members of these groups concentrate on education for their children and the resulting effect on school systems in both countries during the process of what they describe as the 'making up' of the middle-class child. Research on post-liberalisation India has tended to focus on the public sphere such as changes in the media, labour market and political landscape (Butcher 2003; Mankekar 1999; Rajagopal 1999; Sridharan 2004). Barring Donner's (2006, 2008) ethnographic study of middle-class women in Calcutta, little attention has been paid so far to the effects of globalisation on middle-class Indian families, their lifestyles and their experiences of education, marriage and parenting. Based on data collected for my doctoral thesis I examine the gendered aspects of middle-classness in India, drawing on the experiences of a mother and daughter who have lived through the changes since 1991. I reflect on their trajectories of education, marriage, careers and motherhood in an increasingly globalised context. Using Bourdieu's concepts of capital I focus on the roles these two women play in acquiring and reinforcing the economic, social, cultural and symbolic capitals they view as necessary to be middle class and the strategies they employ to transmit these capitals to their children, particularly in the educational field (1984). In doing so I draw parallels with extensive research in the UK looking at the educational strategies which middle-class parents, particularly mothers, employ in order to ensure social reproduction and intergenerational mobility.

India's Middle Classes: 'Old' versus 'New'

I begin with an overview of the historical origins of the middle classes in India and interweave them with Bourdieu's concepts (ibid.). The 'old' middle class, as documented by Liddle and Joshi (1986) arose in the pre-independence period when officials in the British Raj felt the need for English-educated Indians to administer the country. Misra (1961) argues that India's traditional emphasis on literary education and Britain's rule and imperialist economy combined to make the intelligentsia the dominant element of the Indian middle classes during colonial rule. The East India Company's establishment of trading relations with local merchants in the early 17th century, followed by political rule, led to the creation of a middle-class social order. Cannadine (2002) describes how the administration looked on the existing Indian caste structure as something to be promoted and preserved, and an essential feature of the Indian social system.[1] He writes, 'Just as the British local government had always depended on the resident aristocracy and gentry, so their chosen partners in South Asia were the "natural leaders", large landowners, men of property and rank, of power and importance' (2002: 43). Due to their traditional status and authority, these landowners were able to fulfil the role of English notables. From circumstances of their origin, the membership of the educated middle class came to be largely dominated by the traditional higher castes who constituted professions such as medicine, teaching and law.

In his historical study of the creation of a middle class in colonial north India, Joshi (2001) points out that the power of this group was based not on economic capital alone but on the ability of its members to be 'cultural entrepreneurs' (2001: 4), the middlemen who were conversant in English and acted as the interpreters and financiers for the British, thus amassing high levels of economic, social, cultural and symbolic capital. The creation of this group also led to a new understanding and discourse on ideal 'middle-class' women, as documented by Walsh (2004) in her work on domesticity in colonial India. One mechanism of communicating this idealised middle-classness was the women's journal *Stribodh*, which portrayed women as active housewives and mothers, providing information on child care, arranging their homes 'neatly and aesthetically' (Walsh 2004: 23), dressing well to receive their husbands on their return from work and interaction with wider family members. Bourdieu's theory of habitus is instrumental in understanding this response to the creation of a middle class in India during this period; the emphasis is on daily practices of home and family life (1984). More significantly, his concept of symbolic capital, relating to respectability and power (in the context of colonial rule) is key to understanding the acceptance of these customs by women during this time.

Although there was some breakdown of caste structures following independence from Britain, it was members of the professional, educated group that rose to power (for example, Mahatma Gandhi and Jawaharlal Nehru, two of India's leading figures, both before and after 1947, were barristers). The post-independence period also saw new opportunities becoming available for women, particularly in professions such as medicine and teaching in response to demands for healthcare and education. Further opportunities became available in government service and the public sector, establishing a solid, middle-class group who were seen as performing 'patriotic work for the betterment of the nation' (Radhakrishnan 2008: 197).

Economic reform in the 1990s gave rise to a 'new' middle class of entrepreneurs and professionals working in the private sector, most notably those in the information technology field. The rapid expansion of this new group during the last decade of the 20th century constitutes one of the most significant changes in India's contemporary landscape. However, this is still a relatively unexplored area in academia, leading us to question how this new middle class is characterised, how it is described and how it perceives itself

(Ahmad and Reifeld 2001: 13). The most comprehensive, and largely positive, account of this expansion is by Gurcharan Das (2001), a former CEO of Procter & Gamble India, in his book *India Unbound*. Das's book begins shortly before independence and takes us up to the early 21st century, with particular focus on the 'golden summer of 1991' when, with foreign exchange reserves worth only two weeks of imports, India unveiled a series of economic reforms, devalued its currency and lowered import tariffs. This resulted in economic growth at an average rate of 7.5 per cent in the mid-1990s and the creation of a new, consumer middle class. While Das's work is a useful insight into the events leading up to economic reform, it offers little by way of theoretical analyses of the changes experienced by members of the Indian middle class since then.

Bourdieu (1984) asserts that class groups can be defined on the basis of the amount and type of capital that they possess as well as their past history. Groups who are considered upwardly mobile through education or economic means may be seen as lacking the taste to fit in with those who have been considered as belonging to a higher class for more than a generation. This is clearly illustrated in Das's (2002) description of two picnicking families he observed in a New Delhi park.

> I watched the first picnicking family and it was immediately clear that they belonged to the new middle class. They spoke roughly and aggressively. From their talk I gathered that the family had a flourishing export business in garments. All the adults, including the women, worked hard in the business. I admired the ease with which they talked about their customers in Sydney, Toronto and Brussels. They insisted on sprinkling their conversations with English words that they did not understand too well. They were newly prosperous. Yet, they were less than a generation away from the village well, dust-raising cattle and the green revolution of Haryana. (2002: 280)

> I turned to look at the other, quieter family. Three generations were enjoying the afternoon sun after a tidy lunch. The grandmother watched her young grandson roll in the grass; her stern-looking husband, from his self-important manner, had probably just retired as a senior civil servant. Their son, an IIT-IIM trained manager, was on his way up. They were the old middle class. (ibid.)[2]

Das's narrative highlights his view that the first, 'newly prosperous' family is found lacking in taste when compared to the older middle class that existed in India prior to liberalisation in 1991, particularly in his description of the first family speaking 'roughly and aggressively' as opposed to the 'other, quieter family' after their 'tidy' lunch. More significant is his comment on the first family 'insisting' on using English words in their conversation despite not knowing their meaning (the reasoning behind this statement is not made explicit), underlining the ability to speak English fluently as a mark of respectability and prestige. Despite their economic success, the lack of this symbolic capital means they are unable to fit in with the second family who are perceived as more genteel and well-established. On the other hand, while the second family possess higher levels of cultural capital they have lower levels of economic capital than the first family, leading to differences in lifestyles of the 'old' and 'new' middle class.

Defining Class in Contemporary India

Definitions of the 'middle classes' in India have been mainly based on purely economic terms. However, as Deshpande (2003) points out, determining class groupings on the basis of mere consumers does not involve any detailed analysis of the levels or types of consumption. Market surveys have sought to divide 'the middle class' into upper, middle and lower middle-class fractions, arguing that it is only logical to refer to these segments as part of a larger, single middle class if they have more in common with each other than with other groups. Deshpande notes:

> This is a matter for empirical investigation in each given context, but is often forgotten or deliberately ignored. For example, a group that is actually part of the upper class (in terms of lifestyle, income levels, attitudes or other criteria) may prefer to conceal or play down this fact by insisting on calling itself the 'upper-*middle* class'. On the other hand, a group that is actually part of the lower class may wish to pass itself off as 'lower middle class', and so on. In short, the every day term 'middle class' is more of a symbolic than a factual description. It is chosen or avoided for its social connotations, just as the 'right address' indicates social status rather than mere geographical location. (2003: 135–36)

How then, can we come to an understanding of what constitutes middle class/classes in contemporary India? While discussing possible alternatives to income when defining class/es in the Indian context, Deshpande (1998, 2003) privileges both cultural capital and the middle classes' role in the state and historically in the ruling Congress political party with the Nehru–Gandhi dynasty at its core. In doing so he highlights the link between cultural capital and power. He argues that this cultural capital may consist of identities (caste, community and region) or capabilities (educational qualifications, linguistic abilities and other social skills). These forms of cultural capital have tangible and psychological benefits, they can be privatised (by excluding others from their benefits) and they can be passed on from generation to generation. This leads him to conclude that the main function of the middle classes is to build hegemony, and its elite fraction specialises in the 'production of ideologies' while its lower, mass fraction consumes these ideologies thus 'investing them with social legitimacy' (1998: 159), in other words, symbolic capital.

Béteille (2002) uses habitus and capital in order to examine the role Indian families play in the reproduction of inequality. He asserts that while Indian families are moving from joint to nuclear in make-up, they still maintain strong links with their wider kinship network and continue to exert influence over children during their education and beyond. To understand inequality in the Indian context requires an understanding of the differences between families. These cannot be narrowed down to mere differences in economic capital but also social and cultural capital. Béteille argues that each family possesses a different 'stock of cultural capital' (2002: 152) in terms of knowledge, skills and tastes and has its own network of relationships (social capital) which are based both on previous and newly acquired connections. This point is significant to my research with middle-class mothers and daughters in urban India. While they all loosely defined themselves, one way or another, as 'middle class', their economic, cultural, social and symbolic capitals varied to the extent that they are by no means a truly homogeneous group and no attempt must be made to categorise them as such. It also provides a useful tool in understanding and analysing the different experiences of education, marriage and careers that came through in each woman's narrative. The following extract from an interview with Madhuri, a mother who participated in my study, illustrates the intricacies of defining the middle class in contemporary India:

Madhuri I suppose middle class would be divided into upper and lower middle class. Upper middle class would be if you're earning anything above 1 lakh[3] per month. You maintain a certain lifestyle, you have a car, your children attend good schools, generally English-medium schools. You go on vacations once or twice a year. Er . . . you're fluent in English apart from your mother tongue, you read English-language dailies and magazines . . . all those kinds of things.

AK   Okay. And the lower middle class?

M   Lower middle class is people who work in factories, clerks in government offices, jobs like that. They are the majority of people in India, after the poorest classes. It's difficult to say because I could tell you that a farmer is a member of the poorest class but then you have some very rich farmers also. So it's hard to classify.

AK   Would you say class was defined by profession?

Madhuri   Again it's difficult to say. You might say a university lecturer is upper middle class because they speak English, they read English newspapers, their lifestyle generally. But if you see their salary, at least in government colleges, then you wouldn't say they were upper middle class. So I think there are different ways of defining class, different . . . different factors which you can consider. But salary and profession would probably be the most important.

AK   What class would you say you and your family belong to?

Madhuri   We are upper middle class, because we live that kind of lifestyle that I was mentioning just now, the upper middle-class lifestyle. We are not elite, but we are definitely in a privileged position as compared to the majority of Indians. We do not have to struggle to make ends meet, is what I am trying to say.

AK   Would you say that members of these classes have different views about education, marriage, careers, etc.?

Madhuri   Yes I think so. Now my maid, she earns about Rs 3,000 per month so you could say she is amongst the poorer classes. She lives in a *jhopadpatti*, she has studied up to fourth standard.[4] Her son has done up to twelfth standard and now he's working in a factory. She has just arranged his marriage and I don't think he had much say in it, he is only 20. He's not earning enough to support a family but she is adamant that he get married and has taken a loan to finance the wedding. But on the other hand you see people from all classes spending money on weddings.

AK   And differences in terms of educational aspirations?

Madhuri   There I would say that the differences are more. The higher classes will push for education for all their children and they will have money to provide private tuitions and get extra support for their kids if they need it. The lower classes may not have that. They may push for education for boys because the boys will lift them out of poverty, but maybe not so much for girls. If it comes to choosing on spending on a boy's or girl's education, they will mostly, if not always, choose the boy.

Madhuri's views underline the arguments made by Béteille and Deshpande about varying stocks of cultural capital and class differentiation respectively. A salient point emerging from these arguments outlined in this section is that they are all underlined in some way or another by Bourdieu's concepts of capital (1984). A key, unexplored question is the role of women in establishing and preserving these ideologies as socially acceptable and desirable, something this essay seeks to address.

Education and Marriage: A Mother and Daughter Recount their Experiences

My research involved interviews with a total of 27 women based in two major Indian cities. The younger women ranged between the ages of 20 and 35 years. The mothers involved were between their early 40s and late 50s. Some of the single women were in their late 20s, while some in their early 20s were recently married, or had been for some years. One of the mothers was divorced. In terms of religious affinities, four women self-identified as Parsi, two as Muslim and one as Roman Catholic. The rest broadly identified themselves as Hindu but with different cultures and ethnicities based on their caste, regional background and language.

While all the women loosely defined themselves as 'middle class' in some form or the other, their financial, educational and professional backgrounds varied greatly. Some came from affluent families while others had more modest financial backgrounds. Educational qualifications and professional occupations also differed with some mothers holding first degrees but choosing not to work outside the home and others having pursued their careers to various levels following marriage and the birth of their children. This was also true for the young women whose qualifications ranged from higher education diplomas to Masters Degrees and working as flight attendants, call centre employees, software engineers and medical professionals. Here I recount the experiences of a mother and daughter who participated in the research to see whether and how, in the post-liberalisation Indian context, there has been a reworking of cultural and symbolic capital for these two women. I have outlined this information in order to give readers a sense of the context in which the data was collected and, for the purpose of this essay, I focus on the experiences of Naureen and her daughter, Sharmin.

Naureen, a mother in her early 50s, is a teacher by profession. She was married by her early 20s. Living in a joint family meant she was able to draw on her mother-in-law's support for child care which allowed her to continue teaching. She describes her experiences of education and marriage and managing motherhood in conjunction with her career as a teacher:

On her Education and Marriage

In my day there wasn't so much emphasis on education for girls beyond degree level. You shouldn't get me wrong, education was considered important, it gave you that . . . that respectability, people would say 'she is an educated girl', especially when it came to the time of looking for a suitable boy [to marry]. Of course this was not the case for everyone, there were a few high-fliers. Amongst the girls I went to school with, one became a doctor and still practises today. Her father was also a doctor so he very much encouraged her. Apart from her and me, generally the rest of us got married soon after graduation and stayed at home to raise their families. Once the children were old enough they started doing things from home, like one of my friends would run a beauty parlour from her house. It fitted in with the children's school hours and brought in some extra cash. Many of my friends play a supporting role in their husbands' profession, like if the husband is a doctor they help out in his clinic, or if he runs a business they help in the shop/office.

On being 'Middle Class' and Teaching as a Career

I would say the family I grew up in was just average, just 'middle' middle class if you can use that term. My father worked in a bank and my mother was a housewife. Education was considered important, particularly convent-school education, it was thought to instil good values and also convent schools are English-medium, which was again thought good because it would help you find a suitable husband.

My husband is an engineer with [a national company]. His salary was adequate but my mother-in-law encouraged me to continue with teaching. She knew I enjoyed it and also the extra income was helpful. School was five minutes' walk from our house, I could come home at lunchtime and see the children and I was back just after 3.30 p.m. when the day ended. And once they started school our holidays would match. But without my mother-in-law to take care of them I would not have been able to manage work and home. While we have not enjoyed a lavish lifestyle, we have been able to educate our children well and get them into good, well-paid professions. We wanted them to be able to enjoy things that we could not afford, like travelling abroad, gaining exposure to different countries and settings.

On how her Daughter Sharmin's Life Might be Different from her Own

Sharmin went to the same school as me but there was a definite expectation that she would be educated for a purpose other than marriage in mind. We sacrificed a lot for her education, saving so that we could afford to send her to [a well-established, private college] for her studies. I wanted her, my husband and I wanted her to be independent and to enjoy her career. Teaching is considered a very respectable profession, but it is not very lucrative in terms of remuneration. At one time I was earning just ₹ 3,300 per month and Sharmin's starting salary was more than ten times that amount. The boom in the computer industry meant she was able to secure a very well-paid job, that wasn't the case when I was her age. Her education for marriage was also important, you want your child to find the best possible partner in life. Her qualifications were on par with her husband's, so they helped her find someone like-minded and compatible in terms of education and outlook. He was going to study at [an Ivy League institution] in America, so they went together. She worked while he studied, so she was able to support both of them. Now they are back in India. They have a lifestyle that her father and I could not afford on our salaries. Her kids go to a private school whereas she attended [a local convent school] like me, they take trips abroad like Mauritius, Dubai and all these places. So our lives are very different. The software profession has allowed them to live a very upper middle-class lifestyle.

Sharmin, Naureen's daughter is in her late 20s. She is married with two young children and a software engineer by profession. She shares her experiences of education, marriage and a career:

On her Education and Marriage

My mom had a very traditional wedding. She was barely out of college when she got married. I knew I didn't want that. I met my husband at work. We were together for a few months and then my parents started searching for a husband for me. I had been seeing someone before but they were very much against that, his career prospects weren't good, in the sense he wouldn't have been able to travel abroad with his qualifications and I always knew I wanted to work outside India, even if just for sometime. They were happy when I met my husband and they knew he was going to study in the US. They felt our educational backgrounds matched very well.

On being 'Middle Class' and Software Engineering as a Career

I suppose you could say we [her husband and herself], are now upper middle class. He comes from a wealthy family, they own a business and have properties all over [our home city]. So in that sense our backgrounds were a little different, my parents were educated but in service professions whereas his were not so educated but were financially very well-off. But educationally, my husband and I were at the same level.

I wanted to pursue a career to be independent. I wanted to know that I had that backup, you know then that you are able make your own choices and nobody can impose anything on you. But now we are financially very secure so I will give up work soon so that I can spend more time with the children and run the home. Maybe when they are older I can go back to work.

On how her Life might be Different from her Mother's

My parents really worked hard to give me the best education possible. They always had that in their minds. Now I want to make sure I can do things for them, so that they are comfortable. We travel a lot now, and it's something I just didn't do as a kid. My kids have been abroad with us already, Singapore, Dubai and places like that. That's different from my childhood when going abroad was seen as something really special. Education is still important though, the reason I'm thinking of staying at home is to be able to spend time with the children on their schoolwork. It's getting very competitive now and we have to try as hard as possible to get the kids into a good school, like one of the ones with an International Baccalaureate syllabus. I've lived abroad and seen the environment, I want my children to be able to participate in that environment and an IB school will prepare them to do that. The preschool I send them to prepares children for the entrance exam for those IB schools. And I also send them for elocution classes. An examiner will come from [a London-based institution] to examine them. Some people say, 'They are so young and doing an exam?' but it's not like an exam, more like role plays and they enjoy it. And it will help them, you need to speak English confidently, especially if you want to go abroad. In today's world you need that.

Naureen and Sharmin's narratives demonstrate how mother and daughter now belong to different sections of the middle class given their different professions and the variance in their earnings. This was by and large true for most women I interviewed, with mothers either choosing to stay at home or to pursue 'old' middle-class careers in teaching and the banking sector while their daughters studied subjects such as information technology, a profession frequently associated with the so-called 'new' Indian middle class (Radhakrishnan 2009). Naureen sees her education as instrumental in finding a husband. She initially shares her desires for her daughter to be educated in order to be independent but also highlights the importance of a good education, seen as desirable when looking for a life partner. Sharmin further elaborates on this point when she first asserts that she wanted more agency than her mother when it came to finding a husband but then speaks of the unsuitability (as viewed by her parents) of a young man she was dating previously, and their approval when she married someone with higher educational qualifications and the ability to study and work overseas as well as in India. Naureen also pinpoints the flourishing computer-related industries in India and how this gave her daughter the opportunity to earn a comparatively higher salary and travel abroad, something which she herself did not have.

Education in convent schools was previously aspired to because of the opportunities for marriage through migration, to men settled particularly in the United Kingdom and North America. Naureen's convent school education gave her the cultural and symbolic capital required to secure a good marriage to an engineer. What, if anything, changed for her daughter? Marriage continued to be an important factor and Sharmin, like her mother, was also able to use both the cultural and symbolic capital she had acquired in order to find a suitable husband. She was also able to accumulate higher levels of economic capital than her parents which gave her more financial independence. Whereas her parents' status and respectability came from their professions of banking and teaching, Sharmin's concern for her children was getting them an education in elite, private schools for the cultural and social capital this would provide, including the ability to travel, study and perhaps settle abroad. This was perhaps the most striking difference between mother and daughter; Sharmin's keenness to educate her children at a private school and her preparations for this at a time when the children were still very young. Thus while such aspirations for education are not new — both Naureen and Sharmin are well-educated — they have taken on a different form in the sense that they are now truly global. This is clearly demonstrated in Sharmin's desire for her children to speak fluent English and having them take elocution lessons, which she sees as a way of ultimately ensuring their participation in the global economy. As Ganguly-Scrase and Scrase note:

> There is the intrinsic relationship between a command of English and future professional employment, a relationship forged in the colonial history of India and reinforced by the dictates of a globalised economy. English proficiency . . . endows a person with a significant social advantage by securing his or her cultural capital. (2009: 177)

Deshpande (2003) examines access to languages amongst the different fractions of the Indian middle class. He divides these into three groups: monolingual English speakers, those with English as their first language with strong links to a second, Indian language and those fluent in Indian languages with little or no access to English. Naureen and Sharmin's families come under a slightly different category — they speak Gujarati, their first language, at home but are also fluent in Hindi and English. The implicit assumption, Deshpande notes, is that English-speaking fractions have greater levels of cultural and symbolic capital, leading to Sharmin enrolling her children in private English elocution lessons in addition to the English-medium schools they were attending at the time. She spoke of plans to perhaps return to the United States which in turn has led to an emphasis on education for her children in a school following the International Baccalaureate system. In her view, such an education — in contrast to the previously sought-after convent school education which usually offers the local state board of education curriculum — would allow her children to become truly global citizens with the ability to 'fit in', as she sees it, should they choose to study and/or live abroad. When Sharmin and her husband returned to India from the United States, they did so 'endowed with global experience' (Radhakrishnan 2008: 5) and the option to migrate if they wished. In a study involving Indian IT professionals based in Silicon Valley and Bangalore, Radhakrishnan (2008) highlights the decisions many such individuals take to return to India following stints abroad either for working or studying, or those who travel abroad from India temporarily for specific work-related projects. The interaction between her two groups in India and the United States led to the development of a sense of 'global Indianness' played out in the workplace and universities which Radhakrishnan describes as 'a set of beliefs and practices that are at once tied to a global lifestyle and to a deep sense of belonging to the Indian nation' (2008: 10). While these developments have benefited women in terms of education, employment and career opportunities, they have also reinforced the role of women, both in India and in the diaspora, as agents and transmitters of 'Indian' values and culture to their children.

What also emerges from Sharmin and Naureen's experiences is that the boundaries between the old and the new middle class are not so rigid. As we saw from Das's quote in an earlier section, members of the old middle class viewed cultural and symbolic capital as much more important than economic capital. The distinction between the old and the new middle classes which Das identifies, is linked to the Green Revolution in northern India where the new middle class that he refers to had a sudden growth of wealth but without proportionate increases in levels of education. The deregulating of the Indian economy in the early 1990s saw a distinct kind of economic capital coming in linked to new professions and education, creating a new, rich middle class particularly in the information technology industry (Fuller and Narasimhan 2007) and allowing young Indian professionals the mobility to access education both at elite institutions in India and abroad. Education therefore formed a bridge between the old and new middle classes in a way, by providing the cultural capital earlier gained from a convent/English-medium education. Naureen's view of her convent school education was that it would provide her with respectability and enable her to find a 'good' husband, as she saw it, an educated professional. Sharmin's reflections on her husband's background note that while his family are wealthy property owners they are not 'as well-educated' as her own parents who did not possess similar levels of economic capital but had the cultural and symbolic capitals in 'respectable' professions of engineering and teaching. She does not mind this difference given that her husband's education is on par with hers, he has studied abroad and has good prospects. Continuing in this vein, Palshikar (2001) notes that while the middle classes in contemporary India may still be dominated by the perceived respectability of 'old' middle-class professions, the concepts of lifestyles are geared more towards the 'new' middle class who are more at ease with the idea of a consumerist lifestyle.

Conclusion: Global Links Arising from Education and Marriage

Through this essay I have drawn out two women's experiences of education and marriage and the strategies they use or seek to use in order to maintain their social class. Sharmin was educated through the best resources her family was able to provide for her, had the capacity to pursue her career and have her own ambitions fulfilled. She now seeks to do the same for her own children, working through strategies to maximise their educational qualifications and experiences and strengthening their position as upper middle-class Indians and global citizens. This reflects Donner's (2006, 2008) work with middle-class families in Calcutta looking at strategies employed by mothers to secure their children's futures. She notes that some fractions of the middle class with previously dominant positions in education have had to adapt to new 'strategies and regimes or risk being left behind' (2008: 196). This perceived risk is played out in the manner in which Sharmin negotiates the effects of economic liberalisation through her children's education. She does this by choosing what she views as an appropiate preschool and engaging her children in extracurricular activities in order to give them an advantage when applying for admission to schools offering the International Baccalaureate curriculum. She also acknowledges her mother's role in shaping her own education and her desire to be a similar influence on her children.

> As a teacher, my mom would study with me; make sure I was ready for the exams and unit tests. I really feel her input was so crucial, it's the reason I got to where I am today. I want to do the same for my own kids, that's why I started looking around early for nursery schools, to prepare them in the long-run. I make sure I know what they are doing [in school], the lessons they learn, just so I am completely involved. As an educated woman myself it's so important I pass it on to my kids. I remember one of my school teachers writing in my autograph book when I was leaving school, she wrote something like, 'education commences at the mother's knee', and it's really stayed with me. Because it was true for me, and it will be true for my kids too.

Research by several key academics in the UK has established a space for theorising the (often gendered) roles performed by middle-class parents in managing their children's education (see David et al.

1993; Reay 1998, 1999, 2000, 2005; Vincent and Ball 2007; Vincent and Menon, this volume). Vincent and Ball's (2007) research details how middle-class parents in London involve their children in extra-curricular activities such as music, dance, drama and sport, viewing these as important investments and in doing so seek to guard against downward class mobility. This mirrors Sharmin enrolling her preschool children in private elocution lessons in order to improve their spoken English. Menon (this volume) details similar extracurricular activities which professional middle-class parents in Delhi seek for their children. David et al. (1993) explore how the boundaries between home and school are established and negotiated by mothers, teachers and policy makers in the UK. They research these issues particularly from the family point of view by focusing specifically on mothers' experiences of their children's education at different levels and how educational policy is shaped by constant change and negotiation. Diane Reay's research (1998, 1999) on mothers' involvement in their children's primary education in two London schools illustrates how the nature of this involvement varies according to a mother's class background and the implications of this on social reproduction. Focusing on the power dynamics between mothers and teachers, Reay draws on Bourdieu's concepts of capital to demonstrate how middle-class mothers use their own cultural capital as a tool to ensure their child gets the best out of the education system while simultaneously highlighting how working-class mothers' comparative lack of such capital renders them less able to do so for their children (1984). She does not seek to blame middle-class women for these inequities, rather sees 'all mothers as caught up in educational markets which operate on the (il)logic of "to her who has yet more shall be given"' (2005: 114). Reay (2000) also draws on the concept of emotional capital to problematise the home–school relationship to show how mothers rather than fathers are most often the central figures in the emotional work of daily care-giving to children.

Naureen and Sharmin both speak of the investments they made and are making in their children's education, investments which in fact transcend three generations. Naureen acknowledged her mother-in-law's help with child care, particularly when her (Naureen's) work as a teacher meant she had to be at school later than usual. On these occasions she knew she could rely on her mother-in-law to provide a meal for her young children when they came in from school and study and play with them. Sharmin spoke of her own worries in balancing motherhood with her job as a software engineer with the pressure of working to tight deadlines, one of the reasons for her considering giving up work in the near future. She in turn relies on Naureen to pick up her children from preschool, give them an afternoon meal and spend time playing with them. Sharmin described her husband mainly in terms of his career and being the main breadwinner. While she acknowledged his support in finding information on preschools, extracurricular activities and suitable primary schools, it was clear that she saw his role very much as a supportive one while she had overall responsibility. Her experiences and thoughts also show that while her education and profession give her status outside the home they also increase the obligations she feels as the person responsible for educating her children. This comes through when she quotes her teacher's sentence, 'education commences at the mother's knee'. Research on this topic in post-liberalisation India is still in its infancy, however, Naureen and Sharmin's narratives reflect similar findings from the UK where the role of the middle-class mother is crucial in maintaining social class and ensuring intergenerational mobility. Drawing parallels with the UK context, Sharmin's substantial economic capital as well as cultural resources show how she uses — and plans to use — these to her children's educational advantage.

While education was a strong theme throughout both Naureen and Sharmin's interviews, there was also the expectation that marriage would follow, thereby conforming to 'traditional' expectations that a 'good' middle-class woman would settle down, sooner rather than later. Thapan (2001) uses habitus to illustrate how adolescent women in India constructed their identity through the interplay of so-called 'old' modes of contact (such as religious practices, cultural traditions and social customs) and apparent 'new' ones (most significantly educational processes, and the visual and print media). Both these old and new modes of contact influenced and structured the identities of these adolescent girls, indicating conformity to the old structures but also a continuous questioning of them. In a different study, Thapan (2006) also notes that women's articulation of their identity corresponds with their class, family and community to which they belong. She uses the term 'postcolonial habitus', the 'dominant modality for the exercise of multiple subjectivities shaped by class, age, ethnicity and region' (2006: 199). This post-colonial habitus is class-based, with marked differences between a middle-class woman with privileges such as an English-medium education and social and cultural capital

(Naureen), and a woman with similar levels of education with much higher economic capital (Sharmin). This is also reflected in their understandings of their position within the family and their ambitions. Naureen's career as a teacher was seen as very much supplementary to her husband's income. While Sharmin's career was seen as equal to her husband's she also speaks of her intentions of giving up work in order to spend more time with her children, reinforcing the expectation that, for a middle-class Indian woman, the family must be privileged above a career.

Two important factors to note are the global linkages that come with marriage, education and careers, particularly through the connections which Indians in the diaspora maintain with their homeland; and the fluidity of movement across international boundaries again through marriage, education and careers. Looking at the impact of these global linkages, Shiladitya Bose (2008) outlines the influence the diaspora wields, through monetary remittances or otherwise, in the spheres of politics, development aid, popular culture and the property market in India — for example, the rise of western-style property developments catering to non-resident Indians (NRIs) for investment as well as representations of NRIs in Bollywood films. For Sharmin and her mother, a convent school, English education was seen as the platform on which they built their higher education and, in Sharmin's case, provided access to an international lifestyle by offering opportunities in both the local and overseas market as a software engineer. They viewed a middle-class lifestyle as instrumental in allowing Naureen to continue as a teacher yet devote time to her children in order for them to flourish at school and university, resulting in 'respectable' professions better-paid than her own. Sharmin in turn plans to stop working so she can similarly concentrate on her children's education, albeit in the different setting of private schools and international curriculums.

Marriage, the family, and the 'right' kind of education were still central to both these women's lives although they manifested themselves differently across the two generations. Within these differences both women were negotiating economic, cultural, symbolic and social capital in order to maintain their position as members of the middle/ upper middle class and transferring these capitals to their children in order to give them an edge in a competitive world with the intrinsic economic and cultural flows that come along with globalisation.

+

Notes

1. For more in-depth debates on caste and class in India, see the essays by Marie Lall and Srinivasa Rao (caste) and Carol Vincent and Radhika Menon (class).
2. Indian Institute of Technology/Indian Institute of Management, are prestigious educational institutions.
3. One lakh is equivalent to the sum of 100,000 rupees
4. *Jhopadpatti* is a slum settlement.

References

Ahmad, I. and H. Reifeld (eds). 2001. *Middle Class Values in India and Western Europe*. New Delhi: Social Science Press.

Bourdieu, P. 1984. *Distinction: A Social Critique of the Judgment of Taste*. London: Routledge and Kegan Paul.

Béteille, A. 2001. 'The Social Character of the Indian Middle Class', in I. Ahmed and H. Reifeld (eds), *Middle Class Values in India and Western Europe*. New Delhi: Social Science Press, pp. 73–85.

———. 2002. *Equality and Universality: Essays in Social and Political Theory*. New Delhi: Oxford University Press.

Bose, P. Shiladitya. 2008. 'Home and Away: Diasporas, Developments and Displacements in a Globalising World', *Journal of Intercultural Studies*, 29 (1), 111–31.

Butcher, M. 2003. *Transnational Television, Cultural Identity and Change: When STAR Came to India*. London: Routledge.

Cannadine, D. 2002. *Ornamentalism: How the British Saw Their Empire*. London: Allen Lane.

Das, G. 2001. 'Middle-class Values and the Changing Indian Entrepreneur', in I. Ahmad and H. Reifeld (eds), *Middle Class Values in India and Western Europe*. New Delhi: Social Science Press, pp. 194–211.

———. 2002. *India Unbound: From Independence to the Global Information Age*. London: Profile Books.

David, M., R. Edwards, M. Hughes and J. Ribbens. 1993. *Mothers and Education: Inside Out? Exploring Family-education Policy and Experience*. New York: St Martin's Press.

Deshpande, S. 1998. 'After Culture: Renewed Agendas for the Political Economy of India', *Cultural Dynamics*, 10 (2), 147–69.

———. 2003. *Contemporary India: A Sociological View* New Delhi: Viking.

Donner, H. 2006. 'Committed Mothers and Well-adjusted Children: Privatisation, Early-Years Education and Motherhood in Calcutta', *Modern Asian Studies*, 40 (2), 371–95.

———. 2008. *Domestic Goddesses: Maternity, Globalization and Middle-class Identity in Contemporary India*. London: Ashgate.

Fernandes, L. 2006. *India's New Middle Class: Democratic Politics in an Era of Economic Reform*. Minneapolis: University of Minnesota Press.

Fuller, C. J. and H. Narasimhan. 2007. 'Information Technology Professionals and the New-Rich Middle Class in Chennai (Madras)', *Modern Asia Studies*, 41 (1), 121–250.

Ganguly-Scrase, R. and T. Scrase. 2009. *Globalisation and the Middle Classes in India: The Social and Cultural Impact of Neoliberal Reforms*. London: Routledge.

Joshi, S. 2001. *Fractured Modernity: Making of a Middle Class in Colonial North India*. New Delhi: Oxford University Press.

Liddle, J. and R. Joshi. 1986. *Daughters of Independence: Gender, Caste and Class in India*. London: Zed Books.

Mankekar, P. 1999. *Screening Culture, Viewing Politics: An Ethnography of Television, Womanhood, and Nation in Postcolonial India*. Durham: Duke University Press.

Misra, B. B. 1961. *The Indian Middle Classes: Their Growth in Modern Times*. Delhi: Oxford University Press.

Palshikar, S. 2001. 'Politics of India's Middle Class', in I. Ahmad and H. Reifeld (eds), *Middle Class Values in India and Western Europe*. New Delhi: Social Science Press, pp. 171–93.

Radhakrishnan, S. 2008. 'Examining the "Global" Indian Middle Class: Gender and Culture in the Silicon Valley/Bangalore Circuit', *Journal of Intercultural Studies*, 29 (1), 7–20.

———. 2009. 'Professional Women, Good Families: Respectable Femininity and the Cultural Politics of a "New" India', *Qualitative Sociology*, 32 (2), 195–212.

Rajagopal, A. 1999. 'Thinking through Emerging Markets: Brand Logics and the Cultural Forms of Political Society in India', *Social Text*, 17 (3): 131–49.

Reay, D. 1998. *Class Work: Mothers' Involvement in Their Children's Primary Schooling*. London: University of London Press.

———. 1999. 'Linguistic Capital and Home-School Relationships: Mothers' Interactions with their Children's Primary School Teachers', *Acta Sociologica*, 42 (2), 159–68.

Reay, D. 2000. 'A Useful Extension of Bourdieu's Conceptual Framework? Emotional Capital as a Way of Understanding Mothers' Involvement in Their Children's Education', *Sociological Review*, 48 (4), 568–85.

———. 2005. 'Doing the Dirty Work of Social Class? Mothers' Work in Support of Their Children's Schooling', *Sociological Review*, 53 (Issue Supplement s2), 104–16.

Sridharan, E. 2004. 'The Growth and Sectoral Composition of India's Middle Class: Its Impact on the Politics of Economic Liberalization', *India Review*, 3 (4), 405–28.

Thapan, M. 2001. 'Adolescence, Embodiment and Gender Identity in Contemporary India: Elite Women in a Changing Society', *Women's Studies International Forum*, 24 (3–4), 359–71.

———. 2006. 'Habitus, Performance and Women's Experience: Understanding Embodiment and Identity in Everyday Life', in R. Lardinois and M. Thapan (eds), *Reading Pierre Bourdieu in a Dual Context: Essays from India and France*. New Delhi: Routledge, pp. 199–229.

Varma, P. 2001. 'Middle-class Values and the Creation of a Civil Society', in I. Ahmad and H. Reifeld (eds), *Middle Class Values in India and Western Europe*. New Delhi: Social Science Press, pp. 86–92.

Vincent, C. and S. J. Ball. 2007., '"Making up" the Middle-class Child: Families, Activities and Class Dispositions, *Sociology*, 41 (6), 1061–77.

Walsh, J. 2004. *Domesticity in Colonial India: What Women Learned When Men Gave Advice*. Lanham, Maryland: Rowman & Littlefield Publishers.

4

Disability, Policy and Education: Contrasting Perspectives from India and England

Felicity Armstrong and Pratyasha Sahoo

In this essay we begin to explore how globalisation, in its different manifestations, both creates conditions and is favourable to widening participation of disabled children and young people in education, at the same time as shifting the purposes and frameworks of education systems in ways which are selective and lead to exclusion and marginalisation. Our focus is on policy in England and India and the ways in which policy making in the two countries has been steered by internal and historical factors and the broader international context. We highlight the role of the growing international disability movement and outline some of the principal international statements and instruments which have emerged in recent years, and consider how these have been interpreted in our two countries. These developments are contrasted with policies connected with global movements of a different kind — those connected with the reconfiguration of the purposes of education as tied to economic conditions and global markets — which appear to work against the development of inclusive policies and practices. While recognising some positive advances in policy and practice in both England and India, we interrogate the failure of governments in both contexts to ensure that policies which have been put in place to support the development of inclusive education are carried through effectively.

'Disability' is a relatively recent entrant to international public debate and policy making relating to wider equality and social justice agendas. Historically, in western contexts, impairment has been treated as a natural and justifiable reason for exclusion, and this has been clearly demonstrated in the development of education systems (Altenbaugh 2006; Armstrong 2003). In the context of this essay, globalisation is interpreted as being historically situated in the sense that its roots are embedded in imperialist expansionism, the growth of world markets and sources of labour, and struggles for supremacy. A recognition of these historical antecedents is important in order to understand contemporary relationships (Alexander 2001). In particular, we recognise the crucial and multiple roles played by colonisation and the imposition of systems of governance such as education, and the complexity of the outcomes and the legacies it has spawned. An example of this is the exportation of categories of impairment, and organisational responses to disability which have been overlaid on already existing cultural knowledge and practices in colonised countries. The endemic use, in the Indian context, of categorical terminology and medical discourses, exported from England, to refer to different impairments, legislation and professional roles, is evidence of this and has implications in terms of the kind of exchanges which take place between those working in the field of disability and education in our two countries. One of these is that because the 'shorthand' of a shared lexicon is commonly adopted uncritically ('special educational needs', 'inclusive education', 'integration', 'learning difficulties') it is easy to assume that these terms have a shared *meaning* and to overlook the very profound differences between our two contexts.

Colonisation and Education

Miles and Hossain (1999: 73) argue that the linguistic and ideological domination by the west of international debate and policy agendas concerning disability and education presents a major barrier to equal participation, arising from the

> Western domination of language (i.e. English) and media (i.e. the press, satellite TV, the Internet and educational publishing) and the ideological imperialism that uses the media to obliterate or marginalise cultural and conceptual notions differing from the latest European-mezzo brow trends. . . . In the Western world of education and disability, new terms are rapidly manufactured, consumed, discarded and dumped in used condition on 'Third World' countries. Asian educational policymakers who are still trying to discover whether 'normalisation' and 'special needs' have any meaning for children in their cities and rural schools now meet Western advisers nudging them onwards to 'differentiation' and 'inclusion'.

The colonial imposition of a western system of education on India, based on Christian benevolence and an ideology of racial and cultural superiority derived from eugenics, served the purpose of both fulfilling contemporary liberal humanitarian aspirations, and as a means of anchoring power. Western education, as cultural discourse, was an important tool in the colonial project, and the work undertaken by Christian missionaries in setting up schools for disabled children in India, begun during the 1880s (Julka 2005), was part of this wider project.

The implications of the relationships forged through colonialism — a historically endemic part of globalisation — are continually present and changing and connect to contemporary questions of inclusion and exclusion in education. This is exemplified by the embeddedness of western perceptions including, for example, the assumption that impairment would naturally imply segregation. One of the defining characteristics of colonialism is the denigration and attempted wiping out, on the part of colonising regimes, of existing knowledge, values and practices in the cultures they occupy. As evidence of the wholesale demolition of the existing Indian education system Mahatma Gandhi observed:

> Today India is more illiterate than it was fifty or a hundred years ago because the British Administrators, when they came to India, instead of taking hold of things as they were, began to root them out. They scratched the soil and left the root exposed and the beautiful tree perished.[1]

Attempts to create a historical *table rase* in the newly colonised territories are undermined by research evidence. Thus, Pramila Balasundram (2005: 2) records the humanitarian support of disabled people in India as far back as 187 BC, and India's 'rich cultural legacy for inclusive education', and observes that,

> Even today, small rural schools provide education for all children under one roof, little realizing that they are following a system of education newly rediscovered in the West termed 'Inclusive Education'. The tragic fact seems to be that somewhere on our way towards modernization we have lost this unique system of education.

Education and Globalisation

Government policies in social welfare, health and education are profoundly influenced by changes in the global economy (Dale 2007). The tightening hold of the standards agenda and increasing competition internationally, under the monitorship of organisations such as the OECD and the World Bank, have a profound effect on the ways the purposes of education and questions of equity are understood. At the same time 'equity', in its multiple configurations and interpretations (see Lall and Rao in this volume), has also become part of a globalised agenda, and disability has been drawn into the terrain in which the struggles between equality and the impulsions of a market ideology take place.

Van Zanten (2007: 88) argues that the 'influence of world models tends to produce a gap between official national rhetoric and the real hybridization of global and local processes' but,

> Fragmentation can in fact lead to a restructuring of decision-making processes: the central State lays down essential principles and leaves the burden of connecting them to social environments to local agents at the periphery who are forced to reconstruct their identities, forge new alliances and invent new organizational and pedagogical responses to crucial problems.

These ideas are illuminating in terms of understanding the positioning of disability and notions of inclusion in government rhetoric and policy making, and the ways in which policies are interpreted, reconfigured, or absorbed and lost in other projects and purposes. There are different examples of these in both the English and Indian contexts, and in this essay we hope to show how 'at the periphery' new organisational and pedagogical responses to the competing claims of social justice and 'performance' have emerged in relation to the participation of disabled children and young people in education. In England, for example, there has been a spread in the discourse of inclusion in the development of national policy documents and statements such as the statutory guidance on inclusive schooling (DfES 2001; Armstrong 2005; Dyson and Gallannaugh 2007). There was an apparent commitment on the part of governments to ensure that disabled people 'have the same human rights as everyone else', as evidenced in the Disability Discrimination Act (DDA, 1995) and the Special Educational Needs and Disability Discrimination Act (SENDA, 2001). However, other government discourse and policies, dominated by managerialism, competition and the measuring of narrowly defined outputs, are underpinned by a very different set of values and vision concerning the purposes of education and its structures, organisation and curriculum.

This configuration of the purposes of education has had a powerful influence on school cultures and pedagogical practices, which have often served to exclude students and others who experience difficulties in learning or who do not 'fit in'. In England, the continued reaffirmation of the important role played by special schools in the education system, as evidenced by the New labour government's refusal to ratify Article 24 of the Convention on Human Rights without a codicil protecting segregated special education (2009), is one outcome of this reconfiguration. Squeezed by these apparently conflicting rafts of policies, it is left to parents, children, local government officials, teachers and governors in local communities at the micro-levels of the system to interpret policies, and resolve contradictions and 'invent new organizational and pedagogical responses to crucial problems' (van Zanten 2007).

Developments in education in the UK and in India mark conflicting paradigm shifts. In the UK, on the one hand, there has been a move away from seeing impairment as a rationale for segregation and exclusion to a very different understanding — that full participation in education is a human right for all. In contrast, while education has always been seen as a necessity in terms of countries' economies, recent education policy reflects a radical shift away from a belief in education as a 'good' in itself and as a personal and social human right, to a view of the purposes of education being primarily concerned with contributing to economic performance.

In India there has also been a rapid growth in the use of discourses of inclusion in relation to education and disabled children in government documents, and among researchers and practitioners. In spite of its status as 'official rhetoric', many disabled children, especially those in rural areas, do not go to school, and the emphasis in education policy documents and in approaches and attitudes of teachers continues to be 'impairment led' (Singal 2008a: 3). However, local and regional responses to 'crucial problems' which create opportunities for disabled children to become learners alongside their peers at school, have emerged largely from the work of non-governmental organisations (NGOs), and campaigning and charitable organisations, sometimes with collaboration and funding from other countries. Examples of 'grassroots' initiatives include The Spastics Society of India founded in 1972 by Mithu Alur, Ashay Pratisthan founded in 1988 by Aruna Dalmia, and Amar Jyoti set up as a Charitable Trust in 1982. All of these, while focusing primarily on the education of disabled children, provide opportunities for disabled and non-disabled children to learn together. In many cases, it is community-based organisations which have created solutions in relation to the education of local children. It is they who have taken up the task of connecting national policies and the tenets of international directives (such as education for all [EFA]) to the social environments in their own communities.

Globalisation and the International Agenda for 'Inclusive Education'

Strategies and policies adopted by policy makers internationally concerning disabled children and their education have undergone considerable change in recent years and this has occurred as a result of advocacy and political engagement in local contexts, and the pressure of international campaigns and instruments. There has been a shift away from understanding segregation as a natural and inevitable consequence of impairment, towards a view of the disabled child as having 'special needs' which require particular kinds of intervention and accommodation in order to facilitate their participation as equal members of society. 'Global' organisations such as UNESCO have provided a focus for international concerns about the numbers of children who are excluded from education (Singal 2008a) and contributed to international debate concerning children's rights and advanced global strategies to confront inequalities in education.

An important contributor to changing understanding of impairment and disability is the politicisation of the international disabled people's movement and the development of disability studies 'rooted in the social model of disability and sociological insights' (Barnes 2007). Tundawala (2007: 1) observes that the significance of the social model

> lies in the fact that disability is not viewed as something invoking pity or in need of a cure. In fact, it presents disability as a consequence of oppression, prejudice and discrimination by the society against disabled people. There is a shift in focus from the disabled individual to the society and its disabling environment constructing economic, social, health, architectural, legal, cultural and other barriers in order to deliberately prevent people with impairments enjoy full benefits of the society. The change in sociological attitudes towards disability finds legal recognition in various disability related legislations throughout the world.[2]

The work of disabled activists internationally has provided a theoretical and political framework for the emergence of a 'disability rights' movement which has influenced policy initiatives and programme implementation in ways which include disabled children and their families as part of the larger international community. While the Jomtein Declaration brought Education for All Children centre stage, it was the Salamanca Declaration (1994) which brought global attention to the rights of disabled people and introduced a new perspective and language to the EFA. National commitments to EFA saw greater attention focused on special needs as will be discussed later on in relation to India. The disability movement in India comprises a number of NGOs and activists who have played a crucial role in creating awareness about the rights of disabled people and in making disability a political issue. Among these organisations the National Resource Centre for Inclusion of India and the Roehr Institute of Canada have played a key role at the national level and in building links with the global movement (Bach 2009). A series of three North South Dialogues took place in Mumbai (2000), Kerala (2003) and New Delhi (2006) organised as part of this Indo-Canadian partnership. These conferences, whose stated purposes were to support the implementation of inclusive education and the building of a Global Alliance, were attended by academics, activists, practitioners, including many disabled people, from many different countries. These are examples of the ways in which globalisation is creating arenas and forging new alliances which facilitate the diffusion and exchange of political ideas, legislation and standpoints, as well as fostering the creation of 'new pedagogical responses to crucial problems'. They also exemplify the many levels through which globalisation exercises its influence.

The global engagements referred to here have led to the emergence of advocacy for 'inclusive education' and the participation of disabled children within the regular everyday life of the school. The term 'inclusive education' has itself become a commonly used part of global terminology.

It is important to consider the emergence and impact of international statements and instruments relating to disability and equity, the global dimensions and 'borrowing' of policies and discourses relating to 'special needs', disability and inclusion, and the effects of global economic relationships on education policy making in India and England.

The International Context:
Instruments and Instrumentalism

Although the term 'inclusion' was not used widely before the 1990s, the principles of inclusive education were already emerging internationally. The General Assembly of the UN adopted the Declaration on the Rights of the Disabled Persons in 1973 underpinned by the principle that 'the disabled shall enjoy the same human rights as the other human beings without any exception'. In 1989 the UN Convention on the Rights of the Child was ratified and the World Conference on Education for All drew up the Jomtien Declaration (1990) which upholds the inherent right of every child to a full cycle of primary education and a commitment to a 'child-centred pedagogy, where individual differences are accepted as a challenge and not as a problem' (Rieser 2008). This was followed by the Salamanca Statement and Framework for Action on Special Needs Education (1994) which focused on the rights of disabled children. It stated that

> schools should accommodate all children regardless of their physical, intellectual, social, emotional, linguistic or other conditions. This should include disabled and gifted children, street and working children, children from remote or nomadic populations, children from linguistic, ethnic or cultural minorities and children from other disadvantaged or marginalised areas or groups. (para. 3)

In 2006 the UN Convention on the Rights of People with Disabilities promoted the right of 'persons with disabilities' to inclusive education through Article 24 which was adopted by 117 countries, including the UK and India. India ratified the Convention in 2007, including Article 24 which makes a commitment to developing an inclusive education system in which mainstream schools develop the capacity to include all disabled children and young people. In contrast, the UK has adopted a conservative approach and has declared its intention to append an 'interpretative declaration' to Article 24 which allows for a continued role for special schools within the general education system. Some commentators have suggested that the notion of 'Education for All' is used as if it 'only applied to economically disadvantaged countries or countries in the South, falsely conveying the impression that Northern countries have succeeded in including all students equally' (Alur 2007: 94).

This view is borne out by the paradox that while India has signed up to a commitment, in principle, that all children should learn alongside their peers, the British government claims a dispensation from the full application of Article 24, thus ridding itself of the awkward requirement that disabled children and young people should attend their local community schools as a right.

It has become increasingly accepted that inclusive education presents a powerful approach to achieving the Millennium Goals (Singal 2008a).[3] Although it is argued that UNESCO's EFA programme, and other international statements, continue to marginalise disability and fail to address the lack of education for many disabled children globally (Miles and Singal 2009), international statements and action have been a positive aspect of globalisation in its broadest sense in terms of the opportunities it has opened up for discussion and for the formulation of statements and projects to defend human rights and support, protect and champion children in terms of participation in education.

In contrast, globalisation has also had a profound influence on national policies in education in terms of increasing instrumentalism and a narrowing, and centralising, control of curricula and processes of testing and selection.

These processes present a major barrier to the participation in mainstream schools of many disabled children globally. Not only have they led to greater diversification and stratification in terms of the emergence of different kinds of schools and their governance, but they have had a particular impact on questions of disability and participation because of constraints on the development of inclusive cultures and practices and on the possibilities for flexible and creative responses to diversity and difference.

Disability and Inclusive Education in England

It is difficult to find any statistics concerning the numbers of disabled children in England. This is surprising, given the relatively small size of the population, and the long-standing commitment by governments to the gathering and publishing of statistical data. Unlike India, all children and young people are enrolled in some form of education between the ages of 5–16. According to a report *Disabled Children: Numbers, Characteristics and Local Service Provision*, prepared for The Department of Children, Schools and Families (Maloney et al. 2008) there are between 3 and 5.4 per cent of disabled children out of the total population, and the relative closeness of these estimates to those for India, as noted in the following section, is also, perhaps, surprising. However, there are enormous difficulties in gathering, analysing and comparing data on impairment and disability as there are vast differences in the ways different professionals and organisations identify and categorise different impairments, even within the same national setting.

The history of formal educational provision for disabled children in England is most easily linked to the introduction of mass education through the education acts of 1870, 1876 and 1880 although there are many examples of earlier projects, sometimes seen as 'experiments' of teaching or 'training' of children described today as 'having learning difficulties', as well as the Workhouse and the Asylum where disabled adults and children were among the populations of the destitute and those deemed to be insane. There were also institutions for deaf and blind children, going back to the 18th century, where education, normalisation and Christianity were all regarded as important, and in the 19th century numerous asylums were established for children who, today, would be officially described as 'having learning difficulties'. The development of special education in the late 19th and early 20th centuries was accompanied by the emergent professions of educationists and medics and psychologists in Europe and North America, as well as the growth of official interest in the health of the general population and of school children in particular. Special institutions were more concerned with care and training, although there were some notable exceptions.

The history of special education in England has centred on perceptions relating to sometimes contradictory concerns of identification and categorisation of impairments, and appropriate responses to the 'needs' of disabled children and young people within the education and professional structures and values of the time (Riddell 2002). For example, the 1944 Education Act (UK), while introducing 11 'categories of handicap', also drew large numbers of disabled children into the education system for the first time, making Local Education Authorities responsible for their education. With the implementation of the Education (Handicapped Children) Act, 1970 the responsibility for provision for children categorised as 'mentally handicapped' moved from the health authorities to local education authorities. This represented an important paradigm shift in terms of the emergent recognition that all children should be regarded as learners and as entitled to some form of education.

The Warnock Report (1978) from which emerged the 1981 Education Act, marked a further paradigm shift and important change in perspective in challenging assumptions that the categorisation of impairment was a justification for the 'special' provision. The 1981 Education Act introduced the concept of special educational needs, a term which was intended to focus on children's educational needs, rather than medically based categories of impairment. Provision was made for the introduction of statutory assessment of learning difficulties to establish whether a child had special educational needs — introducing the new label 'SEN' — and if so, what these needs were. 'Statements' of special educational needs, stipulating the nature of the 'needs', how they should be met, and the resources required, were issued for some children as an outcome of the assessment procedures.

More recently, legislation such as the Special Educational Needs and Disability Act (2001) adopted a change of emphasis in establishing a duty to educate children with special educational needs in mainstream schools provided it is compatible with the wishes of the parent and the 'provision of efficient education for other children'. This Act has failed to bring about a radical change for all disabled children in that successive governments continue to support the continued existence of special schools on the grounds of 'parental choice' and an insistence that there is a 'need' for such schools.

The Duty to promote Disability Equality and to provide Disability Equality Schemes was introduced by the Disability Discrimination Amendment Act 2005, and became binding on all public bodies, including education, by December 2007. The Disability Equality Duty requires all educational establishments to ensure that disabled pupils are not treated less favourably than their non-disabled peers; schools must be fully accessible; they must promote positive attitudes to all disabled pupils in all areas of the curriculum; ensure the elimination of disabilist bullying and harassment; promote equality for disabled pupils, parents, staff and members of the community and ensure that disabled pupils, parents and staff play a full part in the public life of the school.

The continued support for special schools on the part of successive governments explains the relatively slight decrease in the numbers of children attending a special school over the past 10 years, in spite of legislation which appears to support inclusive education. Another reason for this is that although, in principle, local authorities are obliged to implement government policies, it is understood and accepted that there will be a wide variation in terms of *interpretation* — reflecting different political and ideological interests. It is also the case that while far more children who have physical disabilities attend mainstream schools than in the past, children and young people who disrupt the smooth running of the school because of their disturbing behaviour, are now more likely to be placed in a special school, special unit or pupil referral unit (see figures in First Release, DfE 2010).

In England, schools which claim, and demonstrate, a serious commitment to inclusion and equality and do not operate formal or informal selection policies, are often to be found in the least economically advantaged areas and they tend to perform poorly in national tests in comparison with schools in wealthier areas. Inclusive schools such a Sharrow Primary School in Sheffield, England (Abram et al. 2009), have an 'open door' policy and welcome all members of the community regardless of disability or level of attainment. Its population includes children 'in transition' who are refugees, seeking asylum, or living in temporary accommodation, and reflects the diversity of the area, with only 8 per cent speaking English as a first language. The school is fully accessible and there is a serious engagement with transforming curricula and pedagogical practices so that every child receives a meaningful education. Scores in national tests are low and, although OfSTED (Office for Standards in Education) has praised the school for its inclusive response to diversity and its close links with the local community, this praise is outweighed by criticism of the school's performance in national tests which are regarded in public reports as the only 'real' indicators of 'achievement'.

In a sense, schools such as Sharrow Primary School function 'at the periphery' of the main system, often developing creative responses to diversity in their local communities which, while enhancing opportunities for participation and the creation of equitable school cultures, come into conflict with the demands of the national curriculum and assessment. Research studies have shown how pressures to improve scores on national tests have distorted the work of schools, especially those seeking to promote inclusive policies and practices (Armstrong 2003; Florian and Rouse 2005; Ainscow et al. 2006). This is, perhaps, an important indication of the ways in which, in the UK context, 'local agents' mediate, or 'resolve', government hybridised policies which are potentially contradictory in appearing to support 'inclusion' while being driven by a more powerful agenda — that of performance on the global arena.

Disability and Inclusive Education in India

In the era of a rising global debate on the issue of disability, India as a signatory to the International Declarations (UNESCO 1994) on Special Educational Needs has committed to the development of persons with disability from a human rights perspective. To estimate the actual magnitude of the disabled population has been a major challenge. Official estimates of the proportion of persons with disability range from 2.13 per cent (Census 2001) to 1.8 per cent (NSSO 2003). These differences could be due to the variations in study design and the different definitions used in measuring each type of disability (cited in Pal 2010). Alternative estimates using broader definitions estimate persons with disability to comprise around 4–8 per cent of the population. Policy formulations are unrealistic as they take into account the lower, official figure rather than the much higher estimates. The picture is made more complex by variations across groups. As evidenced by NSSO (2003) the prevalence of disability, in the general population, among males is greater (2 per cent) than females (1.5 per cent). Similarly, it is greater in rural areas than in the urban areas and there are more disabled people to be found among socially dis-advantaged groups like the scheduled castes (SCs), that is, 2.4 per cent (ibid.). There are wide variations across types of disability showing highest prevalence rate of motor impairments (57 per cent) followed by visual impairments (28 per cent).

It is estimated that 38 per cent of disabled children do not attend school in India. There are also significant gender differentials among attendance rates of disabled children, with disabled boys' attendance rates at 8–10 per cent above those of disabled girls (World Bank 2007). Of those who have access to formal schooling, only 12 per cent complete the primary level of education and less than 5 per cent complete secondary education (NSSO 2003). The non-enrollment of disabled children is seen to be largely due to the distance between home and school and economic conditions.

In India, formal education for disabled children began during colonisation with the support of the Church and the missionary societies. In 1869, Jane Leupot started a school for blind students in Benares and the first formal school for children with intellectual disabilities was set up in Kurseong in 1918 (Balasundram 2005: 2). In pre-independence India, the imposition of western concepts through colonialism, and through medicalised discourses, underpinned the development of segregated special settings through non-governmental sources deemed to be the most appropriate form of education for children with disabilities. The Sergeant Report of 1944 appeared as the first government document to explicitly mention the education of disabled people. It referred to 'integrated' education, but in limited terms and focused on separate special institutions for disabled children — a position which continued well after independence. In the First Five Year Plan (1951–56) non-governmental voluntary organisations assumed increasing responsibility for the education of this disadvantaged group.

The Kothari Commission (1966) identified four categories of 'handicapped persons' and set up a 'realistic target' of providing education to 15 per cent of those with visual, orthopaedic and hearing impairments, and to 5 per cent of those with intellectual impairments by 1986. It made no recommendations on the provision for vocational education/training. There is no rationale given for the basis for setting these targets. Like the Sargeant Report, the Kothari Commission also recommended the adoption of a 'dual approach (special and integrated)' to meet the educational needs of disabled children. However, the Kothari Commission Report specifically observed that 'many handicapped children find it psychologically disturbing to be placed in an ordinary school and in such cases they should be sent to special schools' (Kothari Commission 1966).

The 1960s was the period when Indian policy makers were preoccupied with the restructuring of the entire education system that had emerged during the colonial period — provision, administration, curriculum and so on. During the same period, the UK, with an established and stable system of education and the involvement of Local Education Authorities (LEAs) focused more on teacher training. Thus, while India was still thinking of addressing the question of *access*, the UK was already building resource capacity in order to meet the educational needs of disabled children. It was only with the National Policy on Education in 1986, and more specifically, following the Rehabilitation Council Act 1992, that the educational needs of disabled children received focused policy attention in India.

The debate concerning the education of disabled children was dominated by the 'Special Needs' approach until the 1970s. The early

1970s marked an important paradigm shift towards 'integration' and is reflected in the language and the provisions for disabled children as explicitly emphasised in the Integrated Education for the Disabled Children (IEDC) scheme. Launched in 1974, its purpose was 'to provide educational opportunities for children identified as having mild and moderate disabilities in common/ordinary schools. Disabled children placed in special schools should also be integrated in common schools once they had acquired the communication and daily living skills at the functional level.' This marks an attempt to move away from the focus on 'special education' and towards 'integrating' children with disability in common/regular schools. However, though India launched the IEDC scheme in 1974 and used the term 'integration', focused attention on the special needs of children with disability within the perspective of the 'social model' was more than a decade away. The dual approach (special and integrated education) was reaffirmed in the National Policy for Education (NPE 1986) which for the first time saw focused policy attention on teacher training programmes and recommendations that provision be made for vocational education for disabled people.

Following India's signing of the 'Salamanca Statement (UNESCO 1994)' with its clearest and unequivocal call for 'Inclusive Education', the 1990s saw the rapid incorporation of the term 'inclusive education' in various official documents and reports (Singal 2009: 10). However, while official policy discourse has incorporated international paradigm shifts and changes in terminology, India has been slow to translate these into legislation.

In 1995 India enacted the Persons with Disabilities Act (PWD Act, 1995) which 'endeavours to promote the integration of students with disabilities in the normal schools' and also promotes the 'establishment and availability of special schools across the nation in both Government and private sectors'. It was the first Act which used the concept of 'inclusive education', albeit while also promoting special schools, marking a move towards changing 'the environment to suit the child and not the child to suit the environment'.

Internationally, both access and participation were the main concerns of the Millennium Development Goals (United Nations 2000) on education and inclusion as a strategy for achieving the goals of 'Education for All' which began to gain wide acceptance from the 1990s (Peters 2003, cited in Singal 2008a). In keeping with these trends, in the late 1990s, India adopted the District Primary Education Programme (DPEP). Sarva Shiksha Abhiyan (SSA), a flagship programme of the Government of India to attain Universal Elementary Education (UEE), covering the entire country including specific components for inclusive education for 'Children with Special Needs' (CWSN) was launched in 2001–2. The Persons with Disability Act (2006) declared a commitment to providing every disabled child with free education until the age of 18, and the removal of physical barriers to access to school, as well as the adaptation of the curriculum and the training of teachers. More recently, in 2009, The Right of Children to Free and Compulsory Education Act was passed which includes 'children with disability' as having a right to education, although in the original draft of the Bill in 2009 there was no mention of the education of disabled people. This Act sharpens awareness and the debate on 'inclusive education' and it is hoped that the Disability Section will find a way for its implementation through the SSA within 'a multi option delivery system'. This includes priority areas such as identification/assessment of children with special needs, providing assistive devices, networking with NGOs, barrier-free access, training for teachers on inclusive education, appointment of resource teachers and adaptation of the curricula and pedagogy.

It is noteworthy that India ratified the UN Convention in 2007, including Article 24, which makes a commitment to developing an inclusive education approach. A brief overview of the policy changes and shifts in relation to the education of disabled people in India shows that while India has been relatively quick in adopting discourses of inclusion, there has been a failure to build the necessary institutional capacities and understanding to translate these into school and classroom practices. There has been a transition from 'special' to 'integration' and most recently 'the inclusive paradigm' which emphasises 'recognizing and responding to the diverse needs of the disabled students through systemic changes'. However, as Kalyanpur (2007: 5) argues, this shift may indicate 'a tendency to be politically correct by taking on current discourses circulating in the west without a real or common understanding of their meaning, resulting in dilution of service quality' (ibid., cited in Singal 2008a: 1516). Thus, though inclusion is seen as the most 'appropriate' policy for the schooling of disabled children in India, in terms of the implementation of government policy, it has remained largely at the level of terminology, although there are some notable exceptions at the local level which have evolved through the commitment and work of activists and organisations such as the National Resource Centre for Inclusion of India.

Inclusive Practice at the 'Grass Roots' in India

There is very little research evidence on the practice of inclusive education in India, although a number of schools are being identified as 'inclusive'. There is a relative absence of developments such as child-centred pedagogy, activity-based learning, increasing equity in assessment and in inclusive teaching such as group/cooperative learning. Furthermore, there is little information about the experiences of children themselves in schools described as 'inclusive' in India. A critical review of available government reports suggests that the approach is still largely one of 'integration' in India. For instance, the enactment of the PWD Act of 1995 continued to use the term integration despite India being a signatory to the Salamanca World Declaration (1994) with its call for 'inclusive education'. Further, although the 2006 Policy for People with Disabilities in India mentioned the term 'inclusive education', it lacked a clear cut plan for the development and implementation of inclusive policies in mainstream settings, leaving schools with a 'free hand'. As rightly argued by Tanmoy Bhattacharya (2010: 211), 'The RTE (2009) does little to encourage "inclusive education" . . . it tacitly encourages integration and maintains silence over inclusion'.

A few affirmative measures for disabled children have been introduced such as providing financial incentives, appointing one or two special teachers, having a resource room in a regular school or at times using an NGO school as a resource centre. Identification of children with disability is still a major challenge and many children with hearing and mild visual impairments are likely to be identified as 'slow learners' and 'failures' without their special needs being identified and addressed.

In a study of 12 schools in Delhi described as 'inclusive' (11 private and one government), Nidhi Singal (2008a) observed that although all these schools facilitated the entry of children with various disabilities into the mainstream classroom, they continued to be excluded from opportunities for participation in the curriculum and the culture of the school. Teachers made no changes in their pedagogical approaches and strongly believed that not 'all' children can be taught in the mainstream. Teachers' efforts to provide flexible opportunities for learning, such as adjusting seating arrangements so that a child experiencing barriers to learning can work with more able peers, or giving them additional time to complete tasks, or some adaptations of the curriculum, were examples of small adjustments that they made in response to the needs of these children. There was evidence of a high dependency on parents or special educators from an NGO for teaching children identified as experiencing difficulties in learning. A major constraint in the education of disabled children and young people in regular schools is that of resources. A study of parents of disabled children studying in two IEDC schools in Bhubaneswar showed that schools lacked the ability to provide the necessary academic services and support (Sahoo 2004). Parents wanted the IEDC schools to be better equipped in terms of the provision of specially adapted and equipped resource rooms, well-trained special teachers who could efficiently teach all the subjects in all the classes, increased financial aid and the provision of good quality aids and other equipment which were lacking in these schools. These changes, they felt, would help their disabled children to cope better in the integrated schools (Sahoo 2004). This issue has been given more serious attention in the recent financial budget and there has been a substantial increase in the national budget allocated for disabled people. However, governmental intervention has been very slow in responding to the diverse needs of disabled children, and the role played by community and civil society organisations has been very important in India.

Initiatives of NGOs

With the National Policy (Bhas 2006) and the interventions of DPEP and SSA, there has been an increasing focus on partnerships between the public and the private sectors in order to achieve the goal of inclusive education. The role of NGOs has been recognised over the years for the education of children with disabilities. For example, the Spastics Society of India (SSI) has developed a network of 18 associated schools in India. All these schools work for children with developmental disorders by providing facilities for identification, assessment, education and treatment which works on the inclusion model. Some of the practices adopted include following a normal academic curriculum, providing equipment (callipers, boots, crutches, etc.) and occupational, physio, speech and motor therapies, as well as establishing links with industries and institutions that can help in providing employment to disabled adults.

Other notable NGOs such as Amar Jyoti, Akshay Pratishthan and Astalavista Divine Welfare and Research Foundation are experimenting with the model of inclusive education. By using a variety of approaches, such as child-centred pedagogy, vocational training courses (tailoring, carpentry, beauty culture, refrigeration, home science, etc.) and adopting special teacher training methodologies they have been able to successfully include both disabled and non-disabled children together into mainstream education. Another experiment in mainstreaming disabled children is Dharavi's Noorani Memorial Karuna Sadan School which has spread to 12 anganwadis (play schools). Disabled and non-disabled peers from over 5,000 households study together. The school has provided multiple assessment, motor/physio/occupational therapies, long-term treatment courses, concept building, intellectual stimulation and parent counselling. This shift in focus marks the importance of the role played by local initiatives which is crucial.

States such as Tamil Nadu, West Bengal and Uttar Pradesh have involved NGOs in all the stages of the IED implementation. This has included involving special schools as demonstration centres, using NGO schools as resource centres for children with severe and multiple disabilities, using the special school staff as trainers for teachers in regular schools, etc. A major problem is that most of the NGOs working with disabled children are 'urban centric', though data reveals a larger concentration of disabled people in rural areas.

The foregoing discussion suggests that social justice in relation to the education of disabled children in India may be 'visible' more at the level of intentions as set out in policy discourse rather than at the level of inclusive practices in schools themselves. Hitherto, socially disadvantaged groups such as the Scheduled Castes and Scheduled Tribes and the socio-religious minorities have received greater attention partly because they have a greater voice in the democratic process. Disability groups have been a voiceless minority and their concerns have been more easily marginalised. International pressures and the disability movement have been responsible for issues regarding disability being taken seriously in recent years. Global advocacy has placed the recognition of the rights of disabled people alongside those of other marginalised groups. Discourses and terminologies from the west have influenced policy and strategies. There has been some change in the policies adopted by the Government of India but they are of limited nature found only in some schools as reflected in a few studies mentioned earlier. The 'medical model' has to some extent been replaced by the 'social model' at the level of policy and discourse but there is a long way to go to realise social justice in the practice of schooling in the direction of a human rights perspective where the right to education for all is viewed as a basic human right.

Disability and the Private Sector

It is against this background that we need to understand the continued and increasing importance of the private 'for profit' sector which offers a 'default' alternative to mainstream and state education for disabled children, and others who do not fit into the system. In England the majority of places at these fee-paying schools are paid for out of public funds by local education authorities. Private special schools are frequently run by business consortia such as the UK-based SENAD group ('a brighter day, a brighter future'!) which owns 13 special schools in the country with fees ranging from approximately £39,000 (day pupils) per annum to £125,000 (boarding fees). Colliers CRE is a 'worldwide affiliation of independently owned and operated companies' whose principle interest is real estate and has specialists focusing on the special education real estate sector, with an apparent particular interest in 'learning difficulties'.[4] This is an example of the commodification of disability, and disabled people, through the adoption of marketing strategies:

> Learning difficulties is normally defined as a significant impairment of intelligence and social functioning acquired before adulthood and it has been estimated that approximately 2% of the population (over one million people) can be described as having some form of learning difficulty. A learning difficulty is not an illness and cannot be cured.

> The sector is currently one of dynamic change, influenced by Government initiatives including the White Paper 'valuing People' and introduction of the Supporting People Grant. The sector offer a range of attractive opportunities for those operators possessing the necessary skills and expertise to deliver the required level of service.[5]

It is a curious paradox that as the 'inclusion agenda' appears to be strengthened in terms of national and international rhetoric and legislation, the numbers of disabled children placed in the private sector in the UK are slowly increasing (DfE 2010).[6]

The private sector is also rapidly increasing in importance in India. There has been a dramatic growth in the number of special schools, especially in urban areas (Singal 2008b) with 1,035 special schools in the early 1990s (Ministry of Human Resources and Development 1992) rising to 2,500 special schools in the country by 2000 (Rehabilitation Council of India 2000). It is not clear what proportion of these schools are privately owned, or run by charities and NGOs, and how many are government schools. There are examples, however, of private business–based organisations which have recently moved into the 'special school' market. One of these is the Astalavista Divine Welfare and Research Foundation which is a subsidiary of the Astalavista Infimedia Private Limited (AIPL) which describes itself as a 'front-runner in Internet and Web Technologies allowing Indian Business Concerns to utilize the Internet to its maximum, in opening their doors to International Trade'.[7] The Astalavista Divine Welfare and Research Foundation opened with the purpose of working to improve the 'health and quality of life of socially disadvantaged people especially through its programme, training and research . . . the focus has always been on education of children with Multiple Disabilities, Cerebral palsy, Autism, hearing impairment'. It is interesting to note a further example of the ways in which categories of impairment have become part of a universal language of individual deficit — a further outcome of globalisation.

There is, therefore, a new presence on the 'special education' scene in both India and England — that of globally connected and business-based organisations which merge economic and business considerations with philanthropic projects. Rather than being 'local agents at the periphery', these organisations represent global agents, operating across national boundaries, which assist the processes of selection and marginalisation necessitated by the requirement for schools to function effectively and competitively by providing mechanisms and arenas for the segregation of disabled learners.

Conclusion

In the early stages of writing this essay the task of 'comparing' our two very different settings through the double lens of disability and education seemed a particularly challenging one, and so it has proved to be. However, in exploring the role and reconfigurations brought about by globalisation, some interesting issues and points of connection have emerged. First, the importance of understanding the many levels at which globalisation reaches into questions relating to education, its meaning, structures and purposes. Some of these appear to be pulling in different directions. While international statements and policies, most of which India and the UK have signed, support the full participation of disabled children in mainstream education, the global standards agenda in which the nature and aims of education are expressed in narrow technicist terms, has steered questions of curriculum and pedagogy and assessment in ways which strengthen processes of selection and marginalisation. Similarly, while both India and the UK have passed potentially powerful legislation in support of inclusive education, 'special education' is, in some respects, a 'growth industry' in both countries.

In this essay we have begun to explore how globalisation, in its different manifestations, both creates the conditions and demands for widening participation of disabled children and young people in education internationally, at the same time as shifting the purposes and frameworks of education systems in ways which are selective and narrow and lead to exclusion and marginalisation. We have underlined the role of the growing international disability movement and outlined some of the principal international statements and instruments which have emerged in recent years. These have a con-tinuing powerful and profound influence globally on perceptions, understanding and policy concerning education, rights and par-ticipation of minority and disadvantaged groups, including disabled people. Such developments are in sharp contrast to policies connected with global movements of a different kind — those connected with the reconfiguration of the purposes of education as tied to economic conditions and the global markets — which appear to work against the development of inclusive policies and practices.

✛

Notes

1. 'The beautiful tree' refers to Gandhi's 'tree of education'. The statement was made at Chatham House in London, 1931.
2. Section 2(i) of the persons with Disabilities (Equal Opportunities, Protection of Rights and Full Participation Act) passed in India in 1995, however, seeks to define disability in terms of a medical problem.
3. The eight Millennium Development Goals are: Eradicate extreme poverty and hunger; achieve universal primary education; promote gender equality and empower women; reduce child mortality; improve maternal health; combat HIV and AIDS, malaria and other diseases; ensure environmental sustainability; develop a global partnership for development.

4. http://www.colliers.com/Markets/UnitedKingdom.
5. http:www.colliers.com/Markets/United Kingdom/Services/Practice.
6. Approximately 1 per cent of the school population in the UK attend residential special schools primarily funded through local education authorities.
7. http://www.astalavista.co.in/astalavista-story.

References

Abram, E., F. Armstrong, L. Barton and Lynne Ley. 2009. 'Diversity, Democracy and Change in the Inner City: Understanding Schools as Belonging to Communities', in J. Lavia and M. Moore (eds), *Decolonizing Community Contexts: Cross-cultural Perspectives on Policy and Practice*. London: Routledge.

Ainscow, M., T. Booth and A. Dyson. 2006. *Improving Schools, Developing Inclusion*. London: Routledge.

Alexander, R. 2001. 'Border Crossings: Towards a Comparative Pedagogy', in *Comparative Education*, 37 (4), 507–23.

Altenbaugh, R. J. 2006. 'Where are the Disabled in the History of Education? The Impact of Polio on Sites of Learning', *History of Education*, 35 (6), 705–30.

Alur, M. 2007. 'The Lethargy of a Nation: Inclusive Education in India and Developing Systematic Strategies for Change', in L. Barton and F. Armstrong (eds), *Policy, Experience and Change: Cross-cultural Reflections on Inclusive Education*. Dordrecht: Springer.

Armstrong, D. 2005. 'Reinventing "Inclusion": New Labour and the Cultural Politics of Special Education', *Oxford Review of Education*, 31 (1), 119–34.

Armstrong, F. 2003. 'Difference, Discourse and Democracy: The Making and Breaking of Policy in the Market Place', *International Journal of Inclusive Education*, 7 (3), 241–58.

Bach, M. 2009. 'Scaling Up Inclusive Education: Reflections on Theory and the Practice of the National Resource Centre for Inclusion — India', in M. Alur and V. Timmons (eds), *Inclusive Education Across Cultures: Crossing Boundaries, Sharing Ideas*. New Delhi: Sage Publications.

Balasundram, P. 2005. 'The Journey Towards Inclusive Education in India', paper presented at Seisa University, Ashibetsu Shi, Hokkaido, Japan, 9 July.

Bhas, D. 2006. *National Policy for the Disabled: No Clear Roadmap for Action*, InfoChange India news and features development, News India, http://infochangeindia.org/20060828251/Disabilities/Features (accessed 25 May 2009).

Bhattacharya, T. 2010. 'Re-examining Issue of Inclusion in Education', *Economic and Political Weekly*, 45 (16), 18–25.

Barnes, C. 2007. 'Disability, Higher Education and the Inclusive Society', *British Journal of Sociology of Education*, 28 (1), 135–45.

Dale, R. 2007. 'Specifying Globalization Effects on National Policy', in S. Ball, I. Goodson and M. Maguire (eds), *Education, Globalisation and New Times*. London: Routledge, pp. 64–82.

DfE. 2010. 'Special Educational Needs in England: January 2010', www. education.gov.uk/rsgateway/DB/SFR/5000939 (accessed 3 March 2010).

DfES. 2001. *Inclusive Schooling: Children with Special Educational Needs.* Ref DfES/0774/2001. London: DfES.

Dyson, A. and F. Gallannaugh. 2007. 'National Policy and the Development of Inclusive School Practices: A Case Study', *Cambridge Journal of Education*, 37 (4), 473–88.

Education for National Development. Report of the Kothari Commission (1964–66). New Delhi: Publications Division, Government of India.

Florian, L. and M. Rouse. 2005. 'Inclusive Practice in English Secondary Schools: Lessons Learned', in M. Nind, J. Rix, K. Sheehy and K. Simmons (eds), *Curriculum and Pedagogy in Inclusive Education: Values into Practice*. London: Routledge.

Government of India. 1986. National Policy on Education, New Delhi.

———. 1995. The Persons with Disability Act (Equal Opportunities, Protection of Rights and Full Participation Act), 1995. New Delhi.

Jeffrey, R. and N. Singal. 2008. 'Disability Estimates in India: Implications from a Changing Landscape of Socio-political Struggle'. Research Consortium on Educational Outcomes and Poverty (RECOUP). Policy Brief No. 3. Faculty of Education, University of Cambridge, UK.

Julka, A. 2005. 'Educational Provisions and Practices for Learners with Disabilities in India', Paper presented at the Inclusive and Supportive Education Congress, 1–4 August, Glasgow, UK, www.isec2005.org.uk/ isec/abstracts/papers_i/julka_a.doc (accessed 28 December 2009).

Miles, M. and F. Hussein. 1999. 'Rights and Disabilities in Educational Provision in Pakistan and Bangladesh: Roots, Rhetoric, Realist', in F. Armstrong and L. Barton (eds), *Disability, Human Rights and Education*. Buckingham: Open University Press.

Miles, S. and N. Singal. 2009. 'The Education for All and Inclusive Education Debate: Conflict, Contradiction or Opportunity?', *International Journal of Inclusive Education*, 14 (1), 1–15.

Ministry of Human Resource Development. 1992. *NPE 1986: Programme of Action 1992*. New Delhi: Government of India.

Maloney, A., C. Owen and J. Statham. 2008. *Disabled Children: Numbers, Characteristics and Local Service Provision*. London: Thomas Coram Research Unit, Institute of Education, University of London.

National Sample Survey Organisation Ministry of Statistics and Programme Implementation Government of India (NSSO). 2003. *Disabled Persons in India.* Report No. 485 (58/26/1).

Pal, C. G. 2010. 'Dalits with Disabilities: The Neglected Dimension of Social Exclusion', Working Paper Series, Vol. IV, No. 03, 2010, New Delhi: Indian Institute of Dalit Studies.

PROBE. 1999. *Public Report on Basic Education in India*, New Delhi: Oxford University Press. The Rehabilitation Council of India (Amendment) Act, Government of India, 2000.

Riddell, S. 2002. *Policy and Practice in Education.* Edinburgh: Dunedin Academic Press.

Rieser, R. 2008. *Implementing Inclusive Education: A Commonwealth Guide to Implementing Article 24 of the UN Convention of the Rights of People with Disabilities.* London: Commonwealth Secretariat.

Sahoo, P. 2004. 'Disability, The Family and Education: An Exploratory Study in the City of Bhubaneswar in Orissa', a dissertation submitted to New Delhi, ZHCES, SSS, JNU.

Singal, N. 2008a. 'Working Towards Inclusion: Reflections from the Classroom', *Teaching and Teacher Education*, 24 (6), 1516–529.

———. 2008b. 'Forgotten Youth: Disability and Development in India', Recoup Working paper No. 14.

———. 2009. 'Paper Commissioned for the EFA Global Monitoring Report, 2010, Reaching the Marginalized', pp. 1–42.

Tundawala, Moiz. (2007. *Empowering the Disabled Through Inclusive Education* (February 2007). Available at SSRN: http://ssrn.com/abstract=984742 (accessed 23 March 2009).

United Nations Millennium Declaration, United Nations General Assembly, Washington, USA, 18 September, 2000.

UNESCO. 1994. *Salamanca Statement and Framework for Action on Special Needs Education.* Paris: UNESCO.

———. 2000. *Education for All: Meeting our Collective Commitments. Expanded Commentary on the Dakar Framework for Action*, Para. 33. Paris: UNESCO.

van Zanten, A. 2007. 'Educational Change and New Cleavages between Head Teachers, Teachers and Parents: Global and Local Perspectives on the French Case', in S. Ball, I. Goodson and M. Maguire (eds), *Education, Globalisation and New Times.* London: Routledge, pp. 83–101.

World Bank. 2007. *People with Disabilities in India: From Commitments to Outcomes.* Washington: Human Development Unit.

Sites consulted

http://www.astalavista.co.in/activities-astalavista.html (accessed 3 April 2009).

http://www.independentliving.org/donet/398_the_roeher_institute.html (accessed 26 February 2009).

http://www.disabilityindia.org/disabilitystatus.cfm (accessed 14 March 2009).

www.diplomatist.com (accessed 16 April 2010).

www.IndianNGOs.com (accessed 16 April 2010).

actionforautism@gmail.com (accessed 16 April 2010).

5

Globalisation, Funding and Access to Higher Education: Perspectives from India and the UK

Vincent Carpentier, Saumen Chattopadhyay and Binay Kumar Pathak

Higher Education (HE) empowers a nation to participate in the growing knowledge economy through innovation and skill development along with fostering social mobility and social cohesion. While exchange of ideas, and mobility of teachers and students have been going on in the true spirit of education for long, the current form of globalisation guided by the neoliberal ideology questions continued state patronage for HE which is increasingly being treated as a private good on a global scale. As HE is subject to market forces, the very process of widening access to HE comes under stress. The mode of financing HE assumes critical importance in this regard as it affects pricing of HE and therefore access and equality of opportunity. Furthermore, funding patterns change the extent of public and private participation and quality of education imparted and as a result, the issue of access gets complicated in the process. As India embraces a globalising world of HE gradually, HE is poised for a metamorphosis. In the UK, the transformations are already underway. The proposed fee hike in UK has once again brought to the fore the issue of funding and access to HE. The present juncture is also important for India as the budgetary allocation to realise the three stated objectives of expansion, inclusion and excellence in HE as envisaged in the 11th Five Year Plan (EFYP) witnesses a substantial jump by around eightfold. But a possibility of a trade-off among the objectives emerges with the steady rise in private sector participation. The possibility of formalisation of the entry of the foreign education providers (FEPs) would complicate the emerging scenario in terms of its implications for all the three stated objectives. In the UK, there have been persistent tensions between two elements of the global-isation agenda: the objective to increase and widen participation to compete in the knowledge economy clashes with the tendency to slow down public spending in HE which is a part of the neoliberal agenda. However, the major financial crisis that the world economy is gradually recovering from may change the terms of these debates both in India and the UK. A shift in discourse, which is already apparent with the re-evaluation of the role of the state and that of the market, may be turned into a new set of global practices and compromise with funding and access policies in HE and therefore, their contribution to economic prosperity and social justice.

In this essay we look at the linkages between the funding pattern of HE and access to it in the UK and India. We argue that the context of a globalising world makes it necessary to take a holistic perspect-ive of the sector because of its inherent complexities and the evolving structure in view of changes in the mode of financing (including the mix of private and public funding of existing universities and the entry of private providers including the foreign ones), the wide variations in quality as well as intersecting dimensions of inequalities like gender, region, class and caste.[1] We compare the emerging scenarios in the HE sector in the two countries to unravel the tensions and concerns in two very different contexts in terms of socio-economic conditions but similar in terms of the contemporary challenges that they face. It may, however, be noted that UK and India are at two different stages in terms of extent of globalisation of the HE sector and it would be interesting to examine how they grapple with the role of HE to promote social equality. In the discussion that follows we provide brief historical overviews of the two countries focusing on funding of HE and access to it. We go on to discuss how the funding policy framework is undergoing changes in the UK and India in the face of new challenges that these two nations face. We then bring in the role of the private sector to understand how HE is set to unfold and explore the possible ramifications of privatisation in realising the basic objectives of the HE agenda and potential areas of concerns. We subsequently analyse how the HE sectors in the UK and India are evolving as they grapple with the challenges and tensions of realising social justice in the backdrop of the dominance of the neoliberal policies. We finally draw conclusions in the last section.

Looking back – UK and India

In order to understand the present state of affairs in HE and link it with the question of funding and equity, it is useful to explore how the states historically responded to the question of access in two radically different socio-economic contexts.

Expansion and Democratisation of the UK Higher Education System

There have been significant changes in HE in the UK over the last century. The major transformation has been the substantial expansion of enrollment. There were about 2.4 million students in 2007 compared to 400,000 in 1990 and 100,000 in 1950. Such an expansion has not been only the result of demographic changes but also the outcome of rising participation rates. Anderson estimates the age participation ratio in 1938 (the proportion of the age group attending university) at 1.5 per cent in England (1992: 16). By contrast, the HE Initial Participation Rate (HEIPR) which measures the number in the age group of 18–30 years who entered an HE course reached 43 per cent in 2006 (DIUS 2008a).

While these figures demonstrate a sound process of expansion, a closer look at the patterns and structure of enrollment tells a mixed story of increased opportunities and persistent inequalities along the line of gender, class and age. This indicates a distinction between increasing and widening participation (sometimes concomitant and sometimes not). First of all, a rise in the proportion of women students from 25 per cent in the 1950s to 55 per cent today indicates that achieving gender equality was a major driving force behind the increase in the participation rates (Carpentier 2006a; Dyhouse 2006). However, studies have shown persistent inequalities in relation to women access and experience in HE as well as different prospects with respect to job opportunities and salaries following graduation (Morley and David 2009). Another pattern of the expansion is the undoubtedly growing number of working-class students. However, participation rates by class confirm a persistent trend of social inequalities in the UK (Archer et al. 2003; Reay et al. 2005). The proportion of students from the lowest social group compared to higher income groups has only slightly increased since the mid-1980s (Galindo-Rueda et al. 2004: 86). The proportion of young people from the top three and bottom four socio-economic classes who participate for the first time in full-time HE were respectively 39.5 per cent and 19 per cent in 2006 (DIUS 2008b). The proportion of ethnic minority students has also increased steadily with differences according to ethnicities combined with gender. Studies from the late 1990s show that 'Indian, Chinese and black African groups were well represented in HE. African-Caribbean men, Pakistani and Bangladeshi women were represented least well' (Tomlinson 2005: 163). Another change relates to the number of overseas students whose share of all full-time students increased from 12 per cent in the early 1980s to 18 per cent in 2007 (a third of them are EU students) (Carpentier 2010). Enrollment has also been driven by the development of lifelong learning especially since the early 1990s; the proportions of undergraduate and postgraduate students over 30 years of age were respectively 15 per cent and 48 per cent in 2007. Such changes in students' characteristics have transformed the modes of enrollment: the share of full-time students fell from 80 per cent in the 1960s to 60 per cent at present (Carpentier 2006a).

In short, the traditional image of the young full-time White male middle-class student is not as dominant as it used to be and has vacated space for more diverse forms of enrollments. Clearly, this signals a change in the nature of the links between universities and the elite (Anderson 1992; Halsey 1993). However, it is important to note that while social, ethnic and gender participation rates have all gone up, some important gaps remain. Moreover, mere focus on access rather than retention does not reveal the true picture as differences in dropout rates and achievements are crucial issues for the under-privileged groups. Interestingly, the HEIPR focuses on access and overlooks experience, a crucial issue for under-represented groups.

In addition, successes and limitations in inclusive education must be explored within the context of an 'increasingly diverse sets of institutions that may have responded to, and to a certain extent, exacerbated inequalities between groups of students' (Reay et al. 2005). Lowe defines the historical expansion of HE as a process of accretion of different kinds of universities (2002) which questions whether it is appropriate to talk about a system of HE. The contemporary system agglomerates the medieval universities (Oxbridge, four Scottish universities and Dublin), University College London and Durham (1830s), the University of Wales and the Civic universities (which developed from 1880 to 1909 with strong links with industry), the university colleges which used to award degrees from the University of London (1926–62), the new universities of 1960s (created to match the expansion policy) and the post-1992 universities (polytechnics and colleges of HE which were given university status). These groups have specific rationales and activities (liberal or vocational education, research or teaching intensive, relationship with public authorities, more or less inclusive access policies) which must be considered when mapping out inequalities.

Differences between increasing and widening access can be better understood by exploring the role of the state which has been a crucial driving force behind the consolidation of the HE system. The University Grants Committee (UGC) was set up in 1919 (Shinn 1980). The UGC was mainly composed of academics and considered by many as a buffer between the treasury and universities (Shattock 1994). Its role was to distribute grants at a time when access was still restricted although Dyhouse observes an opening up of the system to working-class students during the inter-War era (2002: 14).

The conservatives were back in power and their doubt about expansion weakened the position of the UGC which, following the 1988 Education Act, was replaced by the University Funding Council alongside the Polytechnics and Colleges Funding Council (which became independent from the Local Education Authorities [LEAs]). Following the 1992 Higher Education Act, the two councils merged into the Higher Education Funding Council for England and poly-technics and colleges obtained university status. This was the formal end of the binary system but institutional differentiations between pre- and post-1992 universities remained active in practice with pro-found implications for access. Many studies have shown that the latter group still welcomes a greater share of women and a larger proportion of under-represented groups including working-class and ethnic minorities (Leathwood 2004; Reay et al. 2005). This suggests that the profile of the students of old universities still corresponds to the elite system and that the inclusion of under-represented groups has been mainly operated by non-elite institutions.

The story of access to HE is a mixed one. First, the expansion of numbers from the under-represented groups masks some persistent differences in participation that act as a deterrent to close the gap. Second, the strong stratification of HE institutions tends to have displaced the problematic of social justice from '*who access*' to '*what kind of access*'. As a whole, this suggests that the system is less elitist than it used to be but still far from being meritocratic.

Modern Indian HE: The Origins and the Question of Expansion and Access

In India, institutions like the Presidency College, Calcutta (formerly Hindu College) and CMS College, Kottayam were established much earlier (in 1817) but the emphasis on HE was given only in the mid-19th century following the recommendations of the Wood's Despatch of 1854. The establishment of the Universities of Calcutta, Madras and Bombay in the provincial strongholds in 1857 revealed the willingness of the British government to establish the HE system in India.

In post-independent India, the central government took a lead in providing HE. Later, education was made the responsibility of both the centre and the states by the Constitution (Forty Second Amendment) Act, 1976, bringing it to the Concurrent List.

The University Education Commission (1948–49) which was set up under the chairmanship of Professor S. Radhakrishnan, laid the foundation for improvement in HE in independent India and recommended the setting up of the University Grants Commission on the lines of the UGC in England. The blueprint for a national system of education was put forward by the Education Commission of 1964–66.[2] On the basis of the recommendations of the Kothari Commission, the National Policy of Education was formulated in 1968 to have built-in flexibility in the system to be able to adjust to the changing circumstances. The National Policy of Education (NPE) was adopted by the parliament in 1986 and modified in 1990 to include the support to the autonomous colleges, setting up of state-level HE councils to improve quality of education in state universities and emphasise on research in social sciences.[3]

As mentioned, HE has been largely the responsibility of the central/state government. The expansion of HE until the mid-1980s was mostly public in nature (Tilak 2008). The government not only supported HE by funding universities and colleges, but also took over the responsibilities of running the institutions set up through the private sector. In addition, private sector institutions, without any aid from the government, flourished to meet the increasing demand for professional education.

Since the 1990s, the government started encouraging own resource generation and private sector participation in HE to lessen its burden. The resource generation by central universities was first discussed by the Justice Punnaya Committee (1992–93). The Committee recommended incentives for central universities following financial discipline and disincentives for central universities not adhering to such discipline. The Committee also recommended an increased role of government funding for research. Another group set up for this purpose by the Prime Minister's Council was the Birla Ambani Group (2000). The Group recommended reduction of government expenditure in HE, and an increase for the primary education and facilitation of foreign direct investment (FDI) in HE. Similar provisions have been advocated by the High Level Group on Services of Planning Commission in 2008 and recommendations of the National Knowledge Commission (NKC) in its two consecutive reports in 2006 and 2007. In terms of recommendations, these three reports have not been averse to an increased private participation in HE, albeit by different extent. The debates are discussed in the next section.

The Indian HE system has undergone significant quantitative changes in terms of the number of educational institutions, enrollments and size of faculty. There were only 20 universities in 1947. By 2008, the number of universities rose to 431, indicating a twenty-one-fold increase. The number of colleges also rose from 500 in 1947 to 20,677 in 2008, a forty-one-fold increase. The faculty strength rose from 15,000 in 1950 to 0.5 million in 2008, implying a rise by thirty-three-fold. The number of students increased from about 0.1 million in 1950 to over 11.61 million in 2008.[4] Professional education has also grown enormously as a result of an upsurge in both the private and public sector.[5] The share of private unaided higher education institutions increased from 42.6 per cent in 2001 to 63.21 per cent in 2006. Their share of enrollments also increased from 32.89 per cent to 51.53 per cent in the same period (The EFYP Document). The generally accepted participation rate is around 11–12 per cent. By the end of EFYP, the Government of India (GoI) targets to raise the participation rate to 15 per cent, expecting that about half of the incremental enrollment targeted will be catered to by the private providers.

The question of access to HE is very complex in the Indian case because of its bewildering diversity and intersecting inequalities in terms of gender, caste and region. As far as the participation of women in HE is concerned, the percentage of women's enrollment has increased from 10 per cent in 1950 to 39.4 per cent in 2003.[6] The enrollment of women increased from 43,000 in 1950–51 to about 3.3 million in 2000–2001 and to 4.23 million in 2004–5, indicating a hundred-fold rise during 1950–51 to 2004–5. The increase in women enrolled in HE increased from 2.57 million in 1993–94 to 4.26 million in 1999–2000 to 5.4 million in 2004–5 while the corresponding figures for men are 5.1 million, 6.9 million, and 8.1 million for the respective periods. In absolute terms, women continue to lag behind men, but because of an accelerated growth rate in women's enrollment, the gap between men and women is getting narrower. The growth rate of women students in HE between 1993–94 and 2004–5 was 7.72 per cent as compared to 4.73 per cent for men.[7] The growth in enrollment in HE is much higher for rural women as compared to their urban counterparts, that is, 13 per cent as compared to 5 per cent respectively — more than twice as faster for the rural women. The corresponding figures for men are about 5 per cent (rural) and 3 per cent (urban) respectively (Raju 2008).

The participation of deprived groups, namely Scheduled Castes (SC) and Scheduled Tribes (ST) in HE has been rising.[8] Total enrollment of SC and ST in HE in 2005–6 stood at 1,614,138 and 610,488 respectively. The participation rate of SC and ST in HE in 2005–6 was 8.39 per cent and 6.61 per cent respectively, well below the national participation rate of 11 per cent. Though their participation is still low as compared to the national average, their participation rate (GER) increased from 5.09 per cent and 6.43 per cent to 7.81 per cent and 7.57 per cent respectively between 1999–2000 and 2004–5. The participation of other deprived groups collectively known as other backward castes (OBCs) also increased from 6.99 per cent to 10.14 per cent during the same period (Raju 2008; Sinha and Srivastava 2008). The GERs of SCs and STs were about one-third with 'others' and for OBCs, it was around half of others with stark rural–urban differences (Sinha and Srivastava 2008). No less significant is the fact that the GER between the non-poor is significantly higher than the poor with rural urban disparities. The GER of the poor in the rural and urban areas was 1.30 per cent and 5.5 per cent respectively compared to 7.1 per cent and 27.1 per cent in the urban area. Low income being a major hindrance for continuing education all the way up to the HE level is evident if we look at the occupation and enrollment interface. The GER for those engaged in farm and non-farm activities as self-employed was about 5 per cent compared with 1.4 per cent for farm wage labour and 3 per cent for the non-farm wage labour. In short, Sinha and Srivastava (2008) bring out clearly how various factors like caste, rural–urban differences and occupation impinge on GER and how many dimensions of infirmities intersect. The enrollment rates are particularly the lowest among the SCs, STs and the OBCs in the category of poor casual wage labourer households in the rural and urban areas (Thorat 2008).

There are variations in enrollment in gender and castes across region and religion. Access would also differ across the government-sponsored institutions and the private sector. Access to HE in the growing private sector has suffered as several court cases would exemplify.

Policy Shifts in Funding: Specific Implications – Social Exclusion and Inclusion

The question of mode of funding including the issue of public–private contribution has always revolved around the issue of classifying HE as a public good or a private good or some combination thereof. The current form of globalisation and the neoliberal framework promote HE as a driver to compete in an increasingly knowledge-dominated economy in the context of fiscal constraint. This led both countries to treat HE more as a private good or at least as a quasi-public good to be able to encourage resource generation (cost recovery) and private sector participation (Tilak 2008). These are debatable issues in education reforms which question whether globalisation is creating new forms and distinctive patterns of social exclusion mediated by local context (Rizvi and Lingard 2010).

The Debate on Financing HE and the Evolution of the Policy Framework for HE

In the UK, and across Europe, there have been growing concerns about the way the expansion of HE should be funded (Chevaillier and Eicher 2002). Funding debates are centred around alternative views on the arbitration between public and private benefits and public and private costs. Higher education is widely seen as an investment for the socio-economic system and a priority in the policy agenda but debates on who should pay for it are ongoing and passionate. They oppose the contribution of HE to the economy through its impact on the productivity and innovation to the substantial private returns it offers to individuals (Blundel et al. 2000). Altbach notes that the 'idea of an academic degree as a "private good" that benefits the individual rather than a "public good" for society is gaining acceptance' (1999: 2). On the other hand, it should be noted that it is easier to measure private returns (wages) and public costs (taxation) rather than the social returns from HE (let alone the non-economic returns) (Carpentier 2006a). These debates have important consequences on the way HE is funded and especially on the question of fees.

Similar debates exist in India, where HE has generally been classified as a public good or at least a quasi-public good to advocate a greater support from the government (Tilak 2004, 2008). In the context of economic reforms initiated in 1991, the White Paper on Subsidies (GoI 1995) questioned subsidisation of HE in general classifying it as a non-merit good while primary education was identified as a merit good as it generates externalities.[9] More appropriately, HE should be classified as a quasi-public good and, therefore, theoretically, the case for government support remains sound because of the externalities it generates and the significance of catering to social demand rather than market demand backed only by purchasing power (Chattopadhyay 2007).[10]

Economic reforms initiated in 1991 in the aftermath of the balance of payment crisis led to a fall in the budgetary allocation for education as fiscal deficit was sought to be pruned in terms of GDP in the face of stagnation of revenue growth. As argued by Tilak (2008), there has been a gradual change in the way HE has been conceived. It has become more of a private good rather than a public good as the government has shown interest in going ahead with structural reforms even in the social sector. Further, the government is virtually at a crossroads with regard to its relative role of market and the state in the provision of HE (Tilak 2008). The decline in the budget also led to a fall in the real per capita expenditure on students (Tilak 2004).[11]

During the second phase of reform with the gradual emergence of knowledge as a factor of economic growth and a strong urge to realise the full potential of India's growing pool of aspiring youth to take part in the economy's supposed march towards prosperity, the government constituted the National Knowledge Commission in 2005. Though the centre has shown keenness to raise budgetary allocations for HE in recent years buoyed by a higher than anticipated tax collection, the majority of the universities continue to suffer from a funds crunch as the states are compelled to comply with the restrictions on borrowing as per the FRBM Act (Chattopadhyay 2010).[12]

The expansion and diversification of HE has become a major strategy in order to compete in a knowledge economy. The constitution of the NKC and an unprecedented hike of almost eightfold in the allocation for education in the EFYP are clear indications of the growing importance of HE in policy making in India. At the same time, the cost of implementation of such policies led to the question as to whether the public sector alone could meet the challenges of expansion, inclusion and excellence. Though this question does not feature in official pronouncements in India, there is an underlying shift towards greater cost recovery through fee hike, promotion of education loans and public–private partnerships (PPP) as per the EFYP document. The state governments continue to face fiscal pressure due to the FRBM Act as mentioned earlier and so the budgetary allocation for HE has remained under stress.

Though there has been an increased allocation for HE under the EFYP, the role of the government in expanding enrollment in HE is still contestable as evident from alternative sources of funding HE that are being explored as per the recommendations of the NKC and CABE Committee Report and the Cabinet approval for the Foreign Educational Institutions (regulation and entry of operation) Bill. Also, the renewed thrust on PPP would have implications for costs of education and therefore on access.[13] Though, at present, tuition fees vary across universities, overall cost recovery from the students has gone up (CABE Committee Report). The EFYP argued in favour of a fee hike to around 20 per cent of the operating cost of general university education since most university students come from the top 10 per cent of the population by income levels. The fees for (technical education) professional courses, arguably, could be much higher. While there is possibly a case for only a reasonable fee hike, adequate safeguards need to be taken so that access does not suffer.[14]

In the context of expansion of enrollment and under-funding, debates about 'cost sharing strategy' have been taking place worldwide (Teixeira et al. 2006) and are still being debated in both the UK and India. Part of this strategy relies on the increase of fees on the rationale that students should support some parts of the cost of a degree which offers them substantial monetary benefits. Again, the 2008 crisis may lead to a change in the terms of the debates in the face of growing unemployment.

We observe therefore striking similarities in the issues and concerns that arose in the context of financing HE in UK and India notwithstanding differences in their socio-economic context and development.

Public/private Substitution of
Resources in the UK and access

Looking at the past is useful to examine potential connections and tensions between funding and access policies in UK's HE. Since 1945, a major pattern stands out: a sustained expansion of enrollment with fluctuating resources for universities. These fluctuations are the result of the influence of long economic cycles (also called Kondratiev cycles) on the public funding available to education (Carpentier 2003, 2006b; Fontvieille and Michel 2002).[15] The amount of public resources directed towards HE accelerated during the post-War upturn (1945–73), only to go into relative decline following the early 1970s structural economic crisis (1973–?) (Carpentier 2006a: 9).

These fluctuations in public funding led to dramatic changes in the composition of university income. From 1945 to 1973, the share of universities' public resources rose from 50 per cent to nearly 90 per cent and has since retreated to less than 60 per cent (Carpentier 2006a: 11). This suggests that the injection of private funding (including fees, private research, endowments, etc.) has acted mainly as a substitute for the slowing down of public funding rather than as a source of additional resources (Carpentier 2006a). Rising private resources haven't therefore led to a significant increase in the total amount of funding available to institutions.

This public/private substitution of resources combined with a continuous increase in enrolments explain partially why funding per student slowed down significantly in the late 1970s and even more after the second wave of expansion of the 1990s. This tension between funding and access policies symbolises the clash of two aspects of the current form of globalisation: the belief in the knowledge economy and the reluctance to increase taxation (Carpentier 2010). Among the private resources of HE, fees are at the centre of the tensions between ambitions regarding access and reluctance regarding public funding.

The re-emergence of fees as an issue has been a central driver of the expansion of private resources. The trend started in 1967 with the increase of fees for overseas students followed in 1981 by the implementation of full cost fees for non-EU international students (Carpentier 2010; Williams 1984). Policy makers then started considering whether such financial contributions could be extended to domestic students whose fees were being covered since 1962 by mandatory grants from the LEAs. Since then the question of 'how to fund a high quality mass higher education' (Barr and Crawford 2005) has generated crucial debates on the alternative funding systems articulating fees, grants and loans and their impacts on access.

The Dearing Report proposed the introduction of fees with means tested grants (1997). The 1998 Higher Education Act only partially followed Dearing's recommendations (Watson and Bowden 2007). It introduced upfront fees (£1,000) but replaced grants by loans at preferential rates. The 2003 White Paper pleaded for a far more substantial contribution from students (DfES 2003) leading to a narrow parliamentary vote of the 2004 HE Act which introduced a totally new system of student finance in England. The £1,000 upfront fees were replaced by deferred variable fees of up to £3,000 to be repaid once the graduate earns more than £15,000. Financial support is offered to students from poor backgrounds with the reintroduction of a grant of up to £2,700 for a family earning up to £20,000 a year (a figure which was initially set at £15,000 but increased following pressure from rebel Labour MPs). Concerns about the impact of funding on access led to the creation of the Office for Fair Access to ensure that universities offer adequate scholarships to students from poorer backgrounds and develop fair processes of admissions. On its arrival in 2007, the Brown government increased the threshold for a full grant to £25,000 and to £60,000 for a partial grant. Surprisingly, not much publicity was made of this positive measure which made a third of students eligible for a full grant (£2,825) and another third eligible for a partial grant. In the post–credit crunch era, the threshold for a partial grant has just been reduced to £50,000. The Brown Review of Higher Education Funding and Student Finance launched in 2009 recommended that the newly elected Conservative–Liberal Democrat coalition government led by Prime Minister Mr Cameron raise tuition fees by almost three times. The students have vehemently opposed such a move but the government has shown no signs of budging. All these changes reflect political uncertainty and the fact that it is difficult to fully assess the impact of fees on access. This includes deferred fee mechanisms as some studies in the UK have shown that students from low-income families are more debt averse (Callender and Jackson 2005). Many other (non-financial) factors can harm access to HE such as policies and practices at the compulsory level which impact on social groups' differences in attainment at the compulsory level (Ball 2008) as well as institutional policies and practices within the HE sector which contradict widening participation (Burke 2005).

What does the historical relationship between HE funding and Kondratiev cycles tell us about the current debate on fees and access? It was argued earlier that since the 1970s crisis, rising private resources were used as substitutes for public funding rather than additional resources. It is possible that the continuation of this public/private substitution through higher fees may only change the structure of funding of universities without necessarily increasing the level of resources available to them. This will not solve the under-funding issue and will not contribute to improve teaching and research quality in order to compete within the knowledge economy (the original objective of the reform) (Carpentier 2006a). Moreover, an increase in fees with insufficient public funding could be detrimental to access which depends on a substantial financial public commitment to student support (scholarships, grants) and widening participation programmes in schools (Aimhigher: Raising aspirations in secondary education) and universities.

The impact of the new funding regime is not known yet and is an open political process. The previous government has already indicated that the target of 50 per cent participation may not be reached. The 2008 crisis may destabilise the current arrangement of fees, grants and loans confronted to new socio-economic realities which may diffuse the pressure beyond the public sector to individuals (rising unemployment, lower salaries, some banks in the US have started refusing student loans). The global (neoliberal) agenda of public austerity (which drives the public/private substitution of HE resources) may have compromised the other agenda of the knowledge economy (which required expansion of access) (Carpentier 2010).

Expansion, Inclusion and Excellence in India: Emerging Trade off

Democratisation of the HE sector in terms of increased participation of the public and private sector has its merits and demerits. Poor quality, lack of relevance of public-supported education and the growing dominance of the private sector contest the true intention of the government to achieve expansion, inclusion and excellence. Though the sheer growth of the HE sector in India since independence has been laudable, private sector–led expansion in absence of proper regulation has led to a compromise with inclusiveness of expansion and its quality.

The government has also sought to reserve seats for the backward section of the population as discussed in an earlier section.

This section deals with the changes in the HE sector with reference to their implications for inclusion and exclusion.

Achieving Inclusion, Expansion and Reservation

The major objective of the EFYP is to expand participation in HE from 11 per cent in the beginning of the plan to 15 per cent by the end of the plan period, by March 2012. This implies that an additional 7 million students need to be accommodated. This requires a substantial hike in the budgetary allocation to expand facilities. In accordance with this, the EFYP proposes an eightfold rise in the budget for HE. New colleges and universities are being proposed to be set up in the regions where the GER falls below the national average. However, the expansion plan as envisaged under the EFYP will be dented to an extent due to shortage of faculty and it seems unlikely that the budgeted amount could be utilised in full by the end of the plan period. The Sixth Pay Commission for the university teachers seeks to make the teaching profession attractive, but subsequent implementation by the state universities may put the budget for HE under severe stress.

To ensure wider access across all the social classes, GoI, after much contestations, has been able to enforce reservation for the Other Backward Castes (OBCs) to the extent of 27.5 per cent of the total intake of government-funded higher education institutions (HEIs). This has made 49.5 per cent of the seats reserved, if the reservation for SCs and STs are taken together. To keep the seats for the general category unaffected, the HE sector was expanded by 54 per cent.[16] To ensure that the rich among the OBCs do not avail themselves of the reservation, the government has contemplated an income limit, called 'creamy layer', to exclude those who can be considered to be privileged amongst the OBCs.

Funding and Access

Of late, to encourage research, students pursuing research in the central universities are being offered scholarships, which are, however, just sufficient for their sustenance. While the move is laudable, the amount and the coverage are limited. The majority of the students in the state universities continue to find pursuing post-graduation and research difficult. The EFYP earmarks ₹ 50 billion for the creation of a corpus of education loans to facilitate provision of subsidised/interest-free education loans.

Private Providers and Implications

Questions of funding and access need to be addressed in the context of a greater participation of the private sector in HE and the opening up of the international borders to foreign providers. The General Agreement on Trade and Services (GATS) seeks to remove barriers to cross-national trade of services and the World Trade Organisation has accordingly pushed towards a commodification of cross-border HE. The emerging trends in both countries are discussed in the following sections.

Emergence of Private Providers in the UK: Trends and Issues

King observed that the most growing segment of HE worldwide is private HE (2004: 4). According to Levy, 'private HE adds enrolment capacity to the HE system, mostly escaping the constraints about public expenditures that now restrict public expansion' (2003: 3). Teferra and Altbach identified the development of private HE as the consequence of 'the burgeoning demand from students for access, the declining capacity of public universities, the retrenchment of public services, pressure by external agencies to cut public services, a growing emphasis on and need for a highly skilled labour force that targets the local market, and the beginning of interest by foreign providers' (2004: 32).

It is important to note that UK universities are themselves major providers of HE abroad and that the physical or virtual export of programmes can be considered as part of the public/private substitution of resources identified earlier. Till now, the UK government's strategy to increase access with a controlled growth of public funding remains largely based on the increase of private resources rather than private providers. However, the UK has witnessed an increase in the number of private providers of HE. This shift is relatively recent and not strong but such debates about private provision of HE are slowly emerging. It is difficult to offer a quantitative picture of UK private HE today because 'there is currently no process for collecting data consistently from those institutions' (Ramsden 2008: 10) and 'private higher education in the UK resists easy characterisation' (Salerno 2004: 1). The Quality Assurance Agency stressed the need to address 'the current lack of knowledge about this element of the higher education sector' (QAA 2008: 27). King identified three main groups of private providers of degrees in the UK. Those having Degree Awarding Powers (there are only four of them — BPP Ltd, The College of Law, the University of Buckingham and Ashridge Business School — but more applications have been made). Those offering their own non-UK awards (mainly American businesses) recruiting mainly international students. Those offering an award accredited by a UK or a foreign partner institution belong to the most common category and bring in income to UK public institutions (King 2009: 11).

The numbers of these providers is expected to grow and it will be important to assess the implications for access and quality. Many studies in South Africa, for example, have shown that the introduction of private provision did not necessarily expand access and raised concerns about quality (Naidoo et al. 2007). The fact that much of this private provision is cross-border raises additional issues. Robertson notes that 'when member states allow education to be included and traded in global agreements like GATS, member state's ability to ensure that education is a right for all, rather than a commodity to be purchased by the well off is considerably diminished' (2006).

Private HE in India

Privatisation of HE: Mitigating 'Inclusion'

As discussed, marketisation of HE continues unabated in India even while the government contemplates unprecedented expansion in the state sector. However, privatisation has taken place mainly in the realm of professional and technical education in response to the growing demand for these courses.

The issue is to what extent access may suffer due to privatisation. The government colleges and universities offer self-financing courses as funding support from the state declines, or, found to be inadequate. Since the self-financing courses charge higher fees by definition, access is bound to suffer in view of imperfections in the education loans market. Privatisation raises the overall fee structure. The actual cost of education in the private sector is exorbitantly high in view of continuation of the illegal practice of charging capitation fees.[17] Even if loans are made available, students from the under-privileged section may hesitate for the fear of debt. Loans work for professional courses and the government has made loans available only for such professional courses including vocational courses. The other pitfalls of education loans are gender-wise and region-wise discrimination. The poorer sections would always be at a disadvantageous position while applying for loans, as they are the most risk-averse people in general. The proliferation of the private institutions has mainly been confined to the relatively rich states. This further accentuates the problem of regional disparities in access.[18]

The government has proposed to introduce several bills to effect radical changes in the higher education sector. One of them is the Bill on Foreign Educational Institutions (The Foreign Educational Institutions [Regulation of Entry and Operations, Maintenance of Quality and Prevention of Commercialisation] Bill, 2010) which will allow foreign universities, the recognised as well as reputed ones in their own countries, to operate in India and offer degrees. In all possibility, the marketisation of HE will negate widening of access to HE as costs of HE would inevitably go up. India seems to be keen to expedite the process of globalisation of Mode 3 variety with the tabling of the Bill in the parliament as global exchange under Modes 1, 2 and 4 has been a part of Indian higher education, albeit on a moderate scale.[19] In a study carried out by Bhushan in 2004–5 (Bhushan 2009), out of 131 institutions, 107 were engaged in vocational courses, 19 in technical courses and only five in general courses and located in the high-income states. There were 59 from UK and 66 from the USA with the remaining six from other countries. The operation of the foreign education providers (FEPs) could be traced to 1991–92. Initially the tendency was to open up study and examination centres followed by twining and student–teacher exchange programmes, programmatic collaboration to offer joint degrees and ultimately provision of complete degrees which entailed deeper involvement on the part of the FEPs. At present, as per the UGC Act, the degree-granting authority rests with the universities established under central and state acts. Without any proper policy framework FDI in education has avoided the Indian market despite the fact that the growing middle class renders the market sufficiently lucrative for the FEPs.[20]

Private initiatives are not new to the Indian education system. Convent missionaries have been running schools since British rule. One of the oldest colleges, CMS College in Kottayam, was established by the private initiatives of a London-based missionary. The Banaras Hindu University and Visva-Bharati (a central university) were also the outcomes of private initiatives in HE. These were essentially philanthropic initiatives. Even after independence, a good number of educational institutions have been established by the private sector. Some of the private educational institutes like Birla Institute of

Technology and Science (BITS), Pilani have established themselves as high quality institutions. But barring a top few, most of the private initiatives have been questionable as far as their motives are concerned. Be it the clustering of private colleges to be adopted by the state of Bihar in the 1970s or be it the mushrooming of fake universities in the state of Chhattisgarh in the recent past, the objective to gain in pecuniary terms is evident in private initiatives. To reap profits, they go to the extent of cheating students either by providing false or little information or hiding vital and relevant information regarding them (Pathak 2008) which is essential for decision making by the students and providing poor quality infrastructure. 'Given the undesirable practices that the private colleges follow, they cannot be regarded as a desirable, alternative and reliable form of funding' (Tilak and Varghese 1991), as they have been conceived of in recommendations of bodies like NKC and HLGSS.[21] The factor behind the growth of private initiatives is the rising unmet demand relevant to the needs of business and industry. The expansion of HE till 1980 was more in the general stream and comparatively less in the professional stream. This gap in expansion and the need to meet the increasing demand for skilled manpower forced the state to allow the entry of private enterprises in the area of HE, particularly in professional education (Agarwal 2009). The institutions of professional education have been mushrooming in the towns and cities of India.[22] There have been shifts from general to professional courses due to a rise in the number of these colleges and also due to increasing careerism (Kumar 2004).

The private initiatives have been given legitimacy by the provisions of Grants-in-Aid (GIA) status to some private colleges and institutions, The National Law School of India University and Indira Gandhi Institute of Development Research, are examples of PPP in HE (Agarwal 2009).[23] Private initiatives have played a major role in the development of the IT and ITES sector in India. The IT/ITES has not only earned foreign exchange for India, but it has created major job opportunities with 1.6 million graduates employed in this sector and nearly 70 per cent of them are engineers. The growth in the supply of IT and engineers from other areas could be attributable to the growth in the private institutions as 80 per cent of the institutions in the professional stream are from the private sector. The level of skill among the workforce is poor as only 5 per cent of the labour force in the age group of 20–24 years had vocational training (Agarwal 2009).

The growing presence of the private sector in HE in India signals the marketisation of the sector and subjecting HE to market forces has serious implications for access and quality due to rampant commercialisation in absence of a monitoring authority (Chattopadhyay 2009). Thus, with increasing private participation in HE, the lower-income strata and under-privileged groups are likely to suffer the most. The success of participating in globalising HE would also depend on English and internet penetration. English is spoken by 125.3 million Indians as per the Census data 2001 (as reported in *The Times of India*, 14 March 2010). With the increasing demand for English for social and economic mobility, proficiency in the language is crucial. India has to traverse miles to overcome the digital divide.[24]

The Emerging Global Market in India: Regulatory Framework

The possible approvals of the bill regarding the entry of the foreign educational providers and setting up of the National Council of Higher Education Research (NCHER) will usher in a radical change in the regulation of the HE market in India. Private colleges having affiliation to the state universities and private universities with affiliation of the domestic and foreign universities exist in India. The regulatory body, namely UGC, lacks sufficient legal rights and authority. There have been disputes between the UGC, the universities and at present between the universities and the private universities.

The growth of private institutions has clearly set the criterion of capability of paying as the most important one for entry into the HE system. Though the regulatory bodies like All India Council for Technical Education (AICTE) enforce fee-rebates and scholarships, these provisions are hardly complied with. Apart from the domestic private institutions, foreign providers are also looking forward to reaping the potential benefit. A good number of them have already collaborated with domestic institutions or are operating independently. Foreign institutions of repute are yet to arrive on the Indian shore. Most of the foreign providers which are operating in collaboration with the domestic ones offer questionable quality of education in absence of an alert regulatory authority to control these Trojan Horses which are infecting the already struggling HE system (Altbach 2008, 2009). These foreign providers and the domestic private sector are averse to investing in high-cost academic infrastructure, rather they are operational in the fields which are in high demand such as management, engineering and other professional courses.[25] The growing private initiatives coupled with a surge in the number of foreign providers have further accentuated the access to HE. With a vast majority of poor population, India can ill afford to depend on private initiatives and foreign providers for increasing access to HE.

A Comparative Assessment of the Role of Private Provision in HE: Questions of Equality and Quality

We observe that there are not only differences in the rationale for privatisation of the HE system in the two countries, but also in the manner in which it is operated and mediated by context-specific characteristics related to society, culture, polity and the economy. In the UK, constraint in public funding is the main justification for the introduction of elements of privatisation in the functioning of the universities. However, the emerging question of excess of demand for HE compared to the traditional supply (more students cannot find a university place) is slowly emerging as a justification for a greater role for private providers.

In India, the growing demand for HE, and in particular, for professional courses in the face of an unresponsive public education system lubricated the entry of the private parties. Confusion prevails in the HE system with regard to the various important aspects such as entry, fee structure and affiliation of the private sector in HE in India. A spate of court judgements and the pending bills introduced by the Government of India would corroborate this. The gradual weakening of the UGC in monitoring standards in HE and the indifferent attitude of the state governments to monitor the private players have rendered the market virtually an unregulated one. The government is contemplating a regulatory body (the bill pertaining to the NCHER) based on the recommendations of the NKC and the Yash Pal Committee Report to regulate the emerging market for higher education in India. In UK, the severity of the problem is much less but quality of HE in the private sector has become a concern for the regulatory bodies such as universities accreditation services and the British Accreditation Council.

The expansion of the HE in India, though it is meant to be inclusive and achieve excellence, may not turn out to be so. There are enough reasons to worry. Though the government in India seeks to expand the HE sector with an unprecedented rise in the Union Budget, there is an unmistakable tendency in the government policies to privatise as evident from the promotion of public–private partnerships, and education loans under the EFYP.[26]

Creating a level playing field for the 400 universities so as to compete with the foreign institutions in the extreme case of a full-fledged globalisation would be nearly impossible in view of faculty shortage and the resource crunch particularly being faced by the state universities. The other way would be to allow for partnership and twining programmes, which would be nearly evenly distributed among the universities which seems to be nearly impossible. This would usher in a sea change in the overall academic ambience where the universities are virtually grasping for breath. A rise in the cost of education would make HE accessible to the privileged few. Given the fact that 76 per cent are 'poor and vulnerable', widening access would increasingly mean that the students would be coming from increasingly under-privileged sections of the society. The government has to be proactive in monitoring the standard and quality of the private players, and providing scholarships to the needy so that access does not suffer. But it is easier said than done. Good quality education is expensive and financial support to the needy should cover three-fourths of the student community. Given profit maximisation being the sole objective of the private players, domestic and foreign, albeit surreptitiously, it would be an arduous challenge for the government to ensure how to expand in the presence of the growing dominance of private players without compromising on the issue of widening access.[27] The import of government support and building up of good quality public institutions remains the most desirable and viable option. Scholarships like the Rajiv Gandhi Scholarships meant for the SC, ST, and OBC reservations would have a salutary impact on access.[28] The role of a regulatory authority in the form of NCHER as being mooted by the central government is critically important in this regard.

There is a conflict between globalisation and massification in the true sense at the basic level. Scott asks whether there is a conflict between massification of higher education and internationalisation of universities (1998: 121). In India, as we observed earlier, rampant privatisation of education with little regulation and associated concern about quality make the government's claim to achieve inclusive expansion in HE a mere rhetoric.

The drive towards widening access gets mitigated to a large extent if quality of education remains poor. What is alarming is that this is not specific to public-funded institutions. The structure of the private sector institutions is also pyramidical with very few quality private institutions. The majority of the private institutions end up proffering certificates not education (Altbach 2009; Jayaram 2007). This is rampant because it is difficult to define and measure what is good quality of education; the providers find it easy to economise on cost by spending less on infrastructure and teachers as there does not exist any well-defined relationship between infrastructure, and teachers and the delivery of quality education (Chattopadhyay 2009).

The majority of the government institutions also suffer from the same disease. Poor governance and financial corruption, and political interference corrode the quality of education. Therefore, benefits of inclusion are largely negated due to low employability arising out of poor quality education and degrees in general streams in government-sponsored institutions. This leads to lack of motivation to participate actively on the parts of both the teachers and the students.

Therefore, mere access to education will be of little help. The participation rate rises with the level of education and the level of education rises with income level. Therefore, in order to increase skill level among the workforce, an increase in the number of private providers offers a poor solution as the cost of education goes up. Imparting good quality education entails higher cost, and access would suffer. If cost is kept at an affordable level, quality of education is seriously compromised which renders the educated youth unemployable.[29]

Conclusions

While the globalisation of the knowledge economy may benefit the world as a whole, the emerging reality driven by neoliberalism fails to inspire to an equitable world as the disparities between the North and South continue to widen and the income disparities within the nations tend to get more accentuated. The current form of globalisation tends to orient HE towards private resources and private providers away from public responsibility which implies a rise in the fee structure and access to be increasingly determined by the ability-to-pay. As HE becomes tradable within the country and across borders, the process of widening access suffers, education struggles in becoming a key force in ensuring social cohesion and reconstruction of democratic citizenship. With branding of the institutions playing a major role in certifying quality as the education system gets more and more differentiated, the students from low-ranking institutions in the job market are also likely to be unfavourably treated.

In India, 1991 marks a new beginning in policy making as the government introduced a series of new economic policies encompassing various sectors. What is disheartening is that higher education is being treated no differently from other sectors despite a rise in budgetary allocation. There are signs that the budgetary allocation would move in favour of skill development for the workforce away from investing in HE institutions to make space for private investment in HE. There are reasons to believe that the objectives of making expansion inclusive and achieve excellence look less credible now with the infusion of market principles in HE policy making. In the UK, the HE budget is being subjected to drastic cuts as the cost recovery is raised and the restructuring process of the HEIs is guided by corporate principles. This is expected to be partly covered by a rise in private funding but recent regulatory changes have opened the 'market' to an increasing number of private providers. In India, policy makers are now discussing cost recovery to an extent of 20 per cent. However, India differs from UK in at least two respects. One, the per capita national income level in India is much lower as compared to that of UK and, two, the extent of subsidisation of government institutions of HE mainly in general streams is much higher in India. However, quite a good number of government-aided institutions have been offering self-financing market-oriented professional courses. Though this has led to a rise in revenue, even the public education system is getting differentiated where ability to pay matters akin to the private institutions. The education system ceases to be an equalising force. Public–private partnerships and the promotion of education loans add fuel to the process of differentiation.

Moreover, access to education suffers in the face of privatisation irrespective of the country-specific characteristics; what is a matter of concern for India is wide prevalence of poor quality of education which nullifies the increase in accessibility to HE. The exorbitant growth of the private sector and arbitrariness in governance and fee structure make the under-privileged section most vulnerable and averse to join HE provided by the private sector. The government's initiative may achieve inclusion to an extent but its salutary/beneficial impact will remain somewhat mitigated in the context of globalisation of the neoliberal variety. It is doubtful that the recent initiative towards governance reform by the UGC in India will succeed to ensure a turnaround in the public-funded colleges and universities.

Giving autonomy constitutes a key reform initiative. The era will therefore be marked by tension, contradictions and challenges in policy making in HE.

Challenging unequal access to HE might be one of the crucial ways out of the current economic downturn through its contribution to an inclusive socio-economy. In both UK and India, this requires putting equal opportunities at the heart of policies across the whole education system. This means to put in place comprehensive and coordinated actions and mechanisms to address inequalities within secondary education, to ensure a viable student financial support and to remove exclusionary practices across the HE system.

As both UK and India embrace the emerging global knowledge economy, they face similar challenges notwithstanding differences in their respective stages of development, socio-economic profiles and polity. As discussed, the mode and pattern of funding HE is central to higher education policy making and the very question of access to HE revolves around cost of education among other factors. Under the dominant force of neoliberal ideology, the forces of globalisation ensure slow but steady marketisation of HE which negates the benefits of massification of HE and accentuates the process of inequity as the market economy cannot guarantee everybody's participation (Chattopadhyay 2009). As privatisation and marketisation commodify HE, the universities cease to serve the larger interests of the society as they get increasingly attuned to the interest of the market forces. The renewed thrust on skill development through provision of vocational training will help integrate a larger skilled workforce but it may go a long way to render the growth process inclusive as argued by the National Council for Skill Development.[30] This may entail a shift in the budget away from creating IITs and IIMs where the private sector is willing to invest to set up of Industrial Training Institutes (ITIs) and polytechnics for skill development to create job opportunities for 70 million people in the EFYP. The rapid expansion in the distance education programme has indeed led to widening of access at a low cost; however, the quality of education and acceptability of such degrees in the job market remain areas of concern. The perspectives from India and the UK are obviously different but point out in both countries some tensions between these two transformations which are about to increase unless HE policy addresses and balances the questions of funding, quality and equality.

✦

Notes

1. In India, caste is the most pervasive dimension of social stratification. It is a hereditary, endogamous social class or subclass of traditional Hindu society, stratified according to Hindu ritual purity (Lall and Rao in this volume).
2. The Education Commission of 1964–66 is also known as Kothari Commission after the name of its chairman Dr D. S. Kothari.
3. Based on suggestions of the Acharya Ramamurti Committee, set up to review NPE.
4. The National Sample Survey Organisation Employment Survey for 2004–5 gives a higher figure of 15.5 million, while the Population Census gives 18.2 million for 2001.
5. India has grown to have 16 Indian Institutes of Technology (IITs), seven Indian Institutes of Management (IIMs), 1,600 colleges of engineering, technology and architecture, 2,000 medical colleges, 1,700 teacher training colleges and 2,600 other professional and technical institutions in areas comprising agriculture, law, management, computer applications and information technology (Tilak 2008).
6. India has the privilege of having the first women graduates in the British Empire. Oxford and Cambridge had been in existence for 600 or 700 years before they began to admit women to their degrees. Calcutta University admitted two women to its B.A. degree in 1883, and they became the first women graduates in the British Empire (Basu 2005).
7. The Census adjusted figures for these two rounds of NSS. The corresponding census years 1991 and 2001 are slightly higher, that is, 8.77 per cent for women and 5.22 per cent for men.
8. The former untouchables or people belonging to low-rank castes in the Hindu caste system were listed under The Constitution (Scheduled Castes) Order, [1950] 1 (C.O.19).

    Detailed discussion on deprived groups and their education has been done by Lall and Rao in this volume.

    The tribal communities were specified and identified from time to time and were first mentioned under the Constitution of India. Article 366 (25).
9. The Report argued that social sciences need not be subsidised while science education should be (Srivastava et al., 1997). The attempt by the government to set the stage for gradual withdrawal of subsidies from HE met with severe opposition in the academia (AIU 2004a and 2004b) which led to some modification of the classification debate which was published in a later report.
10. Even market demand for HE, private or social can be radically different from social need. Needless to say that social need as a concept is more valid for ascertaining the goal for widening access to HE. However,

classification of HE is actually policy sensitive (Marginson and Van der Wende 2007) and policy trends like greater cost-recovery and creation of space for private providers indicate HE is being treated more as a private good. The advocates of economic reforms have tended to push HE more towards a private good by assigning fewer premiums to the externalities defying virtually the literature on endogenous growth theory and externalities generated by education.

11. Per student expenditure has declined at a rate of 2.4 per cent since 1992–93.
12. The Fiscal Responsibility and Budget Management Act which seeks to restrict borrowing by the government so that the fiscal deficit as a percentage of the GDP remains at 3 and revenue deficit is altogether wiped out.
13. The Planning Commission has been in the process of finalising the models to be implemented. At present, it is not clear how the PPP would work. However, we can make some informed anticipations.
14. Any attempt to strictly adhere to a 20 per cent rule would complicate matters as quality of education is linked to cost of education. Moreover, high cost of education does not guarantee high quality in a system plagued by poor governance.
15. Named after the Russian Economist, Nikolai Kondratiev (1892–1938), four Kondratiev cycles of approximately 50 years have been identified, each showing expansion and depression phases (1790–1820/1820–48; 1848–70/1870–97; 1897–1913/1913–45; 1945–73/1973–?). See Louca and Reijnders (1999).
16. How to accommodate the OBCs has been a matter of contestation in the Court.
17. The government has already started taking action after some cases were reported by *The Times of India* during June 2009.
18. Recently the government in its 11th Five Year Plan strategy has taken the initiative to allocate ₹ 4,000 crore for the promotion of educational loans in meeting the financial need of the weaker sections to access HE and budgetary provision has been made in the Union Budget for 2010–11.
19. There are four modes under GATS. Liberalisation of higher education is focused on Mode 3 under GATS which requires commercial or physical presence of institutions: transnational education. Mode 1 (programme mobility), Mode 2 for consumption abroad (student mobility) and Mode 4 for academic mobility (movement of natural persons) are not unduly constrained by government measures to liberalise HE.
20. From the data collected from the British Council there were 12 UK-based universities offering joint programmes with Indian partner institutions with eight offering at the PG level. In total these programmes were expected to enroll 5,000 students with 10–15,000 for all the FEPS together (Agarwal 2009).

21. Planning Commission's High Level Group on Service Sector, headed by Mr Anwarul Hoda.
22. Around 80 per cent of seats in professional education are catered to by the private sector (Agarwal 2009). The growth has been to the tune of 19–20 per cent in some states.
23. Such institutes are not directly dependent on governments — state and central — for funding, rather they get their funding from the established organisations.
24. Only 7 per cent have access to internet in India.
25. The extent of private participation in professional courses would be around 80 per cent (Agarwal 2009).
26. Educational loans are found to be discriminatory. Even if profits are not made under PPP, the fee structure would go up. The self-financing courses offered by the public-funded institutions in the area of market-oriented courses are expensive.
27. Education is not for business in India. As per the Supreme Court judgement, reasonable surplus could be made for the purpose of reinvestment in the same entity.
28. Upheld by the SC, albeit with some modifications.
29. It is argued that 40 per cent of the graduates are not productively employed with the rate of unemployment going up with the level of education (Agarwal 2009). The budgetary allocation for skill development has been enhanced as this is a focus area under EFYP. UK has GER of 64 in HE with India at around 12 per cent. Proportion of labour force with skill in India is merely 5.4 per cent compared to 26.9 per cent in UK (as reported in Agarwal 2009 with data obtained from GER from Global Education Digest 2007).
30. The Council is chaired by the Prime Minister of India. The possible shift in the focus is reported in *The Economic Times*, 17 March 2010, page 13.

References

Agarwal, P. 2009. *Indian Higher Education: Envisioning the Future.* New Delhi: Sage Publications.

Altbach, P. G. 1999. *Private Prometheus: Private Higher Education and Development in the 21st Century.* London: Greenwood Press.

———. 2008. 'Beware of the Trojan Horse', *The Hindu*, 15 July.

———. 2009. 'The Giants Awake: Higher Education Systems in China and India', *Economic and Political Weekly*, 44 (23), 39–51.

Anderson, R. D. 1992. *Universities and Elites in Britain Since 1800.* London: Macmillan Press Limited.

Archer, L., M. Hutchings and A. Ross. 2003. *Higher Education and Social Class: Issues of Exclusion and Inclusion.* London and New York: Routledge.

Association of Indian Universities. 2004a. Access and Equity in Higher Education, Selection from the University News-15, New Delhi.

———. 2004b. GATS and Higher Education Selection from the University News-18, New Delhi.

Ball, S. 2008. *The Education Debate*. Bristol: Polity Press.

Barr, N. and I. Crawford. 2005. *Financing Higher Education: Answers from the UK*. London: Routledge.

Basu, A. 2005. 'A Century and a Half's Journey: Women's Education in India, 1850s to 2000', in R. Bharati (ed.), *Women of India*. New Delhi: Sage Publications.

Bhushan, S. 2009. *Restructuring Higher Education in India*. New Delhi: Rawat Publications.

Blundell, R. L. Dearden, A. Goodman and H. Reed. 2000. 'The Returns to Higher Education in Britain: Evidence from a British Cohort', *Economic Journal*, 110, 82–99.

Burke, P. J. 2005. 'Access and Widening Participation', *British Journal of Sociology of Education*, 26 (4), 555–62.

Callender, C. and J. Jackson. 2005. 'Does the Fear of Debt Deter Students from Higher Education?' *Journal of Social Policy*, 34 (4), 509–40.

Carpentier, V. 2003. 'Public Expenditure on Education and Economic Growth in the UK, 1833–2000', *History of Education*, 32 (1), 1–15.

———. 2006a. 'Funding in Higher Education and Economic Growth in France and the United Kingdom, 1921–2003', *Higher Education Management and Policy*, 18 (3), 1–26.

———. 2006b. 'Public Expenditure on Education and Economic Growth in the USA in the Nineteenth and Twentieth Centuries in Comparative Perspective', *Paedagogica Historica*, 42 (6), 683–706.

———. 2010. 'Public-Private Substitution in Higher education Funding and Kondratiev Cycles: The Impacts on Home and International Students', in E. Unterhalter and V. Carpentier (eds), *Global Inequalities and Higher Education. Whose Interests Are We Serving?* Houndmills: Palgrave MacMillan.

Chattopadhyay, S. 2007. 'Exploring Alternative Sources of Financing Higher Education', *Economic and Political Weekly*, 42 (42), October 20, 4251–259.

———. 2009. 'The Market in Higher Education: Concern for Equity and Quality', *Economic and Political Weekly*, 44 (29), July 18, 53–61.

———. 2010. 'An Elitist and Flawed Approach towards Higher Education', *Economic and Political Weekly*, 1 May, 45 (18), 15–17.

Chevaillier, T. and J. C. Eicher. 2002. 'Rethinking the Financing of Post Compulsory Education', *Higher Education in Europe*, 27 (1–2), 69–88.

Dearing, R. 1997. *The National Committee of Inquiry into Higher Education: Higher Education in the Learning Society*. London: H.M.S.O.

Department for Education and Skills. 2003. *The Future of Higher Education*, White Paper, DfES, January, London.

Department for Innovation, Universities and Skills. 2008a. *Participation Rates in Higher Education*, National Statistics, London.

———. 2008b. *Full-time Young Participation by Socio-Economic Class*, DIUS, London.

Dyhouse, C. 2002. 'Going to University between the Wars: Access and Funding', *History of Education*, 31 (1), 1–15.

———. 2006. *Students: A Gendered History*. London: Routledge.

Fontvieille, L. and S. Michel. 2002. 'Analysis of the Transition between Two Successive Social Orders: Application to the Relation between Education and Growth', *Review*, 25 (1), 23–46.

Galindo-Rueda, F., O. Marcenaro-Gutierrez and A. Vignoles. 2004. 'The Widening Socio-Economic Gap in UK Higher Education', *National Institute Economic Review*, 190, 75–88.

Government of India. 1966. 'Education and National Development: Report of the Education Commission 1964–66', National Council for Educational Research and Training, New Delhi.

———. 1968. 'National Policy on Education', Department of Education, Ministry of Human Resource Development, Government of India, New Delhi.

———. 1986. 'National Policy on Education', Department of Education, Ministry of Human Resource Development, Government of India, New Delhi.

———. 1995. Government Subsidies in India. New Delhi: Government of India.

———. 1998. 'National Policy on Education', Department of Education, Ministry of Human Resource Development, Government of India, New Delhi.

———. 2000. 'Report on A Policy Framework for Reforms in Education', Prime Minister's Council on Trade and Industry, April, New Delhi.

———. 2007a. 'Report on Conditions of Work and Promotion of Livelihoods in the Unorganised Sector', National Commission for Entreprises in the Unorganised Sector, August, New Delhi.

———. 2007b. 'Report to the Nation 2006, National Knowledge Commission', January, New Delhi.

———. 2008a. 'Approach Paper to the 11th Five Year Plan', Planning Commission, New Delhi.

———. 2008b. 'Report of the High Level Group on Services Sector', Planning Commission, March, New Delhi.

———. 2008c. 'Report of the UGC Pay Review Committee', University Grants Commission, New Delhi.

———. 2008d. 'Report to the Nation 2007, National Knowledge Commission', January, New Delhi.

Halsey, A. 1993. 'Trends in Access and Equity in Higher Education: Britain in International Perspective', *Oxford Review of Education*, 19 (2), 29–40. http://www.bris.ac.uk/education/research/centres/ges/publications/ 04slr.pdf (accessed on 18 August 2010).

Jayaram, N. 2007. 'India', in J. J. F. Forest and P. G. Altbach (eds), *International Handbook of Higher Education*. Dordrecht: Springer.

King, R. 2004. *The University in the Global Age*. Basingstoke and New York: Palgrave Macmillan.

———. 2009. *Private Higher Education: Private Gain or Public Interest?* Presentation to the All-Parliamentary Group: House of Lords, 16 June.

Kumar, A. (ed.). 2004. 'Challenges Facing Indian Universities', Jawaharlal Nehru University Teachers' Association (JNUTA), New Delhi.

Lawton, D. 1992. *Education and Politics in the 1990s: Conflict or Consensus?* London: Falmer Press.

Leathwood, C. 2004. 'A Critique of Institutional Inequalities in Higher Education: (Or an Alternative to Hypocrisy for Higher Educational Policy)', *Theory and Research in Education*, 2 (1), 31–48.

Levy, D. C. 2003. 'Expanding Higher Education through Private Growth, Contributions and Challenges', *The Observatory on Borderless Higher Education*, Report 11.

Louca, F. and J. Reijnders. 1999. *The Foundations of Long Wave Theory*. Cheltenham: Edward Elgar Publishing.

Lowe, R. 2002. 'Higher Education', in R. Aldrich (ed.), *A Century of Education*. London: Routledge Falmer.

Marginson, S. and M. van der Wende. 2007. 'Globalisation and Higher Education', *OECD Education. Working Papers*, No. 8, Paris: OECD Publishing.

Morley, L. and M. David. 2009. 'Special Issue — Celebrations and Challenges: Gender in Higher Education', *Higher Education Policy*, 22 (1), 1–118.

Naidoo, P., M. Singh and L. Lange. 2007. 'Private Provision, National Regulatory Systems and Quality Assurance: A Case Study of Transnational Providers in South Africa', *Journal of Higher Education in Africa*, 5 (2–3), 67–84.

Olssen, M. and M. A. Peters. 2005. 'Neoliberalism, Higher Education and the Knowledge Economy: From the Free Market to Knowledge Capitalism', *Journal of Education Policy*, 20 (3), 313–45.

Pathak, B. K. 2008. 'Information Asymmetry in Higher Education Market: A Case Study of Two Engineering Colleges in West Bengal', M.Phil. Dissertation submitted to the Jawaharlal Nehru University, New Delhi.

Punnayya, K. (Chairman) 1993. 'Report of Justice Punnayya Committee of UGC Funding of Institutions of Higher Education'. New Delhi: University Grants Commission.

Quality Assurance Agency. 2008. *Annual Report to the Higher Education Funding Council for England*, QAA, January.

Raju, S. 2008. 'Gender Differentials in Access to Higher Education', in UGC, *Higher Education in India: Issues Related to Expansion, Inclusiveness, Quality and Finance.* New Delhi: University Grants Commission.

Ramsden, B. 2008. 'Patterns of Higher Education Institutions in the UK', *Universities UK,* Seventh Report, September.

Reay, D., M. David and S. Ball. 2005. *Degrees of Choice: Class, Race, Gender and Higher Education.* Stoke-on-Trent: Trentham Books.

Reddy, J. (Chairman) 1992. 'Report of Janardhanna Reddy Committee of Higher Education and management of Education', Central Advisory Board on Education, New Delhi.

Rizvi, F. and B. Lingard. 2010. *Globalizing Education Policy.* New York: Routledge.

Robbins Committee on Higher Education. 1963. *Administrative, Financial and Economic Aspects of Higher Education,* Appendix 4, H.M.S.O.

Robertson, S. L. 2006. 'Globalisation, GATS and Trading in Education Services', published by the Centre for Globalisation, Education and Societies, University of Bristol, Bristol BS8 1JA, UK.

Salerno, C. 2004. 'Public Money and Private Providers: Funding Channels and National Patterns in Four Countries', *Journal of Higher Education,* 48 (1), 101–30.

Sanderson, M. 1972. *The Universities and British Industry 1850–1970.* London: Routledge and Kegan Paul.

Scott, P. (ed.) 1998. *The Globalization of Higher Education.* Buckingham: Society for Research into Higher Education and Open University Press.

Shattock, M. 1994. *The UGC and the Management of British Universities.* Guildford: Society for Research into Higher Education.

Shinn, C. H. 1980. 'The Beginnings of the University Grants Committee', *History of Education,* 9 (3), 233–43.

Silver, H. 2003. *Higher Education and Opinion Making in England in Twentieth Century.* London: Woburn Press.

Sinha, S. and R. S. Srivastava. 2008. 'Inclusiveness and Access of Social Groups to Higher Education', in UGC, *Higher Education in India: Issues related to Expansion, Inclusiveness, Quality and Finance.* New Delhi: University Grants Commission.

Srivastava D. K., T. K. Sen, H. Mukhopadhyay, C. Bhujanga Rao and H. K. Amarnath. 1997. Government Subsidies in India, New Delhi: National Institute of Public Finance and Policy.

Teferra, D. and P. G. Altbach. 2004. 'African Higher Education: Challenges for the 21st Century', *Higher Education,* 47 (1), 21–50.

Teixeira, J., B. Johnstone, M. J. Rosa and H. Vossensteyn. 2006. *Cost-sharing and Accessibility in Higher Education: A Fairer Deal?* Dordrecht: Springer.

Thorat, S. 2008. 'Emerging Issues in Higher Education: Approach and Strategy in the 11th Plan', Keynote Address delivered during Conference on Higher Education and 11th Plan, 11 November, Vigyan Bhawan, New Delhi.

Tilak, J. B. G. 2004. 'Public Subsidies in Education in India', *Economic and Political Weekly*, 39 (4), January 24, 343–59.

————. 2008. 'Transition from Higher Education as a Public Good to Higher Education as a Private Good: The Saga of Indian Experience', *Journal of Asian Public Policy*, 1 (2), 220–34.

Tilak, J. B. G. and N. V. Varghese. 1991. 'Financing Higher Education in India', *Higher Education*, 21 (1), 83–101.

Tomlinson, S. 2005. 'Race, Ethnicity and Education under New Labour', *Oxford Review of Education*, 31 (1), 153–71.

University Grants Commission. 2008. *Higher Education in India: Issues related to Expansion, Inclusiveness, Quality and Finance*, November. New Delhi: UGC.

Watson, D. and R. Bowden. 2007. 'The Fate of the Dearing Recommendations: Policy and Performance in UK HE, 1997–2007', in D. Watson and M. Amoah (eds), *The Dearing Report: Ten Years On*. London: Bedford Way Papers.

Williams, P. 1984. 'Britain's Full-Cost Policy for Overseas Students', *Comparative Education Review*, 28 (2), 258–78.

6

Advocacy Networks, Choice and Private Schooling of the Poor in India*

Geetha B. Nambissan and Stephen J. Ball

The two main axes of global trends in education policy are parental choice and the role of 'private' schooling, and the reform of state education systems along market lines. The first rests on a set of neo-liberal arguments about more or less radical 'destatalisation' (Jessop 2002), subjecting state organisations to competition and/or the handing over of service delivery to the private sector. The second is post-neoliberal and re-asserts the role of the state but in a new form and with new modalities involving a reformist 'destatalisation' — a shift from government to governance; from bureaucracy to networks; from delivery to contracting. In the pragmatics of reform the two are typically blended together and both axes have strident support from powerful transnational agencies — the World Bank, the International Finance Corporation (IFC), WTO and the Organisation for Economic Cooperation and Development (OECD) in particular. Both are firmly embedded in the generic nostrums of international management consultancies and education businesses (see Ball 2007, 2009).

The dissemination of such policies entails both 'policy entrepreneurship' *and at the same time* a process of policy transfer, and is a mechanism of 'policy convergence'. Consultants and education businesses are delivering 'development' and aid policy (for a potential profit), developing local policy infrastructures, and embedding prevailing western policy discourses, directly or as 'spillovers' into the local policy systems, working with various 'partners'.[1] This is what Kelsey (2006) calls 'regulatory re-territorialisation', which increases the political power and regulatory influence of state, societal and transnational agents who are able to exert control over territorial assets, as well as producing infrastructures which are amenable to further business penetration. In general terms the UK and the USA are probably the most active sites of both axes of reform, and are reform laboratories from which experiments are exported around the world. They are also important sites for the articulation and export of the rhetorics and discourses of reform.

In this essay, we are interested in the flows of these rhetorics and discourses, particularly those which advocate school choice and private schooling as solutions to the problem of achieving universal, high-quality primary education in India. In particular we will identify the role played by transnational advocacy networks (TANs) and the particular activities of one individual policy entrepreneur (IPE) based in the UK — James Tooley — in managing and driving those flows. This involves the mapping of a set of network relations between advocacy groups in the UK (and the US) and local 'choice' advocates in India. In doing so we hope to show how these particular policy networks 'work'. We also want to indicate some of the complex and blurred relationships between advocacy, philanthropy and business within these networks. We then go on to sketch some of the emerging impacts of local and transnational advocacy on the politics of education and education policy in India and also finally indicate some of the ways in which local and international businesses are taking up the spaces and opportunities created by the advocacy discourse for involvement in educational services delivery. We do not set out here to debate the issues of private schooling or choice — one of us has researched them extensively in other settings (see Ball 1997, 2001, 2003) — or seek to interrogate the evidence mobilised in the processes of advocacy although we voice our concerns about some of the knowledge claims made.

Our data here involve the use of secondary sources of various kinds mostly accessed through internet searches. These include the websites of advocacy groups, business information websites and newspapers reports. The range and variety of sources was extensive and we were able to draw upon multiple sources for virtually all of the examples and events referred to. The materials that refer to nodal and influential individuals within the advocacy networks were all drawn from sources in the public domain and in many instances employ direct quotation from the individuals themselves. Our 'method' relies on simple network mapping techniques and the attempt to identify the capacities of the network actors in terms of relationships, finance, 'research' and promotion and publicity, etc. In this respect we are guided by Dicken et al. (2001: 93) who point out that the task of network methodology 'must be to identify the actors in these networks, their power and capacities, and the ways through which they exercise their power through association within networks of relationships'.

Transnational Advocacy Networks

Transnational advocacy networks are typically discussed and portrayed within a paradigm of progressive policy solutions, vulnerable constituencies and community empowerment related to human rights and environmental issues in particular. The Centre on Law and Globalisation defines them as 'fluid and open relationships among knowledgeable, committed actors (individuals and organisations). These relationships span nation-state boundaries. They differ from other types of networks in that they exist to promote principled causes, ideas and values. They exist to change international policy as well as make these changes real in the day-to-day lives of ordinary people.'[2] Transnational advocacy networks are 'communicative structures' organised around the 'shared values' of their members (Keck and Sikkink 1998). These definitions clearly apply to the advocacy work of 'policy entrepreneur' James Tooley, which draws directly on his commitment to the Hayekian argument that markets are both liberatory and progressive. Furthermore, TANs can be part of a reshaping of political processes at supranational, national and subnational levels, although as a number of analysts have pointed out, their activities and impacts vary between nations in relation to institutional arrangements, policy settings and degrees of democratisation, especially when considering transitional or late developing societies (Dalton and Rohrschneider 2003; Held and McGrew 2004). We argue that such a re-shaping is occurring in relation to the politics of education in India. Transnational advocacy networks provide a network of relations for the diffusion of knowledge and information and typically seek to pluralise political authority. They are a 'third force' (Florini 2000) and often an extension of domestic social or political movements. Keck and Sikkink (1998: 25) see TANs as changing national government behaviour through the exchange of norms, ideas and discourses, and working to change public perception of social problems — which again are very apposite in the case we discuss in which, in part at least, there is a contribution being made to the construction of consent in relation to the neoliberal project (Cavett-Goodwin 2008; Harvey 2005). Keck and Sikkink identify four types of TAN strategy: information politics, symbolic politics, leverage politics and accountability politics (see later). Transnational advocacy networks work 'underneath, above and around the state' (Wapner 1996) but their success, according to Keck and Sikkink, depends on the strength and depth of their networks and the vulnerability of the target state or organisations.

The TAN literature tends to neglect the role of individual policy entrepreneurs. Mintrom and Vergari (1996) suggest that policy entrepreneurs perform three functions. They identify needs and offer innovative means to satisfy them; they bear financial and emotional risks in pursuing change where consequences are uncertain; and they assemble and coordinate networks of individuals and organisations with the talents and resources needed to achieve change. The personal resources needed by the IPE 'include intellectual ability, knowledge of policy matters, leadership and team-building skills, reputation and contacts, strategic ability, and tenacity' (Mintrom and Vergari 1996: 424); James Tooley would score well on all counts. The role of financial power is only indirectly alluded to in the mainstream literature on TANs but is a crucial factor in our case.

The Context

Unlike the UK, India is a late 'liberaliser'; policies of structural adjustment and liberalisation were initiated in the early 1990s and only recently has this country been recognised as a key economic player in the global arena. The spread of market relations and discourses has been relatively slow. Nonetheless, there are immense possibilities for the transfer of policy/discourse through the activities of 'policy entrepreneurs', who are strategically positioned and backed by powerful financial and political interests in the early globalising countries. Krishna Kumar has sketched out a set of relations between liberalisation, privatisation and modernisation in the Government of India and suggested that education has become 'a significant arena to study liberalisation' (LaDousa 2007: 139) and that 'privatisation has become a major force'.

India is a long way from achieving universal elementary education. Around 8 million children in the 6–14 year age group are still estimated as being outside of any form of school provisioning. Further, the enormous network of over one million state-run elementary schools (NUEPA 2011) is generally seen to be of poor quality and in need of financial and academic support. India is hence struggling to meet its

Education for All (EFA) goals. This provides fertile grounds for the use of forms of 'accountability politics' by choice advocates. There is a small but expanding market in private unregulated (officially 'unrecognised' by the state) elementary schools that has emerged in response to the growing demand for better quality (English-medium) education by lower middle-class and poor parents who are willing to pay for this education for their children. All of this creates 'opportunities' for private investment in elementary education in India — both in expanding the market for private schools for the poor and 'improving' the quality of state-funded schools. Also important is the fact that state resources for elementary education as well as aid from international organisations/donors are directed to government schools. A discourse of 'school choice' that incorporates concerns of equity and quality for the poor can help create a policy environment that redirects funds from the state and donor organisations to private schools, for instance, through vouchers. It can also encourage private markets in schooling for the poor if there is evidence to project such educational entrepreneurship as a profitable venture. 'For-profit schools are presently illegal in India.

Advocacy for school choice and the market to meet the demand for schooling by the poor has hence a critical role to play in India. Since 2000 the involvement of the private sector along with NGOs and corporate players has received guarded mention in a couple of policy documents — but official policy still fights shy of openly acknowledging the role of the market in schooling for the poor. It is only very recently that some statistics on private, 'unregulated' schools have been collected and their existence formally acknowledged. Acknowledging/encouraging the private market for elementary education for the poor remains politically sensitive and are likely to be met with considerable opposition within the main political parties. Thus, two of the key tasks for advocacy groups have been to destabilise the opposition to private provision of schools, and to bring some credibility to the existing extra-legal (unrecognised) schools.

In the following sections we outline some of the key features of the complex local and transnational advocacy network that is articulating choice and privatisation policies for Indian education. What is important in all of this is the inter-locking relations, re-iteration of ideas, flows of funds, opportunities for promotion and publicity and points of access to arenas of education politics and policy making. These are features of the strength and depth of this network, focused around a clear set of shared values and common goals. All of the strategies identified by Keck and Sikkink are evident here.

India's 'Policy Entrepreneurs'

A key 'nodal' intellectual in choice advocacy in India is British academic James Tooley, a professor from the University of Newcastle, UK. He is deeply embedded in the infrastructure of neoliberal think tanks and institutes in the UK and USA and has important links to various businesses, business philanthropists and charities which promote the market. Tooley is an IPE par excellence. He has played a key role in building and shaping the school choice discourse in India and also occupies a variety of roles and positions in the networks that link organisations and individuals who are presently pushing the 'project' of neoliberalising India's schools (see Figure 6.1). He also has access to considerable financial resources. A former consultant of the International Finance Corporation, Tooley directed the global study of investment opportunities for private education in developing

Figure 6.1: Advocacy Networks, Choice and Schooling of the Poor in India

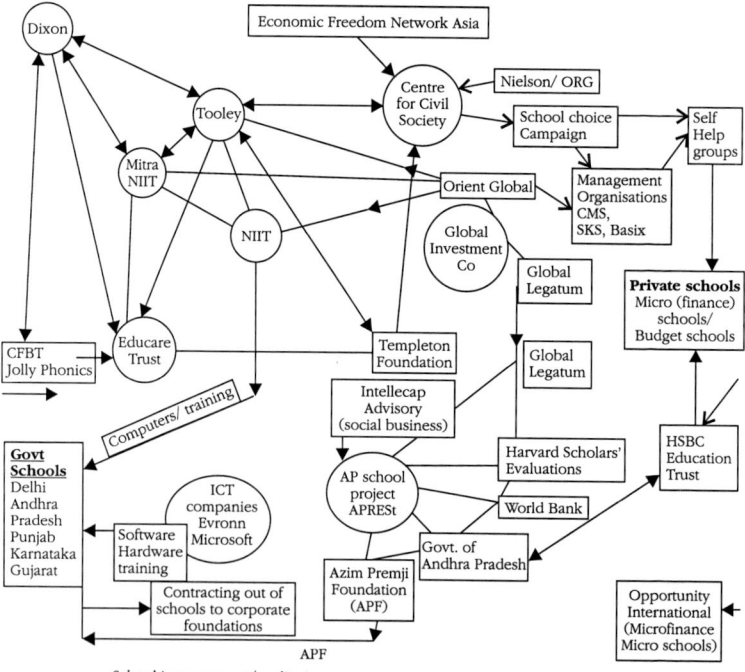

Source: Prepared by Geetha B. Nambissan. Based on information from websites cited in the text.

countries for the IFC — the private finance arm of the World Bank — which led to the publication *The Global Education Industry* (Tooley 1999).[3] One of the sites where research was carried out for that publication was in the poor settlements in the city of Hyderabad in the southern state of Andhra Pradesh in India. Tooley's objective was not merely to show that state-run schools there were not performing, but that the poor were accessing private schools (a fact he felt was not being adequately acknowledged), that they were willing to pay for education, that these schools were low cost but more efficient and better performing than government schools and were also socially committed (they provided free places to the needy). Also he argued that private schools were making profit and if invested in or supported financially, for instance, with low-cost innovative technology, they would be a potential area for business expansion.

One of the ways the pro-market, pro-choice advocacy works is through the circulation and re-circulation of ideas and joining up of points of articulation. Foundations and think tanks and the media are important in the take up and dissemination of ideas and their establishment within policy-thinking. Using a very narrow base of research findings, Tooley has been able to reach a wide and varied audience through academic journals (he has published versions of his findings in, among other places, the *Oxford Review of Education, Journal of Education Policy* and the *International Journal of Educational Research*), a huge range of on-line sites, media interviews, as well as through the lectures and talks that he has given including to parliamentarians (in the USA and UK) and policy makers and other groups in India. There has been extensive media coverage of his exploits (particularly among pro-market newspapers and magazines and websites). In 2006 James Tooley won an essay competition sponsored by the *Financial Times* and the International Finance Corporation for his essay 'Educating Amaretech' (called the 'Gold Essay') which summarised his research on the role of the private sector in the education of the poor (Tooley 2007). He received a prize of $US 30,000. The prize and his main findings regarding the poor and private schooling were reported widely. The Templeton Foundation provided a grant of $US 800,000 for Tooley's comparative study of private schools in five countries that included an Indian component, upon which the essay is based. This essay is a good example of what Keck and Sikkink (1998) call 'symbolic politics' which involves the use of stories or symbols which make sense of advocacy claims for distant audiences.

A number of US, UK and Indian foundations which espouse the philosophy of the free market have drawn attention to and disseminated Tooley's work which has provided a key point of focus for their efforts in relation to India, and other countries. Almost all of these are inter-connected through the Atlas Economic Research Foundation 'Freedom Network' 'the means for free market organizations to share information and connect with like-minded organizations throughout the world'.[4] The Heritage Foundation, The Philanthropy Roundtable and *The Wall Street Journal*, among others, have reported and commended Tooley's work. Andrew J. Coulson, director of the Cato Institute's Center for Educational Freedom (part funded by Atlas) and author of Market Education (1999), has also given fulsome praise to Tooley's research (Coulson 2007). Tooley's writings about his private school projects or features on his work have also been published by the Hoover Institution, The Fraser Institute, The Mackinac Center, Institute of Economic Affairs (of which Tooley is a member), and the National Center for Policy Analysis. His work has also been reported by the Centre for Civil Society, India, in its School Choice Campaign (strapline — Fund Students, Not Schools! — which features on the website of Atlas Economic Research Foundation), *Policy* (published by the Centre for Independent Studies), the Mont Pelerin Society (at its regional meeting organized by the Centre of Civil Society in Goa), The UNESCO Courier, Opportunity International, India Together, The Educare Trust and the Liberty Institute.[5] Tooley's paper (2001) 'The Enterprise of Education Opportunities and Challenges for India', has been published by the Liberty Institute.

The Liberty Institute, the Centre for Civil Society and the Educare Trust are the key sites for school choice and privatisation advocacy in India. Increasingly, school choice/private schooling advocacy networks also include investment companies and venture capitalists that are looking to new market opportunities in India. Tooley argues that: '[c]rucially, because the private schools serving the poor are businesses, making a reasonable profit, they provide a pioneering way forward for investors to get involved too' and that 'investing in a chain of schools — either through a dedicated education investment fund or through joint ventures with educational entrepreneurs — could help solve the information problem for poor' (2005: 1). He also suggests that the 'micro finance' model can be used to fund small entrepreneurs who can be encouraged to set up schools that will give adequate returns. In 'Educating Amaretech' Tooley cites Prahlad's observation that the founder of Aravind Eye Care System in India (which provides cataract surgery for large numbers of the poor in India) was 'inspired by the hamburger chain, McDonald's, where a consistent quality of hamburgers and French fries worldwide results from a deeply understood and standardised chemical process' (Prahlad 2004, cited in Tooley 2005: 9). According to Tooley, 'there is every reason to think that a similarly "deeply understood and standardised" learning process could become part of an equally successful model of private school provision, serving huge numbers of the poor' (2005: 9). Further, since private entrepreneurs already provide, 'free and subsidized places for the poorest, sensitively-applied targeted vouchers could extend access with equity on a large scale' (ibid).

Furthermore, Weidrich points to Tooley's suggestion for setting up of 'Education Quality Zones (EQZs)' where there are 'more relaxed rules and regulations regarding education' along the lines of Economic Priority Zones (EPZs) that have been established by the Indian government 'to foster entrepreneurship and innovation' (Weidrich 2007). Some leaders of Indian industry have also called for 'setting up special education zones' to free education from 'the control of bureaucracies and regulating bodies'.[6]

In February 2007, the 'philanthropic arm' of Orient Global, a Singapore-based investment firm, established an education fund of $100 million. The Orient Global chairman is said to have created this fund after reading Tooley's essay on 'Low-cost Schools in Poor Nations Seek Investors' in the *Financial Times* (17 September 2006). The Global Education Fund is expected to target the market for private schooling for children from low-income families in India; Tooley is designated president of the Fund. Coulson (2007) reports that the education fund 'will follow a three-pronged strategy: invest in publicly listed and private enterprises that will further its mission while helping to sustain it over time (e.g., the Fund has acquired a 9.4 per cent stake in India's NIIT educational chain); conduct research and development for a pilot chain of budget private schools for the poor in India; and make grants to existing private schools to aid in their expansion and protect them from sudden political or economic shocks'. Kalra (2007), writing in the blog *liveMint.com*, quotes Tooley as saying 'we have started looking at investment opportunities in private schools running in slums'. It goes on to say that 'Tooley did not disclose details of his business model, but said he was exploring tie-ups with microfinance providers, such as Hyderabad's SKS Microfinance and Basix, to offer loans to entrepreneurs who wish to open schools in low-income areas' (Kalra 2007).

Two other key PEs in the school choice/private schooling advocacy network are Pauline Dixon and Sugata Mitra, both working alongside Tooley. Dixon is a research associate at the University of Newcastle. Her doctoral degree awarded in 2003 was for her work 'The Regulation of Private Schools for Low-Income Families in Andhra Pradesh, India: An Austrian Economic Approach'. She was International Research Co-ordinator in the Templeton Project (2003–5) directed by Tooley. She has written and published with Tooley and a number of her publications focus on her work in India.[7] She has co-authored (with Tooley) a chapter on private education and the poor for the 2006 *Index of Economic Freedom*, published by The Heritage Foundation and *The Wall Street Journal* (Tooley and Dixon 2005).[8] She was teacher and writer of the course 'Educational Freedom: A Global Perspective', that was a winner of the Freedom Project, managed by the Atlas Economic Freedom Foundation and funded by the John Templeton Foundation.[9] Dixon has also been invited by Capitol Hill, the Heritage and Templeton Foundations to speak on her research on private schooling for the poor and has been associated with the Centre for British Teachers (CfBT)–funded project 'Private Schools for the Poor' (2001–2). Dixon is currently working for the Orient Global Project (2007–9) where she is named project leader along with Tooley and Mitra. Mitra was a research scientist with the National Institute for Information and Technology (NIIT). He received accolades for his 'Hole in the Wall' (HIW)/'minimally invasive education' and is hailed on *Edutopia* (*What Works in Public Education*) (an information Gateway run by the George Lucas Educational Foundation) as the 'Inventor of the off-the-wall idea for Hole-in-the-Wall Education: Put a free computer workstation in the wall of a poor New Delhi neighborhood, and the local children will quickly learn to use it through their own curiosity and experimentation' (Rubenstein 2007). Mitra was named by the George Lucas Educational Foundation as one of the 'Global Six of 2007'.

Mitra argues that HIW education is more effective (and of course far cheaper) than regular government schooling and is appropriate for the poor. 'With backing from NIIT, the Indian government, the ICICI Bank, and the International Finance Corporation, Delhi, Mitra and NIIT founded "Hole-in-the-Wall Education" and set up 250 computers in 110 locations throughout India and later in Cambodia' (NIIT also operates in Africa and Fiji). Mitra asserts that: '[r]esearch shows that Hole-in-the-Wall users performed nearly as well on computer skills tests as children who had learned through a formal class, and their engagement and performance in school improved as well'. In his lectures and writings, Tooley often refers to Mitra's low-cost technology as appropriate for teaching poor children. Mitra is now professor of Educational Technology at the University of Newcastle and he 'aims to spread this model around the world to boost the learning and life skills of children, particularly those living in poverty and with few educational resources'.[10] Mitra's research could be seen as one of many aspects of the use of 'leverage politics', that is, the mobilisation of powerful actors in support of networks goals.

Choice and Schooling: Local Organisations and Advocacy

A number of local organisations have emerged in the last few years with the express objective of promoting school choice and private schooling for the poor in India. The foremost of them is the Centre for Civil Society (CCS) which sees itself as a think tank concerned with ideas:

> [b]ut we don't run primary schools, or health clinics, or garbage collection programs. We do it differently: we try to change people's ideas, opinions, mode of thinking by research, seminars, and publications. We champion limited government, rule of law, free trade, and individual rights. We are an ideas organisation, a think tank that develops ideas to better the world.[11]

The Centre sees its mission as:

> Building a campaign for school choice in India. The need to create a discourse on choice in education, state the case for private schooling among the poor and giving poor parents the freedom to choose.

The case for 'deregulation and delicensing of private schools, legalizing for-profit schools, and microfinance and venture capital for budget private schools' is stressed. The website goes on to say that '[t]oday it is virtually impossible to start a legally recognised school. Also, since many of the schools for the poor are unrecognised, they cannot get a bank loan to improve their infrastructure like any other enterprise'.

The Centre for Civil Society deploys research evidence to bolster its case. Tooley's Hyderabad research and Eva Weidrich's essay

'Vouchers: Is There a Model for India?' can be downloaded from the CCS website (Weidrich 2007). Tooley has also undertaken a study of the access to private schooling among poor families in settlements in East Delhi for CCS along the lines of his Hyderabad study, and come up with similar findings (Tooley and Dixon 2005). The study was supported by Goodrich Foundation, Thomas B. Fordham and Templeton Foundation. More recently, a CCS survey, 'Education for the Poor' was carried out by market research companies AC Nielsen and ORG-MARG, Delhi. The study 'tried to gauge customer satisfaction with government school education'. Tooley is also a Senior Research Fellow with CCS.[12] The Centre for Civil Society is a member of Economic Freedom Network Asia (EFNA) which is linked to the Fraser Institute and the Liberal Institute of the Friedrich Naumann Foundation in Berlin (both part of the Atlas Foundation 'Freedom' network). Figure 6.1 summarises the networks linking intellectual entrepreneurs and advocacy organisations.

The CCS 'School Choice Campaign' was launched in January 2007 as part of the campaign vouchers to be awarded to poor children across seven states in India. In Delhi, applications were invited from parents in poor settlements and around 400 children were chosen through a lottery. The vouchers, worth up to INR 6,000, were awarded at a venue frequented by the cultural elite of the city and this was reported by the media. Significantly, the chief minister of Delhi state was present to give away the vouchers. The CCS website appeals to prospective donors in India, UK and USA to contribute to the voucher fund and has also forms for donations posted on the website.[13]

The CCS claims that the response has been 'overwhelming', their 'biggest support is from dalit and tribal activists', and that the campaign is 'gaining ground in Bihar, Delhi, Jharkhand, Orissa, Tamil Nadu, Uttar Pradesh and West Bengal'. It goes on to say 'Most people realise that the aspirations of the poor are no different from us and they too want their children to attend English medium private schools which will lift them out of their present poverty and give them a decent future. Also, the moment the poor become a bit less poor, they escape the system of government schools' (India Together 2007). The 'campaign' is being managed by a private management company, Cirrus Management Services (CMS) which is taking it to states where the organisation has links with community-based organisations built around micro-finance loan programmes. M. S. Ashok of Cirrus says that his organisation 'hand-holds self-help groups in seven States including Tamilnadu, and has decided to leverage its reach to start a voucher programme'. He goes on to say that they are 'working with a group of individuals and corporates to develop and finance private schools across rural India, initially across 700-plus villages, to be scaled up subsequently'.[14] However, CCS (and other proponents of school choice) realises that it is critical for voucher programmes to have the support of the government if they are to succeed. Raj Cherubal, CCS vice president, observes that 'for the voucher programs to be widely available, the government has to embrace them, or the idea will not scale. . . . If Pilot projects are started in every state, the Government could use them as examples to consolidate and ultimately take over the voucher scheme.'

The Educare Trust (ET)

The Educare Trust is a 'non-profit agency' registered in 2002 by James Tooley (along with 'other members associated with private unaided schools') under the Indian Trust Act, 1882.[15] Tooley carried out his Templeton-funded study (2003–5) through the Trust. The director of the Trust, Gomathi, worked with Tooley earlier on a CfBT project ('Private Schools for the Poor') and subsequently on the Templeton project. Research relating to the use of 'Jolly Phonics' for the 'improvement of English literacy teaching in private unaided schools' was also carried out by the Trust (as a component of the Templeton project). The Trust has a 'marketing manager' who is involved in the marketing of the 'Jolly Phonics English Literacy Programme' and computer programmes along with Sugato Mitra. Director Gomathi 'co-ordinates the scholarship and micro-finance programme. She along with Professor Tooley introduced the voucher scheme and micro-finance in Hyderabad and it is running successfully.' Micro-finance loans are extended to private schools. Pauline Dixon is the International Adviser to ET. It has a scholarship fund called the E. G. West Scholarships which is designed to help economically deprived children in rural and urban India to pursue education in private unaided schools. According to the E. G. West website 'The Educare Trust is the only foundation committed to helping the poor to achieve self-reliance through accessing private education. Professor E. G. West was a renowned British educationalist, who conducted seminal research on private education as a vehicle for helping the poor to help themselves, in Britain, the USA and developing countries. The Scholarships are named in memory of his enduring influence.'[16]

James Tooley is director of the E. G. West Centre, which is based at the University of Newcastle.

Other organisations which contribute to the dissemination of these policy ideas include The Economic Freedom Network Asia mentioned earlier, of which CCS is one of the two members from India. In 2005, the Education Promotion Society of India (EPSI) was established to serve as a 'catalyst Education Promotion Organisation between Government, Academics and the Industry'. Though its focus is higher education, the EPSI has entered the arena of school policy and advocates private schooling for the poor. In 2005, the EPSI organised a dialogue on 'Private Schools Serving the Poor: A Global Perspective' with the Centre for Civil Society. Tooley was invited and he 'shared his findings from Global study of Asia, Africa and China on Private Schools for the poor'.[17]

AP School Choice Project

One of the main tasks of pro-choice advocates is to demonstrate that children involved in the voucher programmes in private schools perform better than their peers in government schools and a study is underway in Andhra Pradesh that seeks to do this. This is the Andhra Pradesh Randomised Evaluation Study (APRESt) that brings together a number of organisations and individuals and reflects the interests that inform the spread of private markets in education in India (Figure 6.1).[18] The project is a 'three-way partnership' between the government of Andhra Pradesh (GOAP), the Azim Premji Foundation (APF is the philanthropic arm of the corporate giant Wipro and is closely involved in government initiatives to improve primary education outcomes) and the World Bank. It aims to 'pilot alternative policy options to improve rural primary education and rigorously measure their impact in rural areas of Andhra Pradesh'. The partners have signed a Memorandum of Understanding: 'to continue to pilot and rigorously evaluate (using randomized allocation of programs) the most promising options in primary education policy over a period of 5 years under the APRESt'.

The APRESt design involves:

> offering scholarships that would allow them (poor children) to shift to schools of their choice (if they wish to) in addition to the option of continuing in the existing government school. Such a program would provide opportunities for children from disadvantaged families to attend private schools. The research study involves a rigorous

evaluation of the impact of school choice both on children who receive the choice as well as on the aggregate impact on education outcomes for all children in villages where the school choice program is implemented.

Both the scholarships as well as the evaluation of the study are being funded by Legatum Global Development, the lead financial partner for the project.[19] The orientation of APRESt is evident in the statement that:

> policies that hope to leverage the existence of private schools for universal quality education need to be designed on the basis of rigorous evidence regarding the relative performance of public and private schools. *The Andhra Pradesh School Choice Project aims to provide such evidence* (our emphasis).

Further, APF, GOAP and World Bank will also be 'instrumental in . . . helping the results *feed into the policy process* [our emphasis] through the institutionalization of APRESt in GOAP's education program' (Educare Trust website). The project will be evaluated by Kremer and Muralidharan of Harvard University (they are both CCS 'School Choice Scholars'), and Sundaram (World Bank).

Advocates of school choice are today building 'research evidence' to show that low-cost private schools are more 'effective' than state-run schools. Studies of Tooley and his associates as well as carefully planned documentation and evaluations of projects such as APRESt are being used to build a discourse to convince policy makers and influential members of civil society of the need for de-regulation and legalising of 'for profit' schools that will meet the educational aspirations of the poor. A case is also being made out that the low-cost school sector can be a good business proposition as well. Studies are presented in a manner so as to suggest that 'objective and sophisticated methodologies' have been used, and their findings can be generalised. We have already referred to research carried out by Tooley and Dixon and those sponsored by Centre for Civil society and the CfBT. The E. G. West Centre at the University of New Castle has also commissioned studies of private unregulated schools in India. The fact that research on private schools in India is informed by powerful economic and political interests but has not been subject to academic scrutiny is of concern.

We have already noted the interests and involvements of business in private schools and school choice advocacy. In the following sections we indicate some of the forms of participation of commercial providers, large and small, in the politics and economics of privatisation, their involvements in the choice advocacy network and some of the ways in which advocacy groups and business interests 'work together' to open up new policy spaces for privatisation and private provision.

Micro Finance and Micro Schools

The nomenclature in relation to schools established by private entrepreneurs for the poor is that of 'budget private schools' or 'micro schools'. Budget schools are described as 'low cost private schools serving the poor' and CCS asserts that '[c]ontrary to popular concerns about their low quality, children from these schools outperform their government school counterparts in key curricular subjects — even after controlling for background variables'.[20] 'Micro schools' is used to refer to schools established by 'educational entrepreneurs' (what the Cato Institute calls 'edupreneurs'). The reference here is to schools established with micro-finance loans and the discourse is primarily one of entrepreneurship and social enterprise.

However, whether as 'budget private schools' or 'micro schools', the driving force behind these schools is profit rather than the broader aims of education. Organisations such as Opportunity International and Global Legatum who are in the micro-finance business, appear to see micro schools as a promising area of investment. Opportunity International was founded in 1971 and was one of the first microcredit lenders, offering small business loans, savings, insurance and training in basic business practices to women and men living in chronic poverty:

> Opportunity International provides small loans — sometimes as little as $50 — and other services that allow poor entrepreneurs to start or expand a business, develop a steady income, provide for their families and create jobs for their neighbours.

The Opportunity International website quotes Tooley as saying, 'I am thrilled that Opportunity International is expanding schools for the poor. I have seen the benefit that these schools bring to an entire community — the parents, the families and especially the children who are getting a quality education from teachers who are dedicated and committed'.[21] In turn Opportunity International refers to Tooley's 'groundbreaking research' to legitimate their loan programme. Crane (CEO, Opportunity International) suggests that microschools can transform the lives of the poor, adding that they 'are usually located right in the neighborhoods where the poor are concentrated. . . . As a result, parents tell us they feel safer sending their daughters to these schools. This will help break the discriminatory cycle that has existed against girls in many poor countries.'[22]

Also involved in the micro finance–micro school advocacy is the HSBC Education Trust and Centre for British Teachers (CfBT) in England. In 2004 the Trust 'signed a memorandum of the CfBT to launch a project called EQUIP (Enabling Quality Improvement Programmes in Schools) that will facilitate private schools to get micro finance from HSBC'. The agreement gives CfBT a lead role in 'identifying schools on the basis of an evaluation of the 'potential of the school for improvement. . . . Schools that are approved by CfBT will receive loans for infrastructure. . . . These schools will have to take a CfBT-designed School Improvement Plan . . . and the progress will be monitored through an Education Management Information System' (The Hindu.com 2004). The loans ranged from ₹ 50,000 to ₹ 5,000,000. The project aimed to enable government-recognised private schools that admitted children of low-income families to get financial aid from the bank to improve their infrastructure. This was in the nature of a 'pilot project, to be implemented in Andhra Pradesh and Tamil Nadu' and 'later be rolled out across the country'. *Business Line* (19 July 2004) reported that 'about 30 private schools in the city have shown interest in joining the initiative. Of them, 16 will be given loans in the first phase.' The Minister for School Education of the AP government was also quoted as asking HSBC 'to expand the scheme to government schools that form more than 80 per cent of the 91,000 schools in the State' (The Hindu Business Line.com 2004).

The micro finance–micro school model has also given a fillip to private companies offering advisory services for social business. Intellecap is one such company that is linked to the Legatum-APRESt project. Intellecap was set up in 2007 with equity investment from the micro-finance company Global Legatum. Other micro-financers SKS Micro Finance and Basix have already been referred to (Figure 6.1).

The State, Public–Private Partnerships and Government Schools

The language of public–private partnerships (PPP) began to appear in education policy documents in India in the late 1990s when corporate organisations expressed their interest in participating in efforts towards Education for All; CCS advocates PPPs on its website. Information Technology is seen by some policy makers in India as the panacea for improvement of the quality of education in state-funded schools and a means of addressing the aspirations of poor parents. As part of PPPs in education, IT companies such as Solaris, Java, Oracle, NIIT and Everonn have easy access to schools. They train both pupils and teachers in IT, signing agreements with state governments. NIIT, Sugata Mitra's parent organisation, is a nodal player in the growth of the state school education business and in educational software development. It is reported to have a 'presence in 2000 Government schools in the states of Andhra Pradesh, Tamil Nadu, West Bengal and Karnataka' (The India Street.com 2007).

Various state governments are formally entering into partnerships and signing memoranda of understanding with companies such as NIIT to supply computers and train students and teachers. Other companies such as Evronn and Microsoft are also finding a foothold in the new education business sector. The official website of the government of Punjab state declares that it is:

> encouraging the participation of private sector for providing good quality education by giving a package of incentives in the form of land at cheaper rates along with other facilities. The Punjab State Government has proposed to set up a chain of *Adarsh Schools*, at least one in each Block, for providing high quality education even at village level. . . . Every school is allowed to lease out spare land to the private contractors, for cultivation. The income so received from this is spent on the development of the respective school.[23]

The Confederation of Indian Industry (CII) is also reported to be involved in initiatives (along with Coca Cola India, Bank of America, and Honda Siel) for 'quality improvement' of education for poor children in slums in Delhi. It is said to have 'facilitated linkages between the State Government and Member Companies for IT-Enabled Education' (which may merely mean bringing computers to schools/training teachers to use them). It has helped in the signing of an MoU between Microsoft and the Municipal Corporation of Delhi

(MCD) for training teachers at 1,000 MCD schools in Delhi. 'The idea is to empower the teachers to use IT as a tool for classroom teaching'.[24] There is today a large and growing market for IT in schools and a policy climate that is beginning to encourage the participation of the corporate sector in this sphere in the name of 'improving' the quality of education.

There is a range of corporate effort in school education especially at the elementary stage and private participation in government-run schools in the provision of infrastructure and facilities, the supply of mid-day meals as well as involvement in the development of curriculum, pedagogy and assessment. Information technology in schools is also a key area of the entry of the corporate sector in the provision of computers and software as well as technical support and training. Foundations established by corporate houses such as the APF (Wipro) and Pratham (ICICI) are an increasingly visible presence in the arenas of education policy making and in initiatives aimed at quality improvement in government schools in some states. Companies such as NIIT and Everonn are more narrowly focused on IT provision and training to schools. In addition, a number of corporate houses have set up philanthropic foundations that specifically state that their interventions in education are 'not for profit'.

A more recent phenomenon is the contracting out of 'under-performing' schools by state governments to corporate foundations. In addition to organisations that work mainly in/with government schools, foundations are also running schools. For example, the Bharati Foundation (funded by the mobile phone company Air Tel) will be running 50 government schools in Rajasthan as part of the School Improvement Programme in that state. The Foundation has a goal of establishing 1,000 Satya Bharati schools across India. *Akshara*, an NGO that runs schools for the poor in Bangalore was established by the wife of the CEO of Infosys (a leading corporate organisation). This is an area that is drastically under-researched and little information is available from websites.

Discussion

The Indian choice and privatisation advocacy network is linked by a complex of funding, exchange, cross-referencing, dissemination, and mutual sponsorship — the latter involving various aspects of what Keck and Sikkink (1998) call 'information politics'. The Centre for Civil Society, the Educare Trust, EPSI and the Liberty Institute

(India) are key points of the local articulation and flow of the choice policy ideas in India but are also engaged directly or indirectly in a bigger enterprise of neoliberal state reform and the re-definition of the boundaries of the policy process — policy channels are being diversified.[25] As the website of the Liberty Institute puts it: 'The Institute particularly seeks to improve our understanding of market processes; to identify the factors that may have restricted the evolution of the market and ways of overcoming those factors; to estimate the costs — social and economic — of curbs on the market forces; to propose market-based alternatives to government regulations in the economy'.[26]

As we have sought to show the Indian pro-choice think tanks are also linked to a number of other co-belief organisations in other countries in a worldwide advocacy network for neoliberal ideas. The Centre for Civil Society, the Educare Trust and the Liberty Institute (India) are members of a global network of neoliberal organisations whose mission is to 'export' choice and markets around the world. They are linked to the Atlas Economic Research Foundation which has its headquarters in Arlington, Virginia. Atlas has launched or nurtured 275 such think tanks in 70 nations around the world and believes that 'the prospects for free societies all over the world depend upon "intellectual entrepreneurs" in civil society, who wish to improve public policy debates through sound research'. Its mission is 'To discover, develop and support "intellectual entrepreneurs" worldwide who can advance the Atlas vision of a society of free and responsible individuals'.[27] This is a formidable network of power, influence, ideas and money which presents a simple message easily understood by politicians and policy makers in diverse locations. The involvement of local business interests adds further strength to the network.

Think tanks often have very specific and effective points of entry into political systems. However, Stone (2000: 216) points out that: '[t]he authority and legitimacy for think tank involvement in global affairs is not naturally given but has been cultivated and groomed through various management practices and intellectual activities'. She goes on to note that '[i]n some cases, however, the think tank scholarly "aura" and independence may be misleading . . . in reality ideas become harnessed to political and economic interests'.

As noted earlier, for the most part research and writing on TANs has focused on areas of human rights and environmentalism. Here we have begun to sketch a particular example of a TAN which is working to disseminate neoliberal ideas and specific neoliberal policies, and in doing so they are, in as yet modest ways, reshaping the Indian state and the governance of education in India. The work of this TAN follows very clearly Brenner and Theodore's (2002) conception of two distinct but dialectical moments in the dissemination of neoliberalism, that is, critique, and attempts to change public perception of policy issues, followed by the 'creation of a new infrastructure for market-oriented, economic growth, commodification, and the rule of capital' (2002: 364). Government education policy and government schools are subject to sustained critique, often on the basis of 'research' evidence (research and evaluations are locked within closed circles created by the privatisers and their allies); alongside this, new educational opportunities are being created for some sections of the poor in India, while at the same time new opportunities are being opened up for small and big business. The shared libertarian values of the network members are a key resource in all of this. The activities of this TAN are interacting with and expanding the discursive and policy spaces within which educational businesses, voluntary organisations and charities can flourish — increasingly supported by commercial and philanthropic micro-finance and multinational investment. These discourses also seek to expand the range of policy choices available to the Indian government and naturalise within Indian politics key neoliberal technologies, including contracting-out and public–private partnerships. Within this field of education in India, what is being attempted through the work of the network is a shift from 'proto' to 'roll-back' neoliberalism (Tickell and Peck 2002), both in terms of the creation of a business infrastructure for private education and pressure for legal changes to enable private for-profit schooling and vouchers. The Indian state is vulnerable in this area of policy given its 'failures' around universal provision and EFA goals and is therefore very susceptible to the politics of a TAN that is very well-funded and backed by a variety of powerful and influential voices local and transnational.

What is also important in the work of this TAN is that the concern and focus on India, especially as far as James Tooley is concerned, is not merely because of the potential for profitable markets in schooling for poor children but that these developments will generate evidence and political support which demonstrate to the west that 'for-profit' education can work and 'if India can do it so can we' and lead to a re-assessment of the role of the state in education in western countries. The E. G. West Centre website[28] has Tooley arguing this quite clearly:

> Certainly stories of the educational entrepreneurs in the slums, battling against hostile government and real poverty, can provide inspiration to the school choice movement in the West. But I also think it can provide more than that .... What West did for the school choice debate in the 1960s and 1970s, the evidence from India and elsewhere can do for the school choice debate now; if the evidence reveals the poorest worldwide achieving better educational outcomes without the state, then this must help inspire and buttress appeals for increased school choice in rich countries now. It also raises anew the question: What is government doing in educationa at all?

This was reiterated by Tooley (2008) on the *Outlook Business* website where he asserts that 'a silent revolution is brewing in low-cost private school chains. In the next wave, they might even "colonise" the West'.[29]

This essay is a first attempt to map and analyse the work of this particular TAN and to adumbrate some critical questions about its activities in India but there is a need for more research into the methods, processes and consequences of this 'silent revolution' in Indian education and its more general effects on and within the Indian state.

✦

Notes

*This chapter is a revised version of G. B. Nambissan and S. J. Ball, 2010, 'Advocacy Networks, Choice and Private Schooling of the Poor in India', *Global Networks*, 10 (3), 324–43.

1. The complexity of these roles, relationships, models of working and underpinning principles makes it difficult to distinguish between public and private in a simple way.
2. clg.portalxm.com/library/keytext.cfm?keytext_id=113 (accessed 24 March 2009).
3. See http://right-to-education-india.blogspot.com/2011/04/8-million-children-still-out-of-school.html (accessed 20 April 2011).

    The World Bank has had more than a decade of close association with state-run primary education in India through the Bank-supported District Primary Education Programme (DPEP). See website http://www.ncl.ac.uk/ecls/staff/profile/james.tooley (accessed 4 January 2010).

4. The Atlas Economic Research Foundation is projected as a 'nonprofit organization connecting a global network of more than 400 free-market organizations in over 80 countries to the ideas and resources needed to advance the cause of 'liberty'. See http://atlasnetwork.org/ (accessed 10 January 2011).

5. Liberty Institute was established in 1996 in Delhi, India, as a 'non-profit organisation'. It sees itself as 'an independent think tank' dedicated to 'empowering the people by harnessing the power of the market'; it declares that 'We seek to uphold the four institutional pillars of a free society — Individual Rights, Rule of Law, Limited Government and Free Market' (http://www.libertyindia.org, accessed 4 January 2010).

6. http://news.education4india.com/2037/nasscom-chief-for-setting-up-special-education-zones/ (accessed 18 December 2009).

7. See http://www.ncl.ac.uk/egwest for list of publications (accessed 22 March 2009).

8. psdblog.worldbank.org/psdblog/2006/01/index_of_econom.html (accessed 24 March 2009).

9. Ibid.

10. For quotes on/by Mitra see http://www.edutopia.org/sugata-mitra-catalyst-curiosity (accessed 4 January 2010).

11. See http://www.ccsindia.org. Quotations are from the CCS web site (accessed 4 January 2010).

12. http://www.ccsindia.org/ccsindia/Newsletter/feb-mar07.htm. J. Tooley, K. Muralidharan, A. Coulson and M. Kremer are also mentioned as School Choice Scholars, see http://www.schoolchoice.in/choice/index.php (accessed 4 January 2010).

13. http://schoolchoice.in/support/fundvoucher.php (accessed 4 January 2010).

14. Ibid. for details and quotes.

15. For all quotes relating to the Educare Trust see www.educaretrust-India.org/about.html, accessed 20 August 2009.

16. See Jamestooley.blogspot.com/2006/01/education-trust-eg-west-scholarships.html (accessed 4 January 2010).

17. http://epsfi.org/about_activities.htm (accessed 18 December 2009).

18. Details about the project and quotes are from Andhra Pradesh School Choice Project Proposal, see http://siteresources.worldbank.org/EDUCATION/Resources/278200-1121703274255/1439264-1178054414297/Karthikmuralidharan.pdf (accessed 18 December 2009).

19. Legatum Global Development is an 'international private investment organisation' and 'part of the Legatum group of companies that has been investing in the world's capital markets for over 20 years and whose mission is to create a legacy of enduring investment success, while applying the same principles of effective capital allocation to promote

sustainable human development', see www.legatum.org/ (accessed 4 January 2010).
20. See www.ccsindia.org (accessed 10 December 2008).
21. See www.opportunity.org/Page.aspx?pid=202 (accessed 4 January 2010).
22. 'Opportunity International Launches Microschools™ — New Frontier in Breaking the Chain of Poverty, Giving the Poor a Working Chance', p. 3. See http://www.communityintl.com/documents/Microschools_Opportunity_092407.pdf (accessed 4 January 2010).
23. See http://punjabgovt.nic.in/education/GovernmentPolicy.htm (accessed 10 May 2008).
24. See http://www.indianamericancouncil.org/afc/education.htm (accessed 10 May 2008).
25. The global networks in which these local organisations are situated carry other concomitant discursive baggage, including conservative religious ideology (e.g., Templeton Foundation and Opportunity International), anti-statism, anti-welfare, radical forms of liberty, the 'enterprise narrative' and in some cases, anti-global warming stances.
26. See www.libertyindia.org/about.htm (accessed 24 March 2009).
27. See atlasnetwork.org (accessed 30 June 2011).
28. See www.ncl.ac.uk/egwest (accessed 30 June 2011).
29. See http://business.outlookindia.com/ (accessed 10 December 2009).

References

Ball, S. J. 1997. 'Markets, Equity and Values in Education', in R. Pring and G. Walford (eds), *Affirming the Comprehensive Ideal*. London: Falmer Press, pp. 69–82.
———. 2001. 'Urban Choice and Urban Fears: The Politics of Parental Choice', Urban education conference, Padogogisches Institut der Stadt Wien, City of Vienna, Austria.
———. 2003. *Class Strategies and the Education Market: The Middle Class and Social Advantage*. London: Routledge.
———. 2007. *Education Plc: Understanding Private Sector Participation in Public Sector Education*. London: Routledge.
———. 2009. 'Privatising Education, Privatising Education Policy, Privatising Educational Research: Network Governance and the "Competition State"', *Journal of Education Policy*, 42 (1), 83–99.
Brenner, N. and N. Theodore. 2002. 'Cities and Geographies of "Actually Existing Neoliberalism"', *Antipode*, 34, 351–79.
Cavett-Goodwin, D. 2008. 'Forces Constructing Consent for the Neoliberal Project, http://culturalshifts.com/archives/206 (accessed 18 December 2009).
Coulson, Andrew J. 1999. *Market Education: The Unknown History*. New Brunswick, NJ: Transaction Publishers.

Coulson, Andrew J. 2007. 'An "Invisible Hand" Up', Philanthropy Roundtable, http://www.philanthropyroundtable.org/article.asp? article=1479& cat=139 (accessed 18 December 2009).

Dalton, R. J. and R. Rohrschneider. 2003, 'The Environmental Movement and the Modes of Political Action', *Comparative Political Studies*, 36 (7), 743–71.

Dicken, P., P. F. Kelly, K. Olds and H. W-c. Yeung. 2001. 'Chains and Networks, Territories and Scales: Towards a Relational Framework for Analysing the Global Economy', *Global Networks*, 1 (2), 89–112.

Florini, A. (ed.). 2000. *The Third Force: The Rise of Transnational Civil Society*. Tokyo: Japan Centre for International Exchange.

Harvey, D. 2005. *A Brief History of Neoliberalism*. Oxford: Oxford University Press.

Held, D. and A. McGrew. 2004. 'The Great Globalization Debate: An Introduction', in D. Held and A. McGrew (eds), *The Global Transformations Reader: An Introduction to the Globalization Debate*. Oxford: Polity, pp. 1–50.

India Together. 2007. 'School Choice Looms for Poor Students', available online at http://www.indiatogether.org/2007/jun/edu-choice.htm (accessed 18 December 2009).

Jessop, B. 2002. *The Future of the Capitalist State*. Cambridge: Polity.

Kalra, A. 2007. 'Education Bulletin: Education Fund Eyes Private Schooling for the Poor', blog posting *liveMint.com* (accessed 10 December 2008).

Keck, M. E. and K. Sikkink. 1998. *Activists Beyond Borders: Advocacy Networks in International Politics*. Ithaca, NY: Cornell University Press.

Kelsey, J. 2006. 'Taking Minds to Market', available at www.knowpol.uib. no/portal/files/uplink/kelsey.pdf (accessed 4 January 2010).

LaDousa, C. 2007. 'Liberalisation, Privatisation, Modernisation and Schooling in India: An Interview with Krishna Kumar', *Globalisation, Societies and Education*, 5 (2), 137–52.

Mintrom, M. and S. Vergari. 1996. 'Advocacy Coalitions, Policy Entrepreneurs, and Policy Change', *Policy Studies Journal*, 24 (3), 420–34.

NUEPA (National University of Educational Planning and Administration) (2011) Elementary Education in India. Progress towards UEE. DISE 2009-10, Flash Statistics New Delhi: NUEPA. Also available at http://www.dise.in/Downloads/Publications/Publications 2009-10/Flash Statistics 2009-10.pdf .

Prahlad, C. K. 2004. *The Fortune at the Bottom of the Pyramid: Eradicating Poverty through Profit*. Upper Saddle River, N.J.: Wharton School Publishing.

Rubenstein, G. 2007. 'Sugata Midra — Catalyst of Curiosity', available at http://www.edutopia.org/sugata-mitra (accessed 18 December 2009).

Stone, D. 2000. 'Think Tanks across Nations: The New Networks of Knowledge', *NIRA Review*, Winter, 34–39.

The Hindubusinessline.com. 2004. 'HSBC Education Trust's Micro-credit Project for Private Schools', 20 July (accessed 15 September 2008).

The Hindu.com. 2004. 'Equip'ping Schools to Clear Hurdles', 20 July (accessed 15 September 2008).

The India Street.com. 2007. 'Analysis of Everonn Systems India Limited IPO', 10 July (accessed 15 September 2008).

Tickell, A. and J. Peck. 2002. 'Neoliberalizing Space', *Antipode*, 34 (3), 380–404.

Tooley, J. 1999. *The Global Education Industry*. London: Institute of Economic Affairs.

———. 2001. 'The Enterprise of Education: Opportunities and Challenges for India', Liberty Institute, Occasional Paper no. 6.

———. 2005. 'Is Private Education Good for the Poor?' Working Paper from University of Newcastle Upon Tyne (England), June 25.

———. 2007. 'Educating Amaretch: Private Schools for the Poor and the New Frontier for Investors', *Economic Affairs*, 27 (2), 37–43.

———. 2008. 'In Letter and Spirit', in *Outlook Business*, http://business. outlookindia.com/print.aspx?articleid=1938&editionid=51&catgid=12& subcatgid=909 (accessed 16 August 2009).

Tooley, J. and P. Dixon. 2005. 'Private Schools Serving the Poor, Working Paper: A Study from Delhi, India'. New Delhi: ViewPoint 8, Centre for Civil Society.

Wapner, P. 1996. *Environmental Activism and World Civic Politics*. Albany: SUNY Press.

Weidrich, E. 2007. 'Education Vouchers: Is There a Model for India?' Centre for Civil Society, New Delhi, http://www.ccsindia.org/ccsindia/policy/ ed/studies/wp0072.pdf (accessed 20 August 2008).

About the Editors

Marie Lall is Senior Lecturer in Education Policy at the Institute of Education, University of London. She is a South Asia specialist with special reference to India, Pakistan and Myanmar. She is an associate fellow at Chatham House and a honorary fellow at the Institute of South Asian Studies at the National University of Singapore. Her research interests cover education, national identity creation and citizenship in South Asia, as well as the wider politics and international relations in the region. She has published widely on all three countries and is the author of *India's Missed Opportunity* (2001) and the editor of *Education as a Political Tool in Asia* (Routledge, 2008).

Geetha B. Nambissan is Professor of Sociology of Education at the Zakir Husain Centre for Educational Studies, Jawaharlal Nehru University, New Delhi. Her areas of specialisation are exclusion, inclusion and the education of marginal groups in India and educational policy. Her current work focuses on the middle classes and educational advantage and the social and educational implications of private schools for the poor. She has published widely in these areas. She is co-editor of *Child Labour and the Right to Education in South Asia: Needs versus Rights?* (2003). She is on the editorial board of the *Contemporary Education Dialogue* and on the advisory board of the *Journal of Education Policy*.

Notes on Contributors

Felicity Armstrong is Emeritus Professor of Education at the Institute of Education, University of London. Her work focuses primarily on policies and practices relating to inclusive education in local, national and international contexts. She is on the editorial boards of the journals *Disability and Society* and the *International Journal of Inclusive Education*. Her recent publications include: *Teaching and Learning in Diverse and Inclusive Classrooms: Key Issues for New Teachers* (Routledge, 2011, co-edited with Gill Richards), *Policy, Experience and Change: Cross-cultural Reflections on Inclusive Education* (Springer, 2007, co-edited with Len Barton) and *Spaced Out: Policy, Difference and the Challenge for Inclusive Education* (Kluwer, 2003).

Stephen J. Ball is Karl Mannheim Professor of Sociology of Education in the Faculty of Policy and Society, Institute of Education, London. His main work is in the field of 'policy sociology'; the use of sociological theories and methods to analyse policy processes and outcomes. His specific research interests focus upon the effects and consequences of the education market in a variety of respects including the impact of competition on provider behaviour; the class strategies of educational choosers; the participation of private capital in education service delivery and education policy; and the impact of 'performativity' on academic and social life. He is a fellow of the British Academy, and a member of the Academy of Social Sciences, FRSA. His latest books include *The Education Debate: Policy and Politics in the 21st Century* (Policy Press, 2008), *The Education plc: Private Sector Participation in Public Sector Education* (Routledge, 2007) and *The Routledge International Handbook of the Sociology of Education* (Routledge, 2010, co-edited). He is also the editor of the *Journal of Education Policy*.

Vincent Carpentier is Senior Lecturer in History of Education at the Institute of Education, University of London. He is the programme leader of the MA in Higher and Professional Studies. His comparative research on the historical relationship between educational systems, long economic cycles and social change is located at the interface of the history of education and political economy. A key area of his research is the political economy of national and global higher education and the exploration of the long-term connections and tensions between higher education funding and access policies. He is associate editor of the *London Review of Education* and a member of the editorial board of *Teaching in Higher Education* and *Reflecting Education*. He has contributed chapters to various edited volumes and papers in journals of repute such as *Higher Education Management and Policy, Paedagogica Historica, History of Education*, etc. He has recently co-edited, with Elaine Unterhalter, *Global Inequalities and Higher Education, Whose Interests Are We Serving?* (Palgrave, 2010).

Saumen Chattopadhyay is Associate Professor of Economics of Education at the Zakir Husain Centre for Educational Studies, Jawaharlal Nehru University, since 2004. He worked as an Economist and Senior Economist at the National Institute of Public Finance and Policy (NIPFP), New Delhi during 1995 to 2004. His research interests include higher education, public finance and black economy in the Indian context. He was involved in projects on higher education sponsored by the UGC and the University of Calcutta. He has several co-authored books in the area of public finance and development and chapters in several edited volumes.

Anjali Kothari is a doctoral student in the Faculty of Policy and Society at the Institute of Education, London. Her thesis explores how women in urban Indian families have responded to affluence and cultural change brought about by economic liberalisation since the early 1990s.

Radhika Menon is Assistant Professor in the Department of Education, Mata Sundri College, University of Delhi. Based on her M.Phil. research she has published 'Global City, Local School and the Disadvantaged Youth: Segregation as an Everyday Experience' (September 2006, *Social Change*). She has worked as a consultant for NUEPA in a project on Quality of Secondary Education, and was a member of the Public Study Group on Central Advisory Board of Education (PSG-CABE) on post-independent education policy in India. She has worked on syllabus and textbook development committees of National Council of Educational Research and Training (NCERT) and District Institutes of Education and Training (DIET). Her research interests include urban educational inequities, sociology of policy, class and critical pedagogy. She is currently working on her doctoral thesis on the sociology of access and participation in secondary education.

Binay Kumar Pathak is a doctoral student at the Zakir Husain Centre for Educational Studies, Jawaharlal Nehru University, New Delhi. He is working on 'information-processing, decision-making and choice in higher education' for his doctoral work. He has worked on a project on higher education sponsored by the University Grants Commission. He was a member of the team preparing *Summary Assessment of E-Governance Projects* for the Department of Information Technology, Government of India. His research interests include economics of information, e-governance, and governance of educational institutions and financing of higher education.

S. Srinivasa Rao is Associate Professor at the Zakir Husain Centre for Educational Studies, Jawaharlal Nehru University, New Delhi. His teaching and research interests include diversity, equity, exclusion and inclusion in education and the impact of neoliberal reforms on school and higher education systems. He has been a recipient of the Faculty Enrichment Fellowship (2011) and the Faculty Research Fellowship (2005) of the Shastri Indo-Canadian Institute and the Asia Fellow Award (2007) of the Asian Scholarship Foundation (ASF). He has published articles in journals and chapters in edited books in the area of sociology of education.

Pratyasha Sahoo teaches Sociology of Education in the Department of Elementary Education at Gargi College, University of Delhi and is a doctoral student at the Zakir Husain Centre for Educational Studies, Jawaharlal Nehru University, New Delhi. She has been instrumental in preparing a report on Ten Years of B.El.Ed. Programme at Gargi College for the Confederation of Indian Industry (CII). She has worked on syllabus and textbook development projects of the State

Council for Educational Research and Training (SCERT). Her research interests include issues on disability and inclusion. She has presented papers in several national seminars in the areas of her interest. She is currently pursuing her doctoral work which includes the identity and education of young disabled people in India.

Carol Vincent is Professor of Education in the Faculty of Policy and Society, Institute of Education, University of London. As a sociologist, her particular research interests include the relationship between parents and educational institutions, and how these relationships are mediated by social class and ethnicity. Other interests include parenting, especially mothering, the operation of markets in education, and education policy. She is currently leading a research project on the educational strategies of Black Caribbean middle-class parents. She is an executive editor of the *British Journal of Sociology of Education*, and on the editorial boards of *Sociology* and *Journal of Education Policy*.

Index

school differentiation: India, in, 65
secondary education, 5
Sikkink, K., 163–65, 167, 179
Singal, Nidhi, 118
social citizenship, 8
social democracy, 4
social imaginary: building of, 2
social justice, 3; education, in: changing discourses and practices, 12–15; commitment by India and UK, 11; India, in, 9–12; social democratic notions of, 4; UK, in, 9–12
Spastics Society of India, 106, 119 *see also* Disable people, in India
Special Educational Needs and Disability Act (2001), 112
Special Educational Needs and Disability Discrimination Act (SENDA), 2001, 105
special education, in England: history of, 111
state education system, in UK: disarticulation of, 12
state power: classical liberalism (*see* Classical liberalism); impact of globalisation on, 4
Stephen Lawrence Inquiry Report, 32
Stribodh, 83
Swann Report, 41
symbolic capital concept, 83

Taylor, C., 2
Thatcher, Margaret, 32
Tilak, J. B. G., 133, 136–37, 146, 153
Tomlinson, S., 31, 33, 38–39, 49, 131
Tooley, James, 162
transnational advocacy networks (TANs), 162; communicative structures, 163; definition of, 163; reshaping of, political processes, 163; third force, 163; types of strategy, 163–64; working of, 164

UN Convention on the Rights of the Child (1989), 109
UN Declaration on the Rights of the Disabled Persons (1973), 109
UNESCO, 107
Universal Elementary Education (UEE): India, in, 116, 164
university: role of, 9
University Education Commission (1948–49), 133
University Grants Committee (UGC), 132
urban middle class: value crisis, 62

Visva-Bharati, 145 *see also* Higher education (HE)

Warnock Report (1978), 112
Weis, Lois, 56
Weisskopf, Thomas E., 39
Wessel, M. V., 62
Western education: cultural discourse, as, 104
White groups, in UK: achievement gap between non-White and, 35
women: new opportunities, after independence, 83
World Bank, 6; support to DPEP, 11
World Congress on Racism, Racial Discrimination, Xenophobia and Related Intolerance (2001), 28
World Trade Organisation (WTO): education agenda of (*see* Education agenda, of WTO); General Agreement on Trade in Services (GATS) [*see* General Agreement on Trade in Services (GATS)]
Wrigley, T., 4

Youth Cohort Study (YCS), 41